Lucy Morgan

Gift from the Hills ❖ ❖

Gift
from the
Hills

❖❖❖❖❖❖❖❖

Miss Lucy Morgan's story of her unique Penland School
with LeGETTE BLYTHE

❖❖❖❖❖❖❖❖❖❖❖❖❖❖❖❖❖❖❖❖❖❖❖❖❖❖❖❖❖❖❖❖

Including an Epilogue

THE UNIVERSITY OF NORTH CAROLINA PRESS
Chapel Hill

TO MY OWN FAMILY
and to
MY CHILDREN ALL OVER THE WORLD

Gift from the Hills ❖ ❖

CHAPTER 1

THE WHISTLE TOOTED, the smokestack belched a round puff of white steam and black smoke, the little locomotive groaned, gasped, lunged and fell back, strained and went forward, and with much bell-ringing, drive wheels clutching at rails, and accelerated puffing, began to catch speed.

And there we stood, our valises at our feet, our heads twisting.

Then from around behind the tiny railroad station a woman came running, arms outflung toward us.

"Lucy Morgan!" she screamed at me. "Mabel!" She grabbed us. "Welcome to Penland!"

Our embraces accomplished, we stood back from each other, and she looked Mabel and me up and down. "We're so happy to have you here," she declared, and then as she noticed our surreptitious glancing about she laughed. "If you look sharply, from here you can see a church and three houses. But in the wintertime with the leaves off the trees you can see *five* houses."

It was June 1, 1920. We were standing beside the tracks of the Clinchfield Railroad at Penland Station in Mitchell County, North Carolina, high in the Blue Ridge Mountains. Our greeter, who had come down from the Appalachian School up on Conley Ridge above the station, was Miss Amy Burt, who in the regular school months was Dean of Women at the normal school at Mount Pleasant, Michigan. She was a friend of my brother, the Reverend Rufus Morgan, an Episcopal minister and founder of Appalachian School, and it was through their friendship that I had been able to take my teacher-training work at her school. Mabel Fauble, who had got off the train with me, was a good friend who had also completed the two-year course at Mount Pleasant. Miss Burt had been spending what she called her summer vacations at Appalachian, an Episcopal institution under the supervision of the bishop of the diocese. We were soon to find, however, that vacation was hardly the word for what she did there.

"While we're waiting for the wagon to get down the hill," said Miss Burt, "I want you to meet some of our Penland neighbors. You'll soon be discovering for yourselves that they are wonderful folk." Whereupon she took us into the station and introduced us to Mr. Henry Meacham, station agent and telegrapher and, we would not be long in finding out, a distinctly unique individual. "A delightful character," Miss Burt said of him as we left. "I'll tell you more about him. But now we must go to the post office and pick up the school mail."

In addition to the station and five houses, Penland had a post office and a general store. The community sat in the heart of a region abounding in mica, kaolin and feldspar, and its people were for the most part engaged in the mines.

At the post office we met Mr. A. C. Tainter. Miss Burt told us that he owned and personally operated the general store. He also kept books for one of the mining companies. If Mr. Tainter had been wearing a red suit trimmed in white fur we would have thought we had found Santa Claus in the flesh. He not only looked like the old gentleman from the North Pole country and had the same proportions, but he also had the same twinkle in his eyes and the same genial countenance; and we were reminded of a bowlful of jelly as he laughed. Through the weeks and months and years ahead we were to learn that Mr. Tainter was not just the keeper of the general store; he was the town's creditor, the community's friend, a friend of everybody, but particularly of the fellow in need, as I myself happily would learn.

He took us over to his store, where we met some other people of the community who had walked down to see the train pull in and to get any mail that might have come on it. About that time the wagon from the school drove up.

"I don't see any place for us to sit," I said.

"Sit?" Miss Burt laughed. "The wagon's for your baggage," she revealed. "We'll walk." She waved her hand in the general direction of Conley Ridge. "It's just up there a little way. The road's too rough for riding. Going up there in a wagon would shake your teeth out."

We loaded the heavier luggage on the wagon, and it started up the hill. We picked up the smaller pieces and started walking. About halfway up the mile slope—and I'm certain that must have been one of the longest miles I had ever walked, though I had been born and reared in the mountains and all my life had been accustomed to walking—we paused for breath under the spreading arms of a giant oak. Then we struck out again up the steep, rocky path, through a blind

5

gate, through a strip of dense woods, and across a vegetable garden that we learned was the school's. Finally, there was the school itself.

We stood a moment and looked at the school. Then we turned and looked down the twisting, tortuous steep path we had surmounted. It had been a hard climb, and we had come a long way up; but we were here. Later I would realize that the climb from the station to the top of the ridge had been only the beginning of the path of my life's work. That path would continue to offer me just as steep a grade, just as many stones over which to stumble, just as twisting and challenging a course. But when I look back now over the way I have come, I see ahead spiritual vistas just as beautiful and rewarding, promising and challenging as I saw in actuality on that first day.

The Appalachian School was a gracious bungalow with a wide porch. Originally built as a rectory, it had grown and developed through the care and efforts of my brother Rufus and his interested friends and church groups. We hastened inside to discover an oak-paneled living room about eighteen by thirty feet in size, with great oak beams overhead. There was a huge fireplace, and on this cheerful day casement windows let in floods of sunlight.

Miss Burt told us that shortly before our arrival bedrooms had been added by completing the second floor, which had been accomplished with the installation of dormer windows. Also, with the aid of government bulletins, Rufus and Mr. George Tim Wyatt, the school's farmer, had recently put in plumbing. They had bought a water wheel for the cold spring and piped the water into Morgan Hall, the name Miss Burt had given the structure in honor of my brother.

Now, ready for the students when they arrived in the fall, was a bathroom! And in the mountains four decades ago a bathroom with running water was something to talk about.

Rufus and I had grown up in another mountain community in far western North Carolina, before good roads and accredited schools had penetrated that region. Even before his high school days were over Rufus had dreamed of such a school for his beloved mountain people. In later years he, together with our bishop, had planned to build a school in some community where the opportunities he wanted to offer were lacking, a community whose people were of substantial stock, the sort in which one might build with success.

I was soon to realize that no happier choice could have been made than Penland. These were great people, choice Americans. Here families of Buchanans still read their Bibles brought from England and traced their ancestors to President Buchanan's brother. The family of our Mr. Wyatt had emigrated from Virginia to Penland, and in the Wyatts flowed the blood of Sir Francis Wyatt, a colonial governor of Virginia. Here was a family in which inherent culture lay, here was a whole community of such blood and bearing.

In these mountains, I hasten to say, is the purest Anglo-Saxon stock in the nation. The people have been isolated in the main for some two centuries and consequently their blood lines from England and Scotland come down unmixed with other people's. Even today you frequently hear in the mountains words and expressions that those who do not know better may think are mispronunciations and bad grammar; actually they have come down, excellent English and Gaelic in their day, from the times of Shakespeare, and even, say the students of language, from Chaucer. Isolation has preserved the blood

7

lines of these people, their language, their inherent naturalness, their basic culture.

The Clinchfield Railroad had come into this country only
twenty years before that June day we got off at Penland Station, and it was the only dependable artery of travel. There
were no hard-surface highways then; the famed North Carolina mountain highways that now carry you on broad strips
of asphalt to the tops of some of our highest peaks, including Mount Mitchell, the loftiest in eastern America, were but
engineering dreams.

It was into such an isolated community that Rufus had
brought his Boston bride. At first they even lived in a one-
room cabin with a lean-to. It was entirely foreign to Made-
line's way of life, as difficult for her as Boston would have
been for me, no doubt. Soon they had the more comfortable
arrangements in the rectory, but even then she was not happy,
especially after the two babies came along. She had become
convinced that it was absolutely necessary for Rufus to accept
work in some city where there were what she termed advantages for the children. So Rufus had moved away from Penland and the Appalachian School, but his heart was still here
in these hills.

Morgan Hall was not our only building; we also had Ridgeway. This was a long, two-story structure resembling a bar-
racks, which had been put up as a boys' shop. But it would
actually serve as a classroom and library, with one room set
aside as a chapel where we could hold Sunday school classes
and Sunday worship services as often as some clergyman could
get to us.

We felt almost wickedly luxurious as we settled in Morgan
Hall with its running water and bathroom, three bedrooms,

office and a study, all on the first floor. With Miss Burt, Mabel and me were two other women who were combining a vacation with hard work. It was to be a busy and interesting summer. We cooked, canned food for the winter, conducted Sunday school, discussed farming problems with Mr. Wyatt, did everything we could toward getting Morgan Hall and Ridgeway ready for the opening of school in the fall. And for recreation we visited the neighbors.

One of these neighbors was Aunt Susan Phillips. Rufus had written me about her. She lived some distance away from the school, Rufus had said, but he didn't say how far. And he had added what he knew would be for me an intriguing note: Aunt Susan had done a sizable amount of hand-weaving. In those years little hand-weaving was being done in this country, and we were growing desperately afraid that if something were not done quickly to revive the craft, it would soon become a lost art.

Rufus had written that he hoped I could learn to weave at the school, and possibly interest others enough to revive an art that had lingered longer in the mountains than anywhere else. He told me that Aunt Susan was the only person he had found in the county who had ever done weaving. And Aunt Susan was in her nineties!

So we determined that at the first opportunity we would go to see Aunt Susan. She lived over on Snow Creek, we found out, but no one seemed to know just where. Mr. Wyatt thought it was about two miles and a half, but he wasn't sure.

The day finally came when we could spare the time, and we started off to visit the venerable old lady. It was just after breakfast when we left Morgan Hall. We walked down hill and up, and down again, over rocky, furrowed roads, through short cuts, along bypaths, around big rocks, over fallen tree trunks. After miles of walking we met a man and asked him how far it was to Aunt Susan Phillips' house. He puckered his brow and studied a moment. "Well," he opined, "from here I reckon it must be nigh on to two miles and a half."

"Well," my friend suggested, "we may be treading water, but we aren't walking backwards anyway."

So we trudged on, relieved when we came to a downhill stretch but discouraged when we began another uphill climb. We crossed small streams, pushed brambles and vines out of our way to keep to the twisting path, and plodded across hollows. Then we met another man. We told him we were on our way to the home of Aunt Susan Phillips.

"Can you please tell us about how far it is from here?" we asked.

The stranger assumed an air of solemnity and carefully considered our question, and only after due deliberation did he answer:

"Right from here, best I can figure it, 'twould be about two miles and a half."

We thanked him wearily, and resumed our walking.

"I've never walked so long and so far in my life to stay in one place," Mabel observed, not too happily. We were sure we had more than walked Mr. Wyatt's two miles and a half and we were confident we had trudged the first stranger's two miles and a half. But we were not willing to turn back, even though we were very footsore and hungry by now.

When we were certain we had walked that third two and a half miles, we came to an open place and saw in the field down below us two sunbonneted women planting corn. We called down to them: "Could you ladies please give us directions how to get to Aunt Susan Phillips' house?"

One of them pointed to the other. "Here she is."

And there she was indeed, ninety-four years old and planting corn!

They came in from the field, put on dinner over the open fire in the fireplace; they hung pots on the crane and laid out bread in a Dutch oven set on the hearth over a bed of bright red coals. And that meal! We were as hungry as bears after having walked so far, and the food was delicious. I shall never forget how good it tasted. There were corn pone and steaming biscuits, ham and gravy, beans and potatoes, homemade cheese, jams, jellies. It was wonderful. Fresh sweet milk and buttermilk, cold from the spring, coffee, and I don't remember what else.

But an even more wonderful treat was awaiting us. When we had eaten until we were stuffed, Aunt Susan showed us all of her hand-woven coverlets, some in blue and white, some in rose madder, blue and white. Most of them were woven in the traditional pattern called Cat's Track and Snail's Trail.

Nor were these the only prizes we were to see that day. Aunt Susan and her two daughters (one of whom had been planting corn with her) were wearing linsey-woolsey skirts and basques; they showed us yardage in reserve for future needs. Aunt Susan had woven all this years before, when her eyes were much younger and sharper.

We noticed that most of the materials were of a brown color, dyed, they told us, with walnut hulls or walnut roots, whichever happened to be handiest at the time. At the bottoms of the skirts there were stripes in various vegetable-dye colors—indigo blue, the yellow of hickory bark, tan from onion skins, green produced by dyeing yarn first in the ooze of hickory bark and then, after it had dried, in an indigo bath. There was nothing harsh in Aunt Susan's colors; all were soft and mellow and rich. For me her coverlets were the greatest attraction; I fairly ogled them, I felt their softness and perfection of texture, I marveled at their color. I yearned to know how to create such materials and such patterns. All the way home I thought of those beautiful specimens, each worthy of immortality in some museum, and of what a tragedy it would be were the art of creating such things lost to succeeding generations.

We got home that night in time for supper, after walking three times the two miles and a half to Aunt Susan's, and the same distance back. It had been a big day. More importantly, it had deepened my determination to do everything I could to help preserve for America and the world the rapidly dying handicraft skills, particularly hand-weaving, that had been for so long a distinctive part of living in our North Carolina mountains.

Later one of our teachers bought a pedometer and we took it along the next time we walked to Aunt Susan's. The distance recorded, we were not surprised to discover, was seven and a half miles. Things are big in our mountains—the hills, the hospitality and genuineness of the people, the love of freedom, the flowers, the trees, yes, and even the miles.

We often took walks in those days. We visited other neighbors who lived in the vicinity of the school, but we also went to see special beauty spots in the region.

Frequently acting as our guide on such occasions was a neighbor whom I shall call by the admittedly fabricated but nevertheless descriptive name of Tippytoe Golightly. I have heard it said that Tippytoe took pride in the fact that the revenue officers had never been able to pin on him any charge related to the manufacture or dispensing of a liquid product derived from corn grown in his vicinity and rather widely known—and, I should add, appreciated—by the name of moonshine. That I can easily believe. Tippytoe knew the woods and all living things in them, and he was familiar with all the hidden places. He and nature were in tune.

Somebody told me a story about Tippytoe, which I like. It went something like this: My brother Rufus was the first Episcopalian to live in this neighborhood, and also the first man these people had known who never wore a hat. Ergo, Episcopalianism and hatlessness were related. Well, Tippytoe was in a secluded spot back in the hills one day, having just run off a batch of moonshine, when the revenue officers came crashing through the bushes. But the moonshiner managed to get away just in the nick of time. Later, however, the officers spotted Tippytoe and arrested him.

"For what?" he innocently asked the revenuers.

"For making moonshine liquor, of course," they replied, and they described the exact location of his still. He protested that he knew nothing about it. Whereupon they produced his hat, which in his hurry to get away he had left behind.

"Tippytoe," one of them said, "we got you this time, and you know it. You ran out from under your hat. We found it right there at the still and the hat puts you there. You know that's your hat; we've caught you not far away and you don't have a hat on. How do you explain not having a hat?"

"Easy," said Tippytoe. "I'm an Episcopalian."

Tippytoe was locally famous for his ability to outrun the revenue officers, many of whom were themselves fleet of foot. A man told me that once Tippytoe was helping prune apple trees in the school orchard when he saw two strange men com-

13

ing around the curve in the road. A sort of sixth sense, perhaps extrasensory perception, told Tippytoe that the men were revenuers seeking him.

"When Tippytoe seen those strangers," my informant declared, "he just sort of riz off the ground and he didn't touch it again till he hit the top o' the Blue Ridge."

That first summer at the Appalachian School was a busy and adventuresome time, as have been all the summers since, in fact. What with getting meals three times a day and attending to the various other household duties, planning social activities for all ages, visiting the neighbors for miles around, supervising the farm operation—which meant saying either yes or no and trying to fit the two words into the right places—the summer days were full and meaningful.

While Miss Burt was with us that summer she very ably took the lead in directing affairs, but I was soon to have to do my own thinking, deciding and managing. It seems to me that ever since that summer, the things I have had to do, the things that have been most worth while, have been those that I have known least how to do. Perhaps that's the way we learn. If it is, I have indeed been exposed to a mountain of learning.

Miss Burt had to leave in time to get back to Michigan for the opening of the fall term of her school, where she was a tremendously important cog in the machinery that ran it. But that fall Mrs. Mabel Evans came from Berwyn, a suburb of Chicago, to visit us. Her little daughter had been one of my pupils there.

As soon as Mrs. Evans arrived in Penland she gave helpful Mr. Meacham, the Penland Station agent, a message to be telegraphed her husband telling him of her safe arrival, and ending, "Love, Mabel." Mr. Meacham always used his judgment in dealing with our telegrams; he would telephone us immediately if he considered the matter urgent but would put the message in our mailbox if time was not important. And often he would give good advice on how to answer telegrams we had received, or even suggest ways of handling the situation involved.

So when Mrs. Evans handed Mr. Meacham her telegram, he carefully perused her writing. Then he scratched his head and asked, "What's that last word there?"

"Love," she replied. "L-o-v-e."

"Ain't necessary," he declared, and scratched it out. Mr. Meacham saw no need of cluttering up the wires.

Shortly after Mrs. Evans arrived several of the young men around Penland suggested an evening's trip up Hoot Owl Hollow to visit the Hoppes family, all of whom were known in our community as musicianers, the term our people used in describing persons who played musical instruments. Mrs. Hoppes, Myrtle and Ledger were guitar players, and Mr. Hoppes played the banjo and fiddle. He was also a natural-born impersonator and, I was soon to discover, one of the rarest personalities I have ever encountered.

To get up to their home we had to walk, of course, and we had to cross a river. And the only way we could get across the stream was on a trestle of the little narrow-gauge railroad used to haul feldspar down from the Hoot Owl mines. The trestle was high above the shallow, rock-filled river.

When we reached the trestle that night we discovered to our great chagrin that the dinky engine had been left on it. We would have to maneuver our way around the little engine in the darkness. There was so little room to get past it that a misstep would send us tumbling to our deaths, most likely, on the rocks below.

Even I, country gal and mountain goat that I was, scrambled around that engine with my heart in my throat. As for Mrs. Evans, to whom even a country road was an adventure, this experience was more than a major operation, for it resulted in complete speech paralysis. Mrs. Evans, as much as anyone I believe I ever knew, enjoyed conversation and could turn it on and let it run endlessly. But this night, as she eased by the engine on the trestle, she uttered not one syllable. I had never known such a situation, and her silence disturbed me even more than my own crossing of the narrow bridge.

In fact, Mrs. Evans hardly spoke again—not more than a few words at most—until after we had returned home; and not until breakfast next morning did she really regain her ability of self-expression customarily demonstrated. Only then did I know that the paralysis had been but temporary.

The visit to the Hoppes family that night was an experience I shall never forget, and the beginning of a friendship that has lasted throughout the years. Mr. Hoppes regaled us with stories about himself, about his neighbors, about Court Week at Bakersville, the county seat, about any number of experiences that appealed to him. But not once did he tell a story with a sting; never did he utter a word that might injure someone's feelings or reputation. Friendly, kindly, believing and telling the best about everybody, he nevertheless was a narrator who never missed an entertaining episode or failed properly to embellish it.

Some of the stories he told were about a delightful character named Uncle Sol. Uncle Sol had died soon after I came to Penland, and I never had the pleasure of knowing him. Uncle

Sol, I had heard, was a great storyteller who delighted even in telling stories on himself. And Penland folk who knew them both declared that Mr. Hoppes in telling Uncle Sol's stories sounded for all the world like the old gentleman himself.

A choice Uncle Sol story concerned his experience with an obstreperous steer calf. I'll try to relate it as nearly as possible the way Mr. Hoppes told it that night in his house.

"One day I was out in the woodshed a-workin' on a ox yoke, en my boy Price come along en he says, 'What you a-makin', Pa?' I says, 'Aw, go on 'bout yer bus'ness en leave me 'lone.' He says, 'Hit looks like you could tell me what yer a-makin'. Hit ain't no secret, air hit?'

"So, jes' to git shet o' him en stop his botherin' me I says, 'Well, if you jes' have to know, hit's a ox yoke.'

" 'A ox yoke?' he says. 'How in tarnation you aim to use a ox yoke when you ain't got but one steer calf?'

"I says, 'I done contracted with Steve Sparks fer another little ol' steer calf, en I aim to break our'n in, en then when I git the one from Steve hit won't be no trouble at all to break t'other one in, en then we'll have us a good team,' I says.

" 'But, Pa,' says Price, 'how in the world air ye a-aimin' to break in one calf by hisself?'

" 'Aw, go on off en leave me 'lone, en by the time I git this here thing done I'll be ready with a plan,' I says.

"So when I got that yoke all shaped up en ready fer use I called Price en I says, 'Price, bring that thar calf 'round here now, en we'll jes' try him out with this here yoke.'

"Price he brung the calf, en I says, 'Now, Price, we'll jes' put one end o' this here yoke over his neck, en put the bow in place en key hit in, en then I'll jes' put t'other end o' the yoke over my shoulders, en I know I can pull as much as this here little ol' calf.'

17

"So that's jes' what we done. We got the yoke over the calf's neck, en the bow in place, en my head in t'other end, en then I says, 'Now, Price, pick up that thar little rope I got tied to the yoke, en walk us 'round en see how we does.'

"Well, Price he walked us 'round the yard, en I says, 'We're a-doin' fine, Price. We're a-doin' real fine. He ain't a-goin' to be no trouble a-tall to break in. Now git that ol' sled thar en the woodshed en hitch hit onto this here yoke, en see how we pulls.'

"Hit worked fine, en then I says, 'Price, we ain't a-goin' to have no trouble with this here calf a-tall. Now le's see how hit'll pull a load. You git on the sled en see how we does.'

"Well, by that time that thar calf had a-done 'bout all he cared to do that mornin', en he started off down the road a-trottin'. Price he tried to hold that thar calf back, but the little ol' rope broke. Then hit was me en that calf down the hill, me a-runnin' to keep up, becuz I had my neck in that thar yoke en hit was either keep up or leave my neck behint. En Price he couldn't do nothin' but look, helpless like.

"But 'bout then I seen my wife Mariah a-comin' 'round the bend in the road. She been down to the store en was a-comin' home. 'Bout then she seen us a-comin', me en the calf.

" 'Ketch us, Mariah!' I hollered. 'We're a-runnin' away!'

"Well, that thar woman come a-runnin' to meet us, en she took a-holt o' my end o' the yoke, en helt on fer dear life.

" 'Turn me loose, Mariah,' I hollered, 'en ketch a-holt o' that thar calf! I'll stop!' "

Another person whom I met about that time was in her way just as unique and charming an individual as Uncle Sol had been. Both had the stamp of the mountains upon them, authentic and immediately recognizable.

I met her early that September. The time drew near for the school session to open, and Mabel Fauble and I went across the mountains for some girls who were to be boarding students. First we went to the Mission House in Linville, presided over by delightful Miss Irene Lazier, who had worked happily and faithfully with Rufus and the little church group in that community.

Linville, one of North Carolina's famed mountain resorts, is about twenty-five miles from Penland. Now you can spin over well-engineered hard-surface highways from one community to the other, allowing for the mountain curves, in considerably less than an hour. But in those days it was an achievement to make the journey. From the school we walked down to Penland Station and boarded a train to Johnson City, Tennessee, some sixty miles away, which took about two hours and a half. The train arrived in the Tennessee city near nightfall, and we spent the night there. Next day we boarded the narrow-gauge little train officially known as rolling stock of the East Tennessee and Western North Carolina Railroad, but more affectionately called Tweetsie, and on Tweetsie we rode to Linville.

We went directly to the Mission House where Miss Lazier greeted us warmly and made us welcome. Early next morning we started on our trek to the homes of two girls who were to be members of our Penland family for the next year.

One of the girls was Maudie. I must tell about her. Of all the wonderful people I have known in the mountains, and I have spent most of my life in the mountains, I'm sure I've never known a more interesting person than Maudie. Au-

19

thentic, genuine, individual and unique, Maudie has been one of my favorites since the day I first saw her.

We found her over on the slope of the Grandmother Mountain. Grandmother is opposite the Grandfather, and it's a gentle slope, more feminine than rugged Grandfather.

We returned to Penland in reverse order from the way we had come, and finally we got back to Appalachian School. The distance across the mountains was actually about eighteen miles, Rufus said, and unencumbered we could have walked it in much less time. Rufus several times has walked it.

Their first train ride was a gala occasion for the girls, and they were especially interested in the news butch and his wares—chewing gum, peanuts, soda pop and the rest. It was on that train ride back to Penland that we began to know each other. I am sure that life has never been quite the same for them or for us since the day we trudged up the hill to end our journey from the Grandmother to Penland.

Maudie was seventeen. At that time mountain girls unmarried at seventeen were beginning to be considered old maids. I don't know how Maudie had escaped matrimony for so long; I don't recall ever having asked her. I wish I had; I know her answer would have been priceless.

After supper that night I took the girls upstairs, put the kerosene lamp on the ledge in the hall and said, "Now, girls, can you see from here to get your nightgowns and get into bed?"

"Whar they at?" Maudie asked me.

I said, "Where did you put your things when you unpacked?" And then I remembered that the only baggage Maudie had brought was a shoebox. "What do you sleep in at home, Maudie?" I asked.

"My shimmy-shirt," she replied.

I could think of no answer to that, so I went on to point out the bathroom. "Turn on the water in the tub," I told them.

Maudie looked, then said, "Lordy, I wouldn't git in thar. I know I'd freeze to death."

One morning, when it was very cold, Mrs. Evans went downstairs and found a big fire roaring in the wide fireplace. The fireplace was our only source of heat until after the frost, when the furnace was put in. There were big logs on the fire, of the size that Mr. Wyatt ordinarily brought in; but Mr. Wyatt wasn't at the school that morning, Mrs. Evans knew, and she wondered how those big logs happened to be there. She asked Maudie, who was sitting before the blaze, "Who brought in those logs?"

"I did," Maudie replied. "I went out and got 'em in my bar' feet."

"Why, Maudie," Mrs. Evans protested, "didn't you know there's frost on the ground this morning? You'll freeze your feet. Why didn't you put on your shoes?"

"Well," Maudie said serenely, "my shoes was upstairs, my feet was down here, and the wood was out yander."

Later that year Maudie had a sore throat and a persistent cold. I took her to Dr. Peterson in Spruce Pine. Even to get to that town, now only six miles away by an excellent highway, we had to walk down to Penland Station and take the train, and then walk back, or walk down and ride back. It would have been impossible to get over the road in an automobile.

Dr. Peterson put his finger into Maudie's mouth to see if she had tonsils, and then I saw him withdraw it quickly and walk over to the basin to wash it.

"I'll never do that again without giving her a general

21

anesthetic," he said. And he showed me where Maudie had bitten through the skin.

When we came back home I was telling one of the teachers about it.

"Maudie," she asked the child, "what in the world did you do that for?"

And Maudie said, "Well, I didn't like the feelin' of his finger in thar, and that's the only way I knowed to git it out."

Maudie is now living back over around Grandmother. She is married to a good man, I have been told, has several children and is doing well. I am happy that she is. As I said, Maudie was one of my all-time favorites. She was always fairly bursting with originality and there was something of the sturdiness and strength of the mountains about her. I believe something would have been lacking in my life had I never crossed paths with her. In our weaving at Penland we like to put in bright threads here and there to give color and sparkle and life to our fabrics. For me Maudie is one of the brightest threads.

We worked especially hard that first year at Appalachian School but there were diversions, too. I shall never forget those Friday and Saturday nights—social nights, we called them. Once a month they meant square dancing and doing the Virginia Reel.

As soon as we could get supper over, do the dishes, and dress ourselves up, the neighbors would begin drifting in. And soon the dancing would begin.

Our best evenings were when the Hoppes family came to play for us. As they began tuning up, I got the same thrill I get before the opening of a grand opera when the musicians assemble in the orchestra pit and start making those investigatory sounds with their instruments. In both instances, to me even the floor boards seem to be charged with an emotional expectancy.

When the musicianers had warmed up their strings to their satisfaction, we would line up and go into the Virginia Reel with everything that was in us. Tall Harry Willis or handsome Dean Tainter, the storekeeper's son, or some other local Beau Brummel would call the figures. And how those mountain boys could call figures! Gertrude Anthony wrote home to her mother in Chicago: "You should hear them call, 'Swing her like you love her,' and see the way they swing me!"

Big, little, old, young—everybody took part in those dances. Our friend Mr. Tainter seldom missed a dance. Many a time when the sets were long and his two hundred pounds began to weigh heavily, I have seen him pick up a stool, carry it through the dance with him and between his turns grab a spell of sitting.

"Lassy" time was another diverting season up in our country. They didn't say 'lasses for molasses, their word was lassy. As cold weather approached, we looked forward eagerly to the time for b'iling lassy.

That year Mr. Wyatt had planted sorghum cane, and one cold morning he came to me with a worried look on his tanned face. He said he was sure there would be frost that night, and if the cane was to be saved, we would have to strip it before nightfall.

I knew that it would take more than Mr. Wyatt and his helper, Mr. Thomas, to pull all that cane fodder. While we were talking about it one of the girls told me that she had pulled fodder at home. "I'd just as soon pull fodder as wash them dishes," she declared, "and maybe a little sooner."

23

It seemed cruel to let a girl go out on such a cold day and do a man's work—and hard work, too—in the field. But I settled my conscience by bundling up and going out with Mandy and the men. Of course, she took it in her stride. Next day I had cramps in my fingers. But we saved the cane.

After fodder pulling came the fun. Mr. Fate Conley—his name was Lafayette but everybody called him Fate—had a molasses mill, the kind with cogwheels into which the sorghum cane was fed. A mule is hitched to one end of a long beam, and the other end is attached to the cogwheels, so that when the mule walks slowly around a circle described by the beam, the cogwheels press out the juice from the cane. The juice is caught in a bucket which is then emptied into a large vat. This vat sits over a sort of furnace constructed of native stone, and in the furnace a steady fire is kept burning.

On molasses-making days we would go over and watch as soon as school was out in the afternoon. Aside from chestnut and chinquapin hunting, what could be more fun in the fall than taking part in molasses-making, even if only to watch? We had a part, however. We would beg a nice stalk of cane from Uncle Fate, dip it into the vat of boiling juice and, when it had cooled sufficiently, run the stalk between our lips. Delicious? There is no other taste like it. The same stalk was used over and over as we redipped it.

I recall one day we had two city guests with us, practical Mrs. Breed from Milwaukee and dainty, correct Mrs. Anthony from Berwyn, Illinois. Mrs. Anthony watched us dipping and redipping.

"Do you really think this is sanitary?" she finally ventured to ask her companion.

I listened for Mrs. Breed's reply. "Oh," she said in a motherly manner, "I think after it's boiled it's probably all right." Then, to my joy, both ladies took Uncle Fate's proffered stalks, dipped them into the vat and sucked them with as much gusto as the rest of us. I agree with Mrs. Breed. I don't believe a germ could withstand a boiling in that bubbling cane juice.

That winter an elderly teacher in the primary department of the school contracted pneumonia. She had often told us that she had had pneumonia before. Her doctor had said that if she ever had it again it would kill her. So when she found that she had contracted it, she chose the hymns to be used at her funeral and made other preparations for shuffling off her mortal coil. Our household was clothed in gloom and heavy dread.

Dr. Peterson came to see her when she first took sick, but told us quite frankly that he had so many influenza cases that he would not be able to take on this pneumonia case. He explained that the old lady's greatest need was adequate nursing. Grace Bailey, a trained nurse who was a native of our section, was home on vacation and the doctor thought we might be able to get her.

So I went begging. I had never met Grace but I knew her family at Penland. She agreed to come, and her arrival changed the gloomy school atmosphere into one of confidence and cheerfulness.

The teacher was getting on fairly well until she developed pleurisy. Again Dr. Peterson came up, and he told us that we should get her to the hospital in Johnson City as quickly as possible.

This meant bundling her up against the rigors of the winter weather and literally carrying her the mile or more down the hill to Penland Station. So Grace fixed her up, and Mr.

25

Wyatt, Mr. Thomas and other neighbors gathered to carry her on a cot to the station. We realized that this presented in itself quite a problem. How, for instance, would we get her through the blind gate? A blind gate, it should be explained to those not familiar with the term, is a gap left in a fence through which persons can make their way by twisting a bit, but cattle, being unable to maneuver in the same manner, are effectively blocked.

I went down to see how the men were going to handle the gate and proceed down the steep hillside without accident. At the gate I watched in wide-eyed amazement as the men lifted the cot up level with the top of the fence, passed it over and then let it down on the other side without a slip or jolt.

The teacher got well. But for the remainder of the year the job of teaching the primary children fell to me. And that was only one of many duties I had. As a matter of fact, I have a notion that if each of the workers during those early years of the Appalachian School were to list only a part of the work they did, every list would include teaching, cooking, washing dishes, scrubbing floors, washing and ironing clothes, gardening and a bit of nursing. Those were busy times.

But I hesitate to mention one of my duties, and I blush even yet when I do so. I have always been allergic to figures, but as so often happens at Penland, I had to do something for which I was poorly prepared. I was the bookkeeper. It was a duty that I just ran up against, and there was nothing for me to do but grapple with it.

I had a good friend named Paul Willis, who kept books for one of the mining companies. Paul, a social asset in our community and a regular guest on Virginia Reel nights, came to realize what a problem it was for me to keep the books. So very generously he agreed to check my books at the end of each month.

Finally he came to me one day and said, "Lucy, if you just will not put down anything in your books, no figures at all, I can do it from the stubs in your checkbook. That will be easier for you, and I'm sure it will be easier for me!" I was delighted to accede to his request.

There were times at Penland when I thought that if I could go back to my old teaching job, even teachers' meetings would be bliss. And to be in a position where I was told what to do, where decisions were made for me and all I had to do was follow them seemed the greatest joy a human could yearn for. I felt that if only there were some way I could shrug off responsibility, where I wasn't being called on every day and hour, it seemed, to make an important decision, how easy and enjoyable living would be.

When in those early days the world seemed to get so heavy on my shoulders that I felt I could not stagger any longer under its weight, I would steal off down the hill to that warm, friendly, understanding new friend whom I already considered an old friend, Mrs. Henry Willis. She seemed to own the wisdom of the ages. And along with wisdom, she had a native wit and an immeasurable faith. A day with her would always send me home with a feeling that all anyone has to do is live one day at a time, live it well and wisely and happily. And surely, I would say to myself, any of us can manage one day at a time.

Looking back, I don't believe I ever discussed with Mrs. Willis any of my problems, as such. I would just spend a quiet Sunday with her and her husband, discussing whatever might come into our minds as we sat by the fire and cracked walnuts on a flatiron. Every time I went to the Willises I came away refreshed in body and mind, renewed in spirit. But for that dear lady, I wonder if there would now be a Penland School of Handicrafts.

Nor must I forget Mr. Wyatt. He brightened our days. If we happened to wake up on the wrong side of the bed, or if someone were homesick—and one can be really homesick back in the hills with the high mountains shutting out the world— or if for any other reason our faces and our spirits were long, Mr. Wyatt's ringing voice, contagious wit and soaring spirits brought sunshine and warmth to us. He would set the world right again. No one but me knows how heavily I leaned on him for moral support and courage.

Now in my personal journey I was coming inexorably to a place where the road forked. I must soon decide, I realized, whether I would remain at Penland or return for a time at least to the teaching position I had left.

As a child I had planned that when I grew up I would teach in Rufus' school. But I had taught in a Chicago suburb, had worked in the Children's Bureau in Chicago and had enjoyed a delicious taste of music, opera and the theater. I had even seen the wonderful Pavlova in three performances in two days. To ease my conscience during that time, I had told myself it was better not to go to Penland the first years of Rufus' being there with his bride, but to let them adjust to marriage and Penland first. Anyway in my mind I had been saying, "One more year; then I will make a decision."

Finally I had come. And I had found a great appeal. Life at Penland was much as it was in my happy childhood in the mountains of western North Carolina. Even just that one home of Mr. and Mrs. Henry Willis had come to mean so much to me; it had so much the flavor of my own home. Many factors weighed in favor of my staying.

But other facts argued that I should leave. Rufus had found it necessary to give up his cherished work. How could I do a job about which I knew so little, for which I felt myself so inadequately equipped, without the direction and help and counsel of my brother? And yet, after the start Rufus had made, how could I leave Penland and allow all his work and dreams to go to naught when there was a chance that I might see them through?

I shall never forget that night. A silvery sheen from a glorious full moon veiled the shadowy Blue Ridge, and in the dark hollows below, whip-poor-wills called. For hours I had been wrestling with myself. Finally I let go for a little. As I sat by my window, the beauty of the scene hallowed the moment and quieted my spirit. Suddenly, my way ahead was clear, and my decision was made. I would stay at Penland.

CHAPTER 2

ITTING HERE TODAY, looking out the front windows of my second-floor apartment in The Pines to the smooth roundness of now denuded Pine Knoll and the rise upon rise of the calmly sleeping Blue Ridge beyond, I am content with that decision made long ago.

In casting my lot with Penland, I had elected to stay in my kind of country with my kind of folk. I am glad I did, for I recognize the truth of the old saying that you can take a mountain boy or girl out of the mountains but you can't take the mountains out of a mountain boy or girl. I've never been away from the mountains for any great length of time, and I never expect to be.

When I gaze west to the symmetrical cone of Bailey's Peak, I can see clearly outlined in my memory the log cabin in which I was born, seven miles from Franklin, North Carolina. I was the sixth of nine children. My parents had moved there from the near-by home of my maternal grandparents, the Albert Silers. And when I was still very young they moved to a home about sixty miles away, near Murphy in the westernmost tip of the state. I often recall the delightful days of my childhood, and these blessed memories have warmed and strengthened me and inspired me to brave tasks at hand and to challenge larger ones ahead.

Beyond old Bailey and the flown years I can listen to Mother and Father reading aloud on long winter evenings as Mother knitted stockings for the children. Amazingly, Mother would read and knit at the same time; it's still a marvel to me how she did it. I remember most their reading Dickens. I recall that my father once asked his friend Colonel Pierson if he had read all the Dickens novels.

"No," said the colonel, "I wouldn't want to keep on living if I couldn't look forward to another Dickens novel I hadn't read."

The older I grow, the more grateful I am for parents such as ours, whose discipline was by love. We could not endure to do things that would grieve our parents.

We lived simply, in a house with no plumbing and no electricity, but I never think of it as having been a difficult way of living. On Sunday mornings there was a great stir as Mother got us washed and dressed, the older ones helping the younger ones, to go to Sunday school and church. We drove there in a buckboard pulled by a white pony. Mother and Papa sat on the spring seat, Mother holding the baby and Papa driving, and we children sat on the floor in the back, with our feet hanging over the sides.

Once a month a clergyman would conduct services, first in

a little upstairs office room and later in a church built by the efforts of the two Episcopal families in our community, the Beals and the Morgans. Neither family had money, but the two must have had persuasive powers, for the clergyman volunteered to match every dollar they raised for building the house of worship. Mother must have written to everyone whose address she could get. In each letter she enclosed a card, made in Papa's printing office, with a hole in it the size of a quarter. The cards came back filled; I imagine a great part of the little church was built with the quarters returned in Mama's cards.

On Sundays when the clergyman was not there Papa served as lay reader. He usually read a sermon by Phillips Brooks. Ordinarily he wore a wing collar and a black four-in-hand tie, but one Sunday which I shall never forget he wore a little grass-green bow tie. Laura, the baby of maybe two years, had not noticed this until he began reading the sermon. When she spied it from her seat in Mother's lap, she leaned forward and spoke out boldly, "Father, where did you get that tie?"

Papa ignored the question, of course, and went on reading. But Laura was not to be denied. "Father," she demanded more loudly, "where did you get that tie?" Mother tried to quiet her, but to no avail. When Father still did not answer, she asked again.

Then Papa paused, looked toward her. "Mother gave it to me," he said, and returned to his reading.

Papa always hitched the pony across the street from the church, in front of the courthouse. On summer days when the church doors were open, the pony could surely hear the Sunday service, but paid no attention to it until Papa began reading the sermon in his strong voice. Then that pony invariably whinnied! This was a part of the ceremony of Sunday's service.

As far as I know, when we were children there were no such things as dime stores, certainly not in our part of the country. Our playthings were much more original—and more appreciated and enjoyed, I'm quite sure—than the things bought for children today. They had a kind of personality that, to me, seems lacking in modern toys. We had outdoor playhouses and made stick-dolls. I wonder if other children made them too. Mountain laurel, which we called ivy, made the best dolls. We broke off little twigs of ivy and used the fork for the legs and the stem for the rest of the body. A wee bit of cloth with a hole in the center made the dress. You just slipped it over the stem and there you were! A few tiny pieces of cloth would provide a whole wardrobe.

We would use tiny twigs to pin together big oak leaves and make hats, trimming them with flowers in season. Sometimes we would make things as complicated as shawls and jackets. With mosses and stones we made all the furniture a playhouse could need. And among the furniture would always be a piano. For our music, besides singing, we would make our own musical instruments by putting pieces of paper over hair combs, loosely. By blowing on these in just the right way we could produce a tune.

We played all kinds of games, too, both original and traditional. The most complicated was "Old Granny Hoop-Scoot." It took all of us, and a like number of cousins, to stage a really good game of this.

One of our favorite outdoor games was playing church. In our yard there was a big rock that made an excellent pulpit, and my brother Ralph was always the best preacher to be had.

He could shout and cavort about, moving his congregation to tears or to laughter—mostly laughter.

In the many years since those dear days I have often wished that I might do again what I did as a child. At times when I knew I had failed to be my best self, when I was discouraged at not having been what I had hoped to be, I have wished I could once again climb into Mother's lap and say, "Mother, I just feel bad all over."

Mother would always say, "What's the matter with my little lamb?"

"I don't know. I just don't know. I can't tell whether my stomach aches," I would tell her, "or whether it's my conscience hurting." And then in a moment everything would be talked over and smoothed out and life would become normal and happy again.

My father was a visionary and a humorist. I do not know when the Blue Ridge Parkway and the Great Smoky Mountains National Park were first thought of and planned. I do know that Papa used to look out over the ravine in front of our house to the blue mountains beyond and talk of the time when our government would seek to protect the wildlife and preserve the forests of our mountains.

Back of our house there was a grove that he trimmed out carefully, a place where he cherished and protected special flowers and ferns. When my younger sister Laura was just old enough to manage the difficult words, he taught her to call this little grove the National Appalachian Park, Forest Preserve and Zoological Garden. He took great delight in hearing the little mite of a girl rattle off the imposing designation.

When I was fourteen our mother died.

After Papa had been a widower several years, he wrote all

his children and asked if we would object to his marrying again. None objected, and Father married Miss Ada Warner, who was just about the age of our eldest sister. She was from Atlanta; they had met when she was summering at Murphy.

Ada was one of ten children. When Papa went down to ask Mrs. Warner for her daughter's hand, she said her only objection was the considerable difference in their ages. He was there on a Sunday and all ten children were at the dinner table. The proposal was being discussed, along with Mrs. Warner's objection, when Father spoke out.

"Mrs. Warner," he said, "if this is going to worry you, I won't say another word to Ada about it. I'll just take you instead."

There was such a burst of laughter over this and so much amusement that after a while the "children" explained to Father that that was just what they had been accusing their mother of trying to arrange.

In later years my sister Laura married Ada's brother Ben and became her stepmother's sister-in-law. This provoked much discussion concerning the relationships of any possible children to each other. Ada had none, but Laura did, and her children called Ada Aunt-Grandma.

Another happy memory has done much, I am confident, to shape my life. I do not remember ever hearing my father say an unkind word to or about anybody. As far as he was concerned, the whole world was good. I still quote to myself, and sometimes to others, some of the things he said to us often: "Never accuse anyone of taking anything unless you see him take it." And again, "We have no right to pray 'Lead us not into temptation' and leave temptation in other people's way."

CHAPTER 3

IN OUR SOUTHERN Appalachians old-time singings still afford one of the favorite forms of
recreation. In recent years over on the slopes
of old Grandfather Mountain, said by geologists to be one of
the oldest in the western hemisphere, the mountain folk have
been having a "singing on the mountain," and to this event
each year come literally thousands who sing and picnic
throughout a long summer day.

But community singings go back beyond my childhood.
In fact, I do not know when or how they started; it may be
that they are traditional in our Anglo-Saxon upbringing.

On our teaching staff the first year at Appalachian School
was Ruth Phelps, who had been in normal school with me at
Mount Pleasant. My sister Esther Freas soon joined us as house-
mother and general household helper. These two quickly became distinct social assets. One of the reasons was that they
were good singers.

Ruth and Esther were able to fit in wherever they might be needed. They joined what was called in those days a singing school, which was held periodically in the various communities, at which a local singer would teach the gospel hymns, using books with an unusual system of notation. The sound of the note was recognized by its shape rather than by its position on the staff. Here is an example:

To explore the history of these notes would be an interesting study. I do not know their origin, but I have been told that monks in the old monasteries of the early Christian era used such notes before the musical staff came into being.

In this old-time singing school the leader explains to the beginners the sounds of the different shapes; he goes through the scales in the do, re, mi language, using the tuning fork to set the proper tones.

When he thinks that they are ready for the first hymn, he sounds the key note, the sopranos, altos, basses and tenors all get their respective tones in a hummed do, mi, sol, do, and the singing begins.

Esther, Ruth and six-foot-five-inch Mr. Jim Turbyfill made a wonderful trio. Mr. Turbyfill's voice was so deep it reached down to his toes.

Singing conventions or all-day singings—progenitors of to-day's "singing on the mountain" with its tens of thousands attending—were great occasions held each fall, with the churches in different communities taking turns as host churches. It's a great pity that these all-day singings are gradually being discontinued, for nothing really takes the place of them. Radio and TV cannot compare, certainly not socially.

They were tremendous occasions, eagerly looked forward to. People would plan and prepare for days ahead of time, baking and cooking. Sometimes a family would take a whole trunkful of food. Nobody ever attended a singing convention in our country without getting his fill of food as well as song.

When the morning of the great day arrived, the choirs, the congregations and the visitors from hither and yon began to gather at the appointed church. The choirs were assigned their turns, the first choir would take its position and the all-day singing would be off to a melodious start.

They began to have competitions and one choir would be voted best for the year, but after a time this competition detracted from the sheer joy of the singing and the fellowship, and it was discontinued.

If one sat through the entire six or eight hours of singing, the day could be long and tiring. But it wasn't the general practice to remain inside the church throughout the singing. Usually there were a bucket of water and a dipper on the rostrum, and from time to time people would stroll up and take a drink. Occasionally a group would get up and slip outside for a little recess. And, of course, the coming of the noon hour was eagerly anticipated, because it brought the social climax of the day, the big picnic dinner.

Tall Mr. Turbyfill was a wonderful spotter. He could lead you straight to a platter of chicken fried by the best-known chicken fryer of the region; or to string beans of a flavor that was just a little better than and slightly different from any others; or to Mrs. Hoppes' checkerboard cake; or to a particularly appetizing layer pie. It was good to have Mr. Turbyfill piloting one about the picnic table. There were too many excellent dishes to even sample every one, and at such a picnic one's capacity was soon reached and often overreached.

After the dinner and a period of conversation and relaxation, the singing convention was reassembled and the choirs sang until late afternoon. When the last song was sung and it was time to go, invitations were extended for spending the night; often invitations had been issued in advance of the convention. There were times when there were not enough visitors to go around and some family would be disappointed and have no company for the night, but it usually worked out very well.

CHAPTER 4

ON OUR Appalachian teaching staff the second year we had a young man who very soon would become one of Penland's most important and widely known assets and, perhaps even more important to us, one who would add greatly to the zest of living in our mountain community. Penland without Howard Ford would never have been the same.

Ruth Phelps, Peggy Breed and Howard taught the upper grades; I taught the first and second. Peggy was a young, beautiful, musical and deservedly popular teacher, another happy addition that year.

In late summer we heard that there would be a fair at Spruce Pine in the early fall, to be known as the Toe River Fair. Our Estatoe River, an Indian name, is known as the Toe. We were offered a free booth and invited to have an exhibit from our school.

We began at once to collect materials for our exhibit, each teacher saving samples of good work done by the school children. The day before the fair was to open Mr. Wyatt took Howard and me in a mule wagon over to the fairgrounds to arrange our display. Significantly, we included certain handicraft projects done by the children.

The exhibits were to be shown in a barracks-like building whose booths were separated only by rough studding. So we had brought hammer and tacks and in Spruce Pine we purchased a small quantity of building paper and a little colored crepe paper for decorating. Howard shinnied up posts and studding and tacked on the paper, and I looked on and contributed my approval. Our work was finished by three or four o'clock, but we were tired, dirty, hungry and more than ready to pile into Mr. Wyatt's wagon to start the two-hour journey home.

That night at the supper table we were talking about the afternoon's work. A funny thing had happened, I told them.

"One of the teachers from the Stanley McCormick School was over there helping get their exhibit set up," I said. "She noticed Howard tacking up paper and scurrying about the place, and she turned to me.

" 'How does it happen that you have an Italian boy over at your school?' she wanted to know."

Well, when I said that, everybody at the table simply squealed.

"Tony Ford," one of them shouted.

And that was where the name Tony Ford was born. There are now few people, even around Penland, who know that Tony is actually Howard Ford.

But to get back to the fair, we won a blue ribbon that year, and a blue ribbon for each of the thirty-one fairs since that first Toe River Fair. This does not mean that our exhibits were best at the fair; it means that the Fair folk purposely classed each school differently so that each would be eligible for a first prize. For example, they might class us as an industrial school and the Crossnore school over in the Linville valley as a vocational school. We were industrial to the extent that the members of our school family learned by doing all the work of our household and school, including sewing for the girls and simple woodwork for the boys.

We had developed a fairly definite routine of teaching, getting our meals and keeping house. The routine was a challenge, and but for certain extracurricular activities and recreational projects it could quickly have become burdensome.

To go back to the meals we had in those days might be considered burdensome now, too, for the Spruce Pine stores did not have the things that they offer now. Nor did we have the money if they'd had the things to sell. No green or fresh vegetables were available in the winter, and if you wanted a steak you either had to order it by mail from Johnson City or wait until someone in the neighborhood butchered a cow.

Soup was routine at noon meals in Ridgeway Hall, and since the kitchen opened off my primary room, I was the soupmaker. Day pupils brought from home whatever their mothers happened to have—a cabbage, an onion or two, a jar of beans. These we would add to our own leftovers—including even cornbread, which we found added body and flavor to the soup—and the whole thing would be dumped into a big pot. But first I would fry a slice of bacon, brown sliced onion in the bacon grease, and lead on with the various additions. The result, I often recall hungrily, was surprisingly good.

Making the soup interrupted lessons, so we began to use soup-making time for learning poems from Robert Louis Stevenson's *A Child's Garden of Verses*. And the youngsters loved it. Poetry and soup seemed to go well together.

There were diversions that kept life at Appalachian School zestful and rewarding as well as challenging and demanding. Sometimes we would attend the plays put on by the public school at Spruce Pine. We would have an early supper, walk down the slope to Penland Station, and then strike off along the railway tracks toward Spruce Pine. By walking the railroad we cut the distance from about six-and-half miles to about four miles each way. The two hours of rest while we watched the play, which usually was itself refreshing, made the walk back home not bad at all, particularly if we had moonlight.

But I'd like to recall another diversion that is not peculiar to our mountains, I understand. It may be southern, it may be even national in scope. But until one moonlight night in those early days of the school, I had never heard of it.

We were sitting on the long front porch when one of the men inquired quite innocently if any of us girls had ever been snipe-hunting. None of us had.

"It ought to be a good night to go," the young man observed. I felt suspicious of a certain tone in his voice, but I looked at dependable, loyal old Mr. Wyatt, who was studying the clear sky, and when he spoke I knew I had been wrong to suspect the visitor.

"Yes," Mr. Wyatt agreed, with a drawl, "this ought to be a good night for 'em to be runnin'."

He went on to discuss the ways of our mountain snipe and where we would most likely find them. He said the old road down by the Cold Spring would be a likely run. He even volunteered for himself and the other men to go back into the woods and sort of shoo them down along the Cold Spring road, where we would station ourselves with tow sacks to catch them.

The men told us that we should hold the tow sacks with our lanterns at the mouths so that when the snipe came down they would see the open mouths of the sacks and run into them in the belief that they were escaping into dark caves. So they hunted up the sacks and we trudged down the hill. With absolute faith in Mr. Wyatt's solemnly proclaimed view on the fitness of the night for snipe-hunting, we took our places in the old road. The men went off to chase the snipe down to us.

Well, we stood there, bent over, holding those open-mouthed tow sacks until our backs ached and our arms were numb. Finally it began to dawn upon our trusting minds that the joke was on us, and we decided to take our bags and head for home. But even then one of the women protested.

"I just don't think it's fair to the men for us to go off now. They were good enough to give us the easy job, and there's no telling how far back in the woods they've had to go to roust out those snipe."

When we got back to the house, of course, the men were there waiting. And they had quite a laugh at our gullibility, even dear old Mr. Wyatt.

That was my first and last snipe hunt.

But not long afterward I did go on another adventure.

During the summer Tony Ford had gone off on horseback with some of the young men of the neighborhood to camp at the top of Roan Mountain. That mountaintop now belongs to the National Forestry Service, and a hard-surface road recently has been completed to the very summit. One can drive the twenty-five miles to it in less than an hour now; it was in those days a long, rough trip to Roan.

Tony's tales of his camping trip were so fascinating that we resolved to include the whole school family and some of our neighbors on a week-end expedition to the top of Roan Mountain. We gathered together mule wagons to carry food and bedding—and us too when it wasn't too steep and rough for the mules.

We made the trip on a golden October day when the air was bracing. However we started so early in the morning that even after going the eight miles from Penland to Bakersville, the stars were still shining. There we started our upward climb. We pushed on until noon, when we stopped for a picnic lunch and relaxation. Then we went on again. There was a scramble to jump from the wagons at Carver's Gap, where the climb became precipitous. The wagons and provisions, we knew, were heavy enough for the mules as they strained to pull the lumbering vehicles over the big boulders along that steep path. In fact, we even contemplated strapping the bedding and provisions onto the mules' backs and leaving the wagons at the gap. But the mules made it, and so, with much huffing and puffing, did we.

We reached the top of the Roan just before dusk, while there was still light enough for us to be able to tell a potato from an apple in preparing supper. The men built the fire, and the girls cooked a quick meal. We ate wolfishly after that long, hard trip, and soon after supper and a little chatting around the camp fire, we were all ready to turn in.

The men went a little way back into the balsam forest to sleep, and we women rolled up in our blankets near the fire.

And how we slept. With our healthy sort of tiredness, the smell of the balsams and wood smoke, the sharp cleanness of the night, the blue-white blazing stars almost within reach, the utter calm and peace of the night, our sleep was relaxed and untroubled.

Until about midnight, when raindrops in our faces awakened us!

It was a gentle little shower. And there was nothing else to do anyway. So we just lay there getting our faces washed. After a while the men came out of the forest looking apologetic, though I couldn't see why. They told us that it usually rained this way in the night on the top of the Roan. But it would last only a few minutes, they assured us. They built up the fire and we waited.

The rain didn't last very long, as they had said. But it turned into sleet! And then the sleet turned to snow.

The boys hurriedly got busy with their axes. They found a place in the balsam groves big enough to make two bedrooms, one for the women, one for the men, and they set to work laying poles from balsam to balsam, placing them in the crotches formed by the limbs to provide a rough framework over which they stretched blankets. Soon they had a cozy shelter for us shivering women.

Out in front they built a roaring fire and heated stones to put at our feet. Soon we were ready to go back to sleep again.

"When you wake up in the morning don't be surprised if you find the mules have come in with you," one of the men said as they told us good night again. And sure enough, when daylight came we saw the mules standing just on the other side of the fire.

We didn't dare try to go down from the mountain top.

Everywhere there were snow and ice, and we knew that if a mule should slip he would very likely break a leg. And we couldn't go far without mules.

But we had enough food to last us three days, and the snow would hardly last as long as our food. So we decided to stay, and not to worry. There was enough wit in that crowd to keep us entertained, and there would be enough work—just feeding and watering the mules and cutting wood and keeping the fire going were major tasks—to keep us busy. No one was bored.

And the Roan was a fairyland of beauty. I have been on that mountain a number of times, but never have I seen it more beautiful. After the snow had stopped falling, the clouds came and sat down on the mountain, and every twig and balsam needle was covered with rime. There is nothing like it. Snow sifts down to cover the tops of things, but rime coats everything all over. Those who have never seen the world thus decorated should come to our mountains and stay until the clouds brush the mountain tops with rime.

We reached home with little trouble and without injury to the mules or to us. For months we continued to enjoy that unusual experience. From time to time we would hear about the house a sudden ripple of merriment and we would all run to see what particular incident of our camping trip to the Roan was being recalled. Then we would live over again those memorable three days.

CHAPTER 5

AMONG THE DAY students in our Appalachian
School were the sons and daughters of the
Wyatts and the Claud Morgans and the two
daughters of the Henry Willises.

Bonnie Willis was a grade-A student with a literary turn of
mind; because of her excellent work she was awarded a schol-
arship to Berea College in Kentucky. Her parents naturally
were pleased, but since Berea was a long way from home Mr.
Willis wasn't willing to let Bonnie go unless someone from
our school could go with her and stay, not for two or three
days, but long enough to see that Bonnie was safely settled
in her college work.

I was elected. Plans were made for Bonnie to enter college
at the beginning of the semester, early in January. Fortunately
work at Appalachian was light at that time of the year, and
I could take my vacation then. But there was another reason
I was glad to go with Bonnie. I had learned that Berea was for

the first time offering a course in hand-weaving that year.

For those who may not be familiar with the program of this fine institution, I should explain that while no tuition is charged at Berea each student must work a certain number of hours each day to "earn his keep." One of the types of work available was that of weaving things for sale. Under the direction of Swedish Mrs. Ernburg the program had been carried on for years. But this year they were beginning a class in which one could learn to assemble a loom, put up a warp, beam it, thread it, learn to read and interpret weaving drafts, and actually weave.

Tony Ford had been hoping to do some work toward his college degree, and he decided to undertake this at Berea. So the three of us went out to Kentucky.

I spent the entire nine weeks of my vacation there learning to weave. I have always been grateful to Mr. Henry Willis for this experience since he was responsible for my going to Berea.

At Penland one may slip over to the loom house as early as one wishes, weave all day and into the night, and even stay until lights are turned off at ten o'clock. But at Berea then the class lasted only two hours a day. However, I bought a loom, put it up in my room and thus got all the experience I could manage.

I was learning to weave beautiful things, such as handsome table linens and gossamer scarves. But more than that, I was weaving beautiful dreams. I was seeing visions of what it would mean to our Penland community and to an even greater area if I could go back and teach our neighbors to weave things as lovely as those I had seen when I visited Aunt Susan Phillips.

Mrs. Matheny, whom I had met at Berea, was teaching the women in her community to weave and was selling their work for them; as they brought it in she would pay them for it by the yard. Why couldn't I do the same thing at Penland?

I suppose I would say, if I had to put my finger on the time and place, that the idea of establishing an institution such as the Penland School of Handicrafts was born then and there. But it would be several years before the school actually could be started.

There were two things I wanted very much to do. The first was to help bring about a revival of hand-weaving, which in our country—I'm speaking of the nation now—had become all but a dead art. Where in the United States could one see hand-weaving being done? I asked people and searched books and magazines, but I found only a very few such places.

As far as I could discover, there was only one book available in this country on the art of hand-weaving. *Foot-Power Hand-Weaving* had been written by Edward F. Worst of Chicago. I read and studied that book avidly. The author's name would come to mean much to Penland and to me.

The other thing I wanted to do was provide our neighbor mothers with a means of adding to their generally meager incomes without having to leave their homes. Thoughts danced through my head nights and days. My mind wove fanciful visions while my tired, sore fingers were weaving tangible materials. I saw innumerable women in modest mountain homes, happily engrossed in weaving beautiful homespuns in delightful old designs, their worries vanishing, their hopes brightening for their children's futures. I saw the education of countless mountain children, even college educations, being clacked out on home looms in the coves and valleys and along the slopes of the Blue Ridge and the Great Smokies.

And I was so impatient to be at it! At night when I went to bed I felt like the child on Christmas Eve who wonders how he can go through a whole night before it is time to get up and see what Santa Claus has put in his stocking. Each day I could hardly wait to be at my loom again.

When my unusual vacation came to an end—it had been a vacation of hard work, but tremendously engrossing—I bought two more looms and had the three shipped to Penland. When I returned to Appalachian School I put up two of them in Morgan Hall. One I threaded with a warp for wool scarves and the other I threaded for rugs.

Everybody who came in to see these little looms marveled at how much smaller and lighter they were than the cumbersome old ones they remembered seeing their grandmothers use. And each wanted to try her hand at weaving, which, of course, was just what I had hoped for.

The thing I had to do now, I realized, was to sell Bishop Horner on the idea of reviving hand-weaving in our community.

Bishop Junius Horner was a gentleman of the old South whom I had known since I was a young child. He was a tall man in every respect, six feet four, gentle, noble, given himself to seeing visions. But his vision, I was disappointed to discover, did not at first embrace hand-weaving. Along with his dreams he had very definite opinions from which he was not easily budged, and he did not approve of weaving as a home industry.

So I invited the bishop to the school, showed him the looms and the things I had been weaving, and then I said to him something like this: "Bishop, I expect to weave on one of these looms myself, but I want to lend the other two to neighbors. I think they would enjoy weaving, and I believe they would be able to produce material for which we could give them a fair price, by the yard. This would provide them additional income, and in turn we could sell what they weave. If it should work out that way it would do what Rufus envisioned when he found the beautiful old coverlets in this neighborhood. It would keep the old art alive, and it would at the same time make life more pleasant for our neighbors. May I try to work this out?"

"No," said the bishop firmly. "The work would be too hard for the women. I have heard too many of them describe the back-breaking job of weaving on those old looms."

"Yes, Bishop," I said, as winsomely as I could, "but those looms had been literally hewn out of the forests. They were heavy and hard to manage. Then, too, the women in those days had harder lives than women do now. Besides doing their housework, they had to help their men with the crops, and often they had to do their weaving by lamplight when the day's work in the fields was over. They had to do it in order to make clothing for their families. But look at these looms, Bishop; they aren't heavy. And today the women would have time to weave."

"No, I don't approve." The bishop shook his head. "Besides, there's no money for such a venture."

I wasn't willing to yield without further effort. "But, Bishop, I have been weaving. Do I look as if it had hurt me? I've been weaving day and night for the last nine weeks, and I've had fun. As for money, I have six hundred and fifteen dollars that I've been putting away for my old age." I looked him straight in the eyes, though I had to look up considerably to do it. "If you don't believe in this weaving, I would like to use my own money to see what I can do. May I?"

The bishop's eyes twinkled. "I'll tell you what you might do," he said, and I knew that he was relenting. "Try weaving eight hours one day. You're a little slip of a girl and if it doesn't hurt you, then go ahead."

So that's what I did; I did weave a full eight hours one day. And not being used to it for that long a stretch, I had a lot of soreness in the muscles back of my knees. And I didn't tell the bishop that the only way I could sit down the next day was to stand before the chair and just flop down into it. Those muscles simply were not willing to lower me gently into the chair!

Not long after this we invited the neighbors in for a rag-rug tacking, and the topic of conversation, of course, was looms and weaving. Mrs. Willis was there, and since she was a person on whom I always relied for help in any important project I was undertaking, I asked her if she would like to have one of the looms in her home. I promised to teach her how to weave, to furnish all the materials and to pay her by the yard for all the cloth she produced. Mrs. Willis agreed to give it a try.

Mr. Wyatt loaded the loom into the wagon, along with all the materials needed to weave off forty yards of warp. We rattled over the mile and a half to the Willis home; Mr. Wyatt unloaded the loom and the weaving materials and returned to the school, but I spent the day there. Mrs. Willis and I assembled the loom, then beamed the warp and began threading. For three days I walked back and forth between the school and the Willis home, helping Mrs. Willis thread the loom and then weave, until she was able to go it alone.

When the rugs were all finished she sent them to me by Mr.

Willis. We figured them up, and I wrote her a check. The check was for twenty-three dollars. Penland was in business!

In those days it was unheard of for a woman to earn that much money in her own home during leisure time. This was indeed something to talk about. When next I saw Mrs. Willis, she reported, with a twinkle in her eye, that all the neighbors knew the size of that check even before her husband got home with it.

And the next morning before I could get up, there were women at our door asking for looms. We sent to Berea for twelve more, and by the time they arrived at Penland they had all been promised. Wagons came from the homes of potential weavers and we loaded on looms and materials. Day after day I went out, sometimes on horseback but more often on foot, to instruct the women. I would stay with each weaver until her warp was beamed and threaded and she had woven enough to know that she could continue without help until another warp would be needed.

How those women learned to weave! It seemed to me that they were learning much more easily than I had learned at Berea, and it wasn't long before they could dress their looms without help from me.

Little by little their husbands began to make equipment for them. Instead of coming to our house to put up their warps on the warping bar that Mr. Wyatt had made by constructing a wooden frame and using broom handles for pegs, these husbands made warping bars like Mr. Wyatt's. One new weaver even made the warping bar herself, using ten-penny nails for pegs instead of broom handles.

At Berea I had bought a Swedish bobbin winder. Our weavers were using their old spinning wheels for filling bobbins. If they did not own spinning wheels they would go to a neighbor who did. In some instances husbands would rig up arrangements for bobbin filling on their wives' sewing machines.

Sadie Grindstaff's husband made the most picturesque bobbin winder I ever saw. Mr. Grindstaff used the water power from the stream running through their yard to turn the wheel that wound the bobbin.

One cold winter afternoon I was on my way home from helping a weaver dress her loom when I decided to stop at a neighbor's house and help her on a new project she was undertaking. She had been weaving scarves which required only two harnesses; I wanted her to try a four-harness operation. So I showed her a four-harness draft, explained how it was threaded. "But I don't have time to start you out on the threading," I told her. "They say it's going down to zero tonight and I want to get home before dark."

She looked at the draft. "Law, Miss Lucy," she said, sighing, "I never could learn how to do that."

"Yes, you can," I said. "You're a smarter woman than I am, and I learned to do it."

"Why, Miss Lucy," she insisted, "I ain't got no education."

"Education doesn't put brains in your head," I told her.

"Well, I reckon it don't," she agreed. "But I guess it helps you use what you got, don't it?"

"Sometimes, I suppose. But you can do it, and I know it."

I didn't really know it. I fully expected to have to return and help her thread the new draft. But I was wrong. Never again did I have to help her with any of the intricate loom problems she was to encounter. To tell her once was all she required.

In fact, I began to feel that I was mentally backward when I saw how readily these women learned weaving with the very little supervision I was giving them. One day I was comforted somewhat when we were exchanging notes on our experiences with looms and weaving. Several of the weavers said there had been times when they had actually wept as they grappled with getting the treadles properly tied to produce the required patterns or wrestled with the eccentricities and perversities of loom-adjusting.

Now there were twelve new looms settled in their homes and our community hummed with new industry and the joys of creating—as well as the joys of earning. But women still came to us with requests for looms and opportunities for weaving. By that time, however, the original $615 was gone, and I had to tell these women that we had no more looms and no more money.

Then one of these women, not to be outdone, had a suggestion. "My husband says that if you will lend him your loom, he thinks he can use it as a pattern to make me one by. If he can, will you let me weave like these other women?" I said yes.

Other husbands began to make looms too. Weavers multiplied. Women whose lives had seemed full already found more time for weaving than they had thought possible, simply because they were eager, I suppose, to do it, and eager for the money that their weaving would bring.

Amy Burt was at Penland permanently now, for she had retired from Mount Pleasant. I was spending all my time with the weavers and weaving problems. And there was no dearth of problems. We had never given thought to marketing, for example. We had supposed that the women would have little time for weaving and that we could sell to our friends what little the weavers would bring in. Our friends had been generous and appreciative, but there were simply not enough of them to buy all that was being produced. Woven scarves, bags, rugs came in until we had a room filled with weaving— and no market. Weavers had been paid as they brought in their work, yarns had been bought and paid for, as long as the money lasted. And now it was gone.

During this experimental time I was working without salary; from the school I was getting only my living. When my savings evaporated, the school paid yarn bills as long as it could. Once we borrowed the Sunday-school collection in order to get a yarn shipment out of the Penland Station. And I remember quite well that we paid it all back.

Our school was receiving little income from the National Board of Missions and the yarn bills were a real hardship. But when the end of the year came and Miss Burt balanced the books, she happily discovered that the small income from weaving had been a little in excess of the outgo. That was encouraging, but even so, there were weavers waiting for their pay and there was that room filled with weaving, and no market. We wrestled and wrestled with our figures and finally came up with the frightening fact that we were some $2,000 in the hole. Something had to be done, we knew; but we didn't know what.

The visions of reviving a dying art and of adding to the incomes of our neighbors had been realized even beyond our dreaming. We knew that. Not only were our weavers producing goods for sale, but there was hardly a weaver who hadn't created things with which to beautify and make more comfortable her own home. They were weaving curtains, towels, table linens, dresses. One weaver had woven her husband a suit. They had revived a cultural heritage.

And the weaving had accomplished things economically,

too. It had brought into numerous homes many extras that would not have been possible without those weaving checks. Added to the scholarships Bonnie Willis' good records had earned her at Berea were her mother's checks from weaving, used for college expenses. In other families, too, children were being sent to school and college, and the weaving was helping bear the costs.

We had given little consideration to another value of weaving, its social value. It is possible for a weaver to put a warp on her loom without help, but it's a difficult feat. So neighbor called on neighbor, and these visits offered opportunities for the exchange of ideas. Housewives discussed the comparative beauties of the different weaving drafts used, talked about the things they had made or were making for their homes, spoke proudly of how little the dress cost that the folk at church complimented so highly last Sunday, or described the washing machine that weaving money had bought and how much time and labor it saved for more weaving.

In fact, we asked ourselves, as we sought to evaluate the coming of hand-weaving to Penland, what phases of living and thinking had not been colored by that weaving?

But nevertheless, however we figured it, from the standpoint of money we owed $2,000, and what could we do to get that money?

I knew we couldn't stop weaving. That would be unthinkable. It just meant too much to our neighborhood for us to throw up our hands and quit. Yet how could we go on unless we figured out some way of bettering our financial situation?

Any way we figured it, we came out with one result. We would have to sell that weaving. If we could sell the stuff in our stockroom and the later products coming from our looms, we would change the color of the ink in our record books from a glaring red to a cheering black. There was no other way.

Finally we sent Bishop Horner an SOS. When he came, and we told him we were $2,000 in the red, he was gentleman enough not to say "I told you so" or to remind us that he had not approved our weaving plans. In fact, the bishop seemed far more interested than he had been when I first approached him with my plan. He had seen that the weaving appeared to be breaking no backs, that it was on the contrary helping everybody who participated in the program except those to whom we owed money.

The bishop told us quite frankly that he was truly interested now in the program. He could see what it was beginning to mean in the lives of many of our people. He optimistically declared that we would eventually find a market for our products. And he asked me to continue the work under the sponsorship of the Appalachian School!

"Pay yourself back the money you advanced," he said, "and also a salary. Do it from the sales of the weaving when such sales can be made."

I agreed that I would, provided I should not be held responsible for the bookkeeping and accounting, and provided further that I should never be required to make speeches! He said there was no reason why I should need to do either. And what experiences I was to have with both, before Bonnie came back to take care of me! The moral is, never refuse to do anything, for that is exactly what is likely to be required of you.

But I was still $2,000 short.

"I don't have two thousand and I don't know what you should do," Bishop Horner said. "But I do know this: Don't stop weaving now, for you can't stay in debt. Keep on for a while and see whether the books begin to look any better. By that time maybe I can think of something. If you could just get out to the resorts . . ."

Even then the western part of our state was known as eastern America's playground during the summer. But, as I have said, transportation was so difficult that we had scarcely considered going to the resorts to show our weaving to tourists and others who might buy it.

"But, Bishop," I said pessimistically, "even to go just the twenty-five miles to Linville takes two days. You know we would have to walk down to Penland Station, take the Clinch-field to Johnson City and spend the night, then take Tweetsie to Linville. And think how much we would have to sell just to make expenses."

The bishop stroked his chin. "How long will it be before the state gets the road finished from Spruce Pine to Penland Station?"

"I don't know, sir," I said, "but you know they are already working on the Spruce Pine end."

"Well, this much I'll promise: As soon as they get a road to you so that you can get an automobile from Spruce Pine to Penland, I'll give you a car. Then you can take your weaving out to the resorts and see what you can do."

So that's what he did. Before the road was entirely finished he gave me a little Model-T Ford roadster with a pickup back. Between us and Spruce Pine there was still a tremendous mud hole; the state kept a team of mules and a driver there, and when a car came along they didn't even wait for it to get stuck. The driver automatically hitched the mules to the bumper and pulled the car through.

60

That little car saved the day for us. Miss Burt and I would load weaving into the back of it and wend our way merrily and hopefully to a resort. Having arrived there, we would go up and down the streets until we had found the best-looking hotel. There we would stop and go in, tell the proprietor who we were, where we were from, and why we had come, and ask his permission to show our wares in the lobby, on the porch, wherever the largest crowds would be.

Now that I know the world a little better than I did then, I marvel that we were never turned away. But not once were we disappointed. The hotels always let us sell. And sometimes they even gave us a free lunch.

Now we were selling things, taking in money and cutting down on that debt. And, more profitable to us perhaps in the long run, we were getting our products and the name of Penland widely known among those folk interested in handicrafts.

The next time Bishop Horner came to see us I related our experiences in selling at the resort places. He was delighted and his enthusiasm gave ours added fire. Then he told us about the General Convention of the Episcopal Church, which was shortly to be held in New Orleans.

"If you want to risk such a venture," he said, "you might go down there and take some of your goods. I believe they would sell pretty well."

I knew that a general convention was held every three years and each one attracted thousands of people. A whole city within a city was set up, with a post office, a Western Union office and a separate telephone system provided to serve the delegates and visitors. Rufus and the bishop were planning to attend, so I would have moral support, at least. I was delighted with the idea.

61

But first Miss Burt and I talked about it and debated back and forth whether we would sell enough to pay expenses and provide a reasonable profit for the trouble. There was no way of being certain what such a venture would bring in. Also we knew that the costs of going to New Orleans would be considerable, with the train fare, hotel bill and other expenses mounting to a sizable figure.

Being good gamblers, or willing ones, we decided it was worth a try. Wonderingly and hopefully we packaged up most of the stock we had, and off I went for New Orleans.

I shall never forget the day I arrived in the great southern city and made my way to the convention's general office. Blithely I went up to the man in charge and asked him where I might display and sell our weaving.

He looked at me somewhat nonchalantly and asked if I had applied for space.

"No, I haven't," I said. It had not occurred to me to do that. I had just followed the bishop's suggestion and had thought everything would be all right.

That man looked at me again, and he didn't need to tell me what he thought of my being so utterly ignorant. The expression on his face plainly told me, even though he was a gentleman and had refrained from putting his thoughts into words.

"All space for exhibits has been applied for and taken," he said, and I was sure I could measure his disgust. "The only thing I can do for you now is to give you a table out in the lobby of the building where the women's meetings are being held."

I thanked him, told him I would be happy to accept that table, and slunk away.

The table was set up for me, and I unpacked and put on

display something of everything we were making at Penland—scarves, rugs, dress materials, shopping bags.

And do you know, I couldn't have had a better place if I'd had my choice? Every woman who attended meetings had to go past my table. The shopping bags on display were just the right size and shape for carrying their convention materials, and it seemed to me that almost every women attending that convention bought a bag.

They were sturdy bags, too, and serviceable. They were made of rug roving in various colors and woven in some of the traditional coverlet patterns such as Pine Cone; Sun, Moon and Stars; and Whig Rose.

Sales were music to my soul, and my spirits soared. Rufus and the bishop were just as thrilled as I, if possible. I would watch for them as they came up the stairs from the street level to the lobby and I could read their eagerness, I was sure, from the time I saw the tops of their heads, and then their eyes, then their whole faces, beaming with anticipation and hope. And when they reached my table, we would gloat over the sales made to that hour.

I wrote home for all the woven stock on hand, and I sold it all—approximately eighteen hundred dollars' worth of weaving. The New Orleans trip had all but brought us out of debt!

When I returned to Penland we paid the weavers and the yarn bills, we ordered more materials and put everybody to work again and started back in the hole. But this time we did not go so far in; we had established something of a market, for we began to get orders from persons who had bought our wares in New Orleans as well as at the resorts in our own section.

Especially at Christmastime church auxiliaries would order

consignments and sell weaving, in part to help us but also to help themselves in their various money-raising schemes. This required a big stock for special seasons. We never knew how much would be sold and how much sent back, but it was another market, and a growing one. Also, as a result of our success in New Orleans we visited other general conventions of our church and there disposed of large lots of our woven materials and products.

CHAPTER 6

ONE DAY SHORTLY after Bishop Horner had given me the little Ford, I had a letter from Peggy Breed in Raleigh. Peggy had left our staff to go to the state capital as a librarian. She had written to tell me about the North Carolina State Fair that was to be held there in the early fall. If we felt that it was worth our taking the chance, she said, we could bring a loom and do some hand-weaving at the fair. If we should decide to do it, she would engage a booth and pay for it herself and she would also take care of us while we were there.

Once more Miss Burt and I weighed and pondered. Despite Peggy's generosity, there would be some expenses in Raleigh, and we had no money. Another thing—and it sounds unbelievably silly from this distance in time—I had learned how to drive the Ford forward but I hadn't yet learned how to back it. The time or two when I had tried, the car had spurted off in a direction opposite to that I had intended.

But we finally decided to take the chance—we usually did, in fact, whenever some adventurous proposal was presented! We loaded the loom and our stock of weaving into the back of the little Ford, and we took off across North Carolina for Raleigh, two hundred and fifty miles eastward.

Roads were being constructed in many localities in the state, and we discovered as we went along that almost the entire section on which we were traveling was under construction. Detours were everywhere, the roads were very rough, and the distance was considerably farther, therefore, than it is today over the wonderful highway that now joins us with the capital city. And the dust was so dense that most of the time we drove with our lights on.

Statesville is about halfway to Raleigh from Penland, and we had planned to get there before nightfall and spend the night.

We did, too, but before reaching Statesville my arms were so tired from twisting the steering wheel of that little car that when I would see a car approaching I would wonder if I could summon strength to pull the wheel enough to the right to pass it. When I finally pulled up in front of the Vance Hotel I was delighted to hand over the car to a bellboy.

All night I was dodging automobiles hurtling toward us! Our room was on the street side and when in my light sleep horns honked, I would say, "I just mustn't go to sleep until I have passed that car!" A city hotel, I found, was no place for inducing sound slumber in a country gal, especially after she had been wrestling detours, dodging broken places in the road and ducking out of the way of approaching cars.

But we slept, even if fitfully, and the next morning we started out again. By nightfall we were in Raleigh. Today we can make this trip easily in five or six hours.

At the fairgrounds we set up our looms and when the fair opened we were ready. Miss Burt was at the front of our booth telling the story of our Penland efforts and selling goods, while I was at the loom weaving. Large crowds stopped to watch us, and they seemed interested. This was 1924; and most of the persons who stopped at our booth actually had never seen hand-weaving done, unless they were old enough to have seen their grandmothers engaged in such a task.

That night we slumped wearily into bed and glanced through the newspaper to see if there was a comment about our exhibit. Sure enough, there was a story saying that our booth had drawn the biggest attendance of the day. I think that was a true report, too, for our booth was the only one where there was activity, with the exception of the booth in which an ultra-modern Jacquard loom—modern for that day certainly—was weaving portraits of the President of the United States and the Governor of North Carolina.

I have always thought of Miss Burt as a superwoman. She was a person of great personal charm who met the public graciously and impressed all with whom she conversed. And since people were curious about our weaving and asked many questions, she was able to make a number of friends for us and our work.

One gentleman, I remember, seemed especially interested, and he asked if we got any state aid for the work we were doing. We told him we did not, but we would certainly be happy to accept it if we could find out how it might be procured. He told us then of the Smith-Hughes Act under which federal and state funds were made available for vocational education. The person for us to see, he said, was Mr. George Coggin, State Supervisor of Trade and Industrial Education.

So later we did get in touch with Mr. Coggin. Soon he came

to Penland and, bless him, said he was just as interested in aiding such work as ours as we were in getting that aid. Of course, we thought that impossible, but nevertheless we appreciated the great interest he did show.

That interest was manifested in the form of half of my salary, but in order to get that half I would have to be given the other half by our county. To qualify for the salary, it was also revealed, I would have to provide a central place to which the weavers could come for instruction rather than go myself to their homes to give them instruction.

I knew that the county could provide no funds toward my salary. But our new county superintendent of schools, Mr. Jason Deyton, was most sympathetic and co-operative, and we talked over the situation until we arrived at the plan that we thought might work. We agreed that from profits on the sales of weaving we would match the state funds.

During the boom years and after we had established a market for our products, this plan worked well. But during the Depression we had no money to pay our half. So when the time for a salary payment was due I would write a check for our half, take it to the county seat and trade it for the whole salary and then rush to the bank to get it there before our poor check arrived. It worked.

From 1929 until 1953, when there were new faces, adjustments and interpretations in Washington, I enjoyed a salary for vocational education work, and that was the only steady regular income that I could always count on. Except for it, I'm sure we could never have weathered the Depression and all the vicissitudes of a growing, evolving, sometimes stumbling handicrafts center.

One of the requirements for qualifying under the state program, as I said, was that we have a central meeting place for our weavers. So for our meetings we decided to use the little, old log cabin that had been the first home of Rufus and his bride. We set aside each Wednesday as "Weaving Day." On that day the weavers would come in, get their pay for work done and receive materials and direction for the next week's work. It was an all-day meeting; problems and methods would be discussed, and we learned much from one another. For instance, we might compare ways of washing and ironing our woven linens so that they looked their best; or exchange recipes for our favorite dishes, or discuss gardening. Once a visiting nurse gave us a short course on home nursing and first aid. Thus we shared experiences in many and varying fields.

The first time we had a wedding in one of our weaving families, I remember, we pieced a quilt for the daughter who was to be married and when the pieces were all put together we had a quilting. The piecing was done on weaving days and the quilting was an all-day affair that was such fun that we established the customs of piecing and quilting a quilt for each son and daughter of a weaver who got married. And quilts were always acceptable.

So Wednesdays quickly became our social days around Penland.

Quickly also we saw that our little cabin was too small for our activities and we discussed the possibility of building a new weaving cabin. The weavers were co-operative, were enthusiastic in fact, and each volunteered to give logs.

During that winter the logs were snaked up from all the different communities in which the weavers lived, some from Wing, some from Rabbit Hop behind the Peak, some from other localities. There were logs of oak, chestnut, maple and locust.

We were going to build our cabin at the edge of the orchard, and we planned the log-raising for the fifth of May in the hope that the apple trees would be in bloom, for what could make a more beautiful setting for the great occasion than an orchard of flowering apple trees?

Of course we would have to have Mr. Coggin as one of our guests for the great day, as well as neighbors and friends from all around.

Sure enough, when May 5 arrived the apple trees were in full bloom and it was a glorious spring day. Mr. Coggin was there, and so were all the weavers and their husbands, and a host of other neighbors.

The cabin would be thirty feet long and eighteen feet wide. The stakes were set, and the work started. The men had organized themselves so that those who had had experience in notching corners took their places at the corners where the stakes had been placed and the others worked elsewhere. Even Mr. Coggin helped. He may never have taken part in a log-raising before, but he was adept with tools and he knew measuring, so he made himself useful.

It was a wonderful day—perfect weather, and happy, busy people. The discordant notes of ringing hammers, rasping saws, banging axes, shouting workmen, shrieking children and barking dogs sounded to me like a symphony. And how those men worked!

The women, who probably outnumbered the men that day, had each brought food. Our old log cabin was the center of feminine activity, and when noon came, the women spread white tablecloths on the grass and laid out a dinner that would compensate any man for a hard day of house-building.

Dear Mrs. Emma Conley, one of our expert weavers from the old days and a grand lady besides, had brought a custard pie with beautiful meringue, toward which she, Mr. Coggin and I were gravitating, when little one-year-old Junior reached out to clutch his mother's skirts and with baby wobble planted his bare little foot right in the middle of that meringue. But what of it? There were pies and cakes and good eating of every sort and in quantities that allowed everybody to gorge himself.

By the end of that day we had built the four walls of our cabin. But more importantly, I felt, we had grown in social stature and had joined ourselves together, as strongly as those log walls had been interlocked, in a sense of achievement and a vision of a creative future.

It wasn't long before we had finished the cabin entirely. A friend of Bishop Horner furnished the oak flooring, and the roof and other materials were paid for from sales of weaving.

CHAPTER 7

GETTING INTO OUR new Weaving Cabin increased almost immediately the community's interest in weaving. And as we progressed in this venture, we learned much, not only about the techniques of production but also about marketing and financing. For those were still our bottlenecks, how to sell and how to finance when we were not selling.

But the weavers knew well our financial ups and downs and they did what they could to help shoulder the burdens. During slump seasons they continued to weave happily even though they did not know when they might be paid.

They had a lot of faith in us.

I once asked a group of them how much of a hardship it was not to get their weaving checks promptly.

"It don't make too much difference, Miss Lucy," one of them said. "We just go to the stores anyhow—over at Wing or Bandanna or Boone Ford, anywhere—and we tell the store-keeper we'll pay him soon as we get our weaving check, and that's all we have to tell him; he lets us have whatever stuff we want."

Often I wished I had that much faith in myself.

With the growth of our market and the ever-increasing number of weavers producing, I now had more work to do than I could satisfactorily handle. So I was greatly pleased when Georgie Morgan, who had completed the course of instruction given at our Appalachian School, came over to help me in the cabin. She did up the packages for mailing, made out the invoices and took care of the yarn supplies. Quickly she became one of my treasures.

Georgie had what I consider one of the first requisites of a Penland worker, a keen sense of humor.

She was quick to laugh and quick to see the humor in any situation. Whether it was the wit of the neighbors—and Penland has an abundance of naturally witty persons—or the remembrance of a certain tourist who came every summer to our shop and had to go to the bottom of every stack of weaving on every shelf and in every chest before choosing for purchase the top towel on the first stack, or of the visitor who was the state's star stutterer, Georgie and I never ceased to be entertained by the scenelets and playlets that were constantly being enacted before our eyes or behind our backs. Sometimes we actually had to turn our backs in an attempt to preserve some dignity.

One Wednesday afternoon when we were piecing a bride's quilt in the Weaving Cabin, Molly Shook, who was not young, nor was she very old, asked me: "Miss Lucy, how many quilts would you give me if I was to get married?"

Somehow in my mind Molly Shook and matrimony just didn't go together, so I felt quite safe in answering, "Oh, Molly, I'd give you two quilts."

Then Sadie Sparks, another weaver who seemed singly settled and self-sufficient, evidenced her interest in what I was confident was unlikely of fruition. "How many would you give me if I got married?"

"Sadie," I told her, "I would give you three quilts."

All the time Georgie had been listening and struggling, I knew, to hold in check the laughter that was threatening to burst out. Now Georgie, with a twinkle in her merry eyes, faced me. "How many," she said, sort of under her breath, "would you give me, Miss Lucy?"

I just couldn't think of the possibility of Georgie's leaving me. Such a thing would be unthinkable, I told myself, and so I spoke out: "Why, Georgie, I'd give you five quilts."

I spoke too fast. Although I have never entered the state, I do thoroughly believe in marriage and I always have to discipline myself to keep from pushing a little when I see romance going slowly. But I hadn't meant to set up a matrimonial bureau. And although the quilts promised could have had nothing to do with speeding the business, I was almost knocked off my feet when a few weeks after that episode Georgie came to the cabin and said to me, "Miss Lucy, will you go with me to Asheville one day this week and help me pick out my wedding clothes?"

"Georgie! You're not going to get married?" I said, amazed. "I don't believe a word of it!"

"I didn't expect you to," said Georgie, grinning, "so just to prove it, I've brought not only my engagement ring but also my wedding ring to show you."

Whereupon she produced them before my startled eyes. Seeing was believing, and immediately I experienced a struggle of emotions. I was happy that Georgie was happy, but I was terribly sorry for myself now that I was going to lose her as a companion in work and fun.

Many helpers have come to Penland to stay a while and then leave, and others have come and stayed, and some seem to have been here always; but no other has given me just the same satisfaction that Georgie did. Georgie, I am happy to say, is still a weaver, and although she lives in an adjoining county we do get together now and then to chuckle over memories of those early days.

But to get back to that quilt-promising rashness. Do you know that before six months had gone by, all three of those girls—Molly, Sadie and Georgie—were married, and we had the job ahead of making ten quilts! And, although it took years of Wednesdays for us to get all those quilts pieced and quilted, we did it. You may be sure I never made any other such rash promises.

It's poor business consigning anybody up here to the permanent status of old maid or perennial bachelor. I do believe there's something in the atmosphere around Penland, though I have never inhaled deeply of it myself, that inspires romance. It may have something to do with nature's lavish beauty, with the unspoiled naturalness of the people, the mountains, the clouds, the flowers. I don't know just what it is; you can't put your finger on it, but it's there.

While I'm discussing Penland and romance and how they seem to complement each other, I want to refer again to two of my very favorite Penland folk. I have told about the year Bonnie Willis, Tony Ford and I went out to Berea College, where during my nine-week vacation I worked and studied weaving and where through the school year Bonnie and Tony did their college work.

But academic pursuits proved not to be their entire interests. In fact, interest in each other grew and flourished, and it continued after Tony had gone on to the University of Minnesota, and after Bonnie had finished her college work and was teaching. So we were not too surprised but nevertheless quite delighted when they announced their engagement and in time were married.

Then, before Georgie left and on what was surely one of the most auspicious days in Penland's history, Bonnie came down to be my assistant and Penland School's Rock of Gibraltar. She came to do—and continues to do—all the bookkeeping and everything else pertaining to figures. She has been and is for me that pillar of strength her mother was before her.

Sometimes I feel downright sorry for Bonnie. I know that my imagination, my eagerness to do the impossible, have been a trial for her, because it is on her desk that the bills are piled and it is her letters that keep our creditors courteous and hopeful. And it is Bonnie's strength that keeps me on the hunt of the rainbow's end, for I know all the time that Bonnie is back of me and somehow will help us keep Penland on its course.

Tony too is a great one. He has been at Penland off and on all these years, and although we have never been able to afford a salary on which he might support a family, he has continued to make Penland his headquarters and has held various supervisory positions for our county and for the state and federal governments. He has spent much time in other countries as a representative of our government, as I shall subsequently re-

76

veal, and has done work of tremendous significance in those areas of the world.

I cannot think of a craft that Tony cannot do and do well. And I don't know anybody more entertaining than Tony.

So I look back. They say that as a person gets older, he lives more and more in the past. No doubt that is true, but for a long time I have been looking back concurrently with looking ahead. I like to gauge and measure the days and the people of our Penland venture in its first years against those of the more recent ones. And looking back to that early chapter when our weaving enterprises were $2,000 in the red and when we had no markets and no automobile roads over which to seek markets, and then to the road-building program that—coupled with the old Model-T Ford and our unorthodox driving—provided means of selling what we had made, and remembering our experiments with salesmanship, and our failures and successes, I don't hesitate to declare I wouldn't have missed it for the world.

But I must admit that chapter looks better from this end than it did when we were writing it. Romances are fun when we can live happily forever afterward, and much more fun when we look back to almost insurmountable difficulties safely surmounted.

CHAPTER 8

At a Mountain Workers' conference held across the mountains in Knoxville in the spring of 1928, Mrs. John C. Campbell, director of the John C. Campbell Folk School at Brasstown, asked some of us who were craft-minded to think with her about the possible values of forming a handicraft guild.

We discussed the idea, considered it from various angles, weighed it, measured it and at length decided that such a guild would be helpful in facilitating our doing together desirable things that we could never hope to accomplish alone. So we proposed to have a meeting in the late fall of representatives of schools and other groups interested in crafts at which we would formulate the procedure.

I yearned for the thrill of having that momentous meeting at Penland, but I realized that we were far off the beaten path and I had little hope that our invitation would be accepted. But I determined to invite them anyway. By that time we had a good-weather road to our hilltop and when there was no rain, snow or ice, an automobile could make the climb in comparative safety. So I said my prayers and invited the group to Penland. And do you know, they accepted!

But when the time came for setting a definite date for the meeting, they changed it from fall to deep winter—two days after Christmas. I was in a quandry. Should I confess that I had no business inviting guests—and outsiders unfamiliar with our community, at that—to come driving up our hill on December 27? Or should I tell myself that I hadn't changed the date of meeting from good weather-time of the year to what would likely be heavy winter weather, and say nothing to them, come what may? Besides, would it be hospitable to uninvite guests?

So I said nothing, and the invitation and acceptance stood.

As December drew near and arrived, I watched, prayed and calculated as best I could. The weather held up, Christmas came and then, the day after Christmas, snow fell. To say the least, the snowfall was heavy enough to make driving up or down our red clay road an exciting adventure.

The first guest to arrive was Mr. Allen Eaton of the Russell Sage Foundation, who later was to write that intriguing volume, *Handicrafts of the Southern Highlands*.

I took my little Ford to meet him at Penland Station and as we drove around our snowy curves to ascend the steep slope, my senses were alert for a tenseness, an anxiety, a pressing of the floor boards by Mr. Eaton. But even as we rounded the Big Turn and the back wheels slithered toward the outer edge of the road, Mr. Eaton seemed as relaxed and calm and happy as if he had been riding these hills every day. In fact, he seemed more composed than I actually felt.

I cannot say that all the guests arrived with as much equanimity as did Mr. Eaton, but at least after they had all had a good night's sleep it was a genial and composed group that sat about the fire in the little Weaving Cabin and discussed organizational details and other plans of what was shortly to become the Southern Highlands Handicraft Guild.

Among those who attended, in addition to Mrs. Campbell and Mr. Eaton, were President William J. Hutchins of Berea College, Dr. Mary Martin Sloop of the Crossnore School in neighboring Linville Valley, and Clementine Douglas of the Spinning Wheel, Asheville. They were the vanguard of a host of interesting people, some internationally known, particularly in the field of the crafts, who would ascend the steep hill to our school.

One who had planned to be present but was unable to attend was Miss Frances Goodrich, a pioneer in the revival of hand-weaving in western North Carolina, of which the Allanstand Cottage Industries in Asheville was a significant result. But she sent Miss Fuller, her representative, to offer to the Guild when it should be formed the facilities of her Allanstand, which was then and continues to be an important outlet for handicraft products.

That meeting, with its developing plans for launching the Guild and the offer of Allanstand, was one of our mountain top experiences.

And we had held it in our Weaving Cabin. Mr. Eaton was immensely pleased with our log meeting place. He spoke about it often and he prowled about it, poking behind stacks of goods and thumping the sturdy walls with his knuckles. When he wrote his book and told of the meeting, he spoke appreciatively of our cabin.

"In all the Highlands there seemed no more fitting place for this pioneer meeting than the Weavers' Cabin on the summit of this mountain ridge," he wrote, and he gave me permission to quote him. "The cabin had been built by the weavers and their husbands, whose homes were scattered about in coves and hollows and on mountainsides within a radius of about twenty miles, as a central place for instructions, receiving supplies, shipping out products, and discussing problems connected with their work.

"The significance to those who were gathered within its walls was that in this remote section, far from the sources usually looked to for help in such instances, these neighbors, all poor in money and goods, had through an inspiring experience in co-operation growing out of their handicraft activities built a cabin of native materials with their own hands and equipped it for their use. Tacked to a log in an obscure place on the wall behind one of the looms was a sheet of paper on which was written in that brevity of expression characteristic of mountain people the legend of the cabin. A part of it ran about like this:

> 3 logs by Henry Willis
> 1 log by Doc Hoppes
> 2 days work by Dave Hoyle
> 2 loads of stone for fireplace
>   by John Maughn
> 4 logs by Sally Sparks

"Some of the logs had been snaked long distances from several mountain homes, and the 'boards' for the roof were rived out of white oak, all materials in the cabin except the nails, glass, and hardware coming from the country around. The labor was, of course, local, and the frame, including the roof, was shaped up and put together in a day by country folk at a 'House Raisin'."

So we formed the Southern Highlands Handicraft Guild. While it was still young and the Great Smoky Mountains National Park and the Blue Ridge Parkway were being developed, we Guild members hoped to interest park officials in helping see to it that only good craft products were shown and sold in these areas. We wanted to prevent the sale of cheap souvenirs often seen along the highways, products in no sense typical of the region.

I evolved the idea of seeing the top man in the National Park Service. I felt that if I could just get someone with influence to help me, I would try to get a meeting with the park man. I had a good friend and fellow Episcopalian in Raleigh, Justice Heriot Clarkson of the North Carolina Supreme Court. I had never gone to Judge Clarkson for help without getting more than I had asked for, so I went to Raleigh, told him what I wanted, and asked him if he would write a letter for me to take to Washington.

He wrote the letter, and he did more. He couldn't leave his office at the time, but he had someone take me over to the governor's office. "Take her over to Governor Gardner and ask him to write Miss Lucy a letter too," he said.

The governor read the letter, handed it to his secretary, and said, "Here, take this and write something similar." Then he told me to return about noon and get it.

When Mrs. Bickett and I went back for the letter—she was the one who had taken me to the governor's office—I read it. It really was similar to the one Judge Clarkson had written, for among other things it said, "I have known Lucy Morgan for years."

I showed it to Mrs. Bickett. "I have never laid eyes on that man before today," I said. "And this is Saturday and his office has closed until Monday; I can't wait that long to get him to correct it."

"Take it on. Take it on," she said. I had misgivings, but I took that letter telling something that was not true. And it worried me. There are times, I think, when a little white lie is justifiable, but I simply can't get by with telling one. And I felt sure that if I took that letter to Washington, those people up there would find me out.

But I took it. And when I got to the offices of the National Park Service I first met Mr. Cammerer, who was then assistant director, and was soon to become director. Not at all what I expected a Washington bureaucrat to be like, he was just as natural and real as someone down under Bailey's Mountain at Penland. I gave him my letters and hoped he wouldn't read them until I was gone, but he did. I was terribly afraid he'd ask me about my long friendship with the governor, but he didn't.

He did ask me why I was so interested in the people and the crafts of the mountain region, and I told him I was a mountain girl myself. "I'm from the sod houses of Nebraska," he said, and right then he won my heart. Mr. Cammerer remained a friend as long as he lived, and he came to Penland often.

He and the other members of the Park Service whom I have met have all been in hearty agreement with the Guild concerning the necessity of requiring that all craft products sold along the Parkway be of high quality, and our relations have been happy and lasting. Mr. Hummel, superintendent of the Great Smoky Mountains National Park, and Mr. Sam Weems, superintendent of the Blue Ridge Parkway, are just as ambitious as the Guild is to have the best handicraft products of the region shown and sold in the areas they supervise.

To further their wish that visitors to the park regions get an authentic picture of the region—the mode of life of its people and their history and general background—a few years ago the park officials established near the North Carolina entrance to the great park the Oconoluftee Pioneer Museum. They brought log buildings from various places within the park area to Oconoluftee and set up a farmstead typical of the pioneer farmsteads of the region. There is the log home, the barn, the smokehouse, the various outbuildings. It is a wonderful museum; it affords the visitor an opportunity to see almost at a glance how the people in the isolated areas of the mountains lived in the early days. Oconoluftee is the beginning of an outdoor museum comparable to so many interesting ones that have been established in the countries of northern Europe.

In order to bring further life and authenticity to this museum, Mr. Hummel and Mr. Arthur Stupka, chief naturalist of the Great Smoky Mountains National Park, asked the Penland School to plan and arrange exhibits in one of the rooms, which they call the Pioneer Handicrafts Room. They also asked us to demonstrate carding, spinning and weaving, which we were very happy to do. And it proved to us again—as we saw with delight the mounting interest of visitors who paused to watch our demonstration—that to see someone actually creating something is far more interesting than to study that same piece of handicraft after it has been made. We noticed, too, that carding and spinning was particularly intriguing, because comparatively few people of our day have seen this fascinating process in the making of homespun.

84

Mr. Stupka is one of our very favorite people. We met him early through our friendship with Mr. Cammerer, and he comes to Penland every year to give an illustrated talk, using many of the colored films he himself has taken, on that most popular of American national parks. His visit and talk are looked forward to by us Penlanders with keen anticipation.

The first year Mr. Stupka came, Rufus was at Penland for a craftsman's service at our little outdoor shrine, held at sunset when the birds were singing their good-night songs. All through the simple but sincere and impressive little service an evening thrush accompanied Rufus, not only for the singing but also through the sermon. Rufus, the birds, Mr. Stupka, all Penland were so harmonious and apparently so pleased with one another that from that day to this we have planned to have Rufus and Mr. Stupka at the same time, Mr. Stupka's illustrated talk following Rufus' annual craftsman's service at the shrine.

Once I asked Mr. Stupka if all Park Service men were choice individuals to begin with or if living close to nature had made them so. He said that they were usually choice men and this prompted them to choose such work, that if they were not the sensitive, appreciative kind they usually soon realized that they did not fit, and withdrew from the service.

All the men from the Park Service and the National Forestry Service who come to Penland to give us programs are the kind that make us realize, or at least feel confident, that no matter what problems we may face, the world can't go to pot with young men like these helping toward the building of a more wholesome tomorrow.

CHAPTER 9

NEWS OF WHAT hand-weaving activities at Penland were doing for our neighborhood financially, culturally and socially was beginning to get around among the people of the nation interested in that ancient handicraft.

One of those who heard about us was Mr. Edward F. Worst of Chicago. Mr. Worst was the author of the only books on hand-weaving published in this country over a long period and he was perhaps the nation's authority on the subject. So it was more than fortunate for us that he learned of Penland and in August 1928 came down to spend his vacation with us. It was stupendous, it was manna from heaven, it was a shot in the arm, to weave a mixture of metaphors. No one can say what his coming that summer, and every summer after that until his death in 1949, really did mean to Penland.

As soon as Mr. Worst arrived, he told us he had come to of-

86

fer himself to serve in any way he could be helpful. Quickly he became interested in what we were doing and from the beginning he found many ways in which to give of himself. And he told us repeatedly that he was having a wonderful vacation doing it.

One of my joyful memories of Mr. Worst pictures him with the group of elderly neighbors who belonged to a generation when one spun and wove in order to be clothed. One such wonderful person, a favorite of Mr. Worst as she was with all of us, was Aunt Cumi Woody of the Deyton Bend community. Aunt Cumi happened to be at Penland the first summer Mr. Worst was with us, and she came every year after that as long as she lived.

I always got a great satisfaction—I might describe it as a soaring lift—seeing Mr. Edward F. Worst of Chicago—North Shore Drive, Art Institute, Marshall Field, Al Capone, stockyards, political conventions, booming business, roaring traffic—happily engrossed in the exchange of ideas and techniques with Aunt Cumi Woody, who dressed in a basque and full skirt, parted her hair in the middle and combed it sternly into a bun at the back of her neck. It always seemed mighty American and so right to me, this man from the great metropolis in serious though lively confab with this dear old lady of the isolated mountain region in the Southern Highlands, each giving and receiving information about a subject in which they were both tremendously interested.

I remember too how sometimes as she sat perched high at one of his multiple-harness looms eagerly working out new methods he had taught her, he would approach her and timidly ask—for Mr. Worst was inherently shy—if she would mind taking time off from her loom to go with him and search

87

out some of the plants, herbs, flowers, leaves and roots she used in making her vegetable dyes. It was in this way, on such a jaunt with Aunt Cumi, that we found the rare madder plant.

In our copy of *A Book of Hand-Woven Coverlets*, by Eliza Calvert Hall, we had discovered two pictures of Aunt Cumi's weaving, which had been taken at the Allanstand Cottage Industries in Asheville. Aunt Cumi had not known that pictures of her coverlets and her name were in that book, and one day I told her about it. "Aunt Cumi," I added, "you should have one of these books." Then I forgot all about it.

But the next year when Aunt Cumi came she went to my desk, picked up *A Book of Hand-Woven Coverlets* and asked, "Is this mine?" Puzzled, I said "No-o." She said, "You said something about getting one printed for me." So I wrote the publishers and told them about it, and ordered a copy. I really thought that they should send her a complimentary copy, but they didn't. They sent me a bill for it. Anyway, it was worth it to me.

Some time ago I saw one of Aunt Cumi's coverlets on display in the Pioneer Museum at Oconoluftee. In this museum, which seeks to re-create a pioneer homestead with authentic furnishings and farm equipment, nothing could have been more authentic than Aunt Cumi's beautiful coverlet. She wove it herself in a pattern called Saint Anne's Robe. But she not only did the weaving. She sheared the sheep, carded and spun her yarn, dyed it with vegetable dyes from plants and roots she had found, and wove it in that beautifully intricate design.

The predominating color of this coverlet is brown, and Aunt Cumi obtained the dye by boiling the hulls of black walnuts. Its secondary color is blue, made from wild indigo.

Indigo is the most temperamental dye I know. It is compounded of wild indigo, wheat bran, lye made from wood ash, and madder. To make it, one borrows, if possible, a starter from some neighbor, just as one does for buckwheat pancakes. If it isn't possible to borrow a starter, then one sets her own bluepot. The pot is usually kept at the back of the stove or in the corner near the fireplace. The time required for ripening depends in general on the "notions" of the blue pot. When it is bubbly on top and smells up the whole house, then the dyer tries it out by dipping in a skein of yarn. If this test reveals that the pot has "come," then one dyes simply by turning the skeins of yarn round and round in the dye bath until they are the desired color of blue. If a light blue is wanted, little of the dye is required; if a darker blue, then more time in the bath and more stirring of the skeins are necessary.

The thing to remember about this dye is that it is not boiled; boiling would upset the equilibrium, and the dye would be spoiled. This type of dye is effective only until it "gets tired," as the mountain dyers describe the chemical reaction that goes on in the pot. Then it must "rest" until it "comes" again. Like our mountain weavers, bluepot dye has temperament and personality. It must be allowed to do its job in its own time and way.

Aunt Cumi's beautiful coverlet also has a little green, and this she got by first dyeing the yarn yellow in the ooze of hickory bark, then dipping the yellow yarn into the bluepot. And she achieved a rose color by dyeing the yarn in the ooze made of the delicate little madder plant which she found in damp meadow places.

Much of the charm of the hand-woven mountain fabrics is attributable to the quality of the dye the mountain weavers concoct from their native plants, including flowers, leaves, stems, roots, bark, nuts. It was the beauty of the coloring, as well as the excellence of the weaving, that had so intrigued Mabel Fauble and me that day we first laid eyes on Aunt Susan Phillips' fabulous coverlets, skirts and basques.

The most experienced dyer in our community was Mrs. Emma Conley, the beloved lady into whose custard pie the one-year-old stepped that memorable day of the Weaving Cabin log-raising. I suspect there's been no one in our mountains surpassing her in the knowledge of plants useful in the dyeing of homespuns and of the processes employed to use them most effectively. One of the most popular little books sold in our gift shop is Mrs. Conley's small volume of instructions on how to use the various mountain plants and their fruits to obtain vegetable dyes. That it came from the printer titled *Vegetable Dying* has made it almost a collector's item. In fact, dropping the *e* in dyeing, either written or spoken, isn't as likely to cause a commotion on our campus as it probably would in other places. For instance, often someone at Penland will yell out, "Where's Mrs. Lewis?" and somebody else will answer with utter equanimity, "She's dyeing this afternoon." Or someone may want to know why So-and-so isn't on hand for lunch or dinner and he'll get the calm explanation, "She dyed this morning and it put her a little late." It must be somewhat disconcerting to persons visiting us for the first time. There's been a lot of living on these up-and-down acres at Penland, but there's also been a lot of dyeing.

Mrs. Conley dedicated her little book to Mrs. Meta Lewis, "who has been so kind in helping me in the Dye House for the last three years, and who helped get these directions ready for printing," she explains. "As a little girl my mother taught me to card, spin and dye the wool for our clothes," she says in the

90

Introduction. "The dyes we got from the plants growing in our neighborhood. We used both the iron and the brass kettles and did our work out-of-doors. The colors and formulas in this pamphlet came from those early experiences and are the ones I have taught at Penland. I hope they will benefit all who are interested in this craft."

Mrs. Lewis likes to tell about the new student who came to the Dye House one day while she and Mrs. Conley were cooking a batch of onion skins.

"Hmm-m-m," she said. "Cooking onions. What you going to do with them?"

"We're going to dye with them after a while."

"Oh," she said, "you have to cook 'em first?"

"Yes, you have to cook 'em first," Mrs. Lewis said.

She went out, but in a little while she was back.

"Where are the onions?" she asked. "What did you do with them?"

Mrs. Conley looked up and with a perfectly straight face answered, "We sent 'em over to the kitchen for soup."

You use only the outer skin of the onion, the deep-brown thin skin. It makes a beautiful gold color.

To dye a pound of wool, Mrs. Conley explains in her book, you use a pound of onion skins—quite a quantity, considering how light they are—and an ounce and a half of alum.

Here is her method: "Put the skins in a brass kettle, cover with water and boil one hour. Strain and return the ooze to the kettle, adding enough water to make a generous dye bath. Now add the alum, stirring until thoroughly dissolved. Then add the wool and let it simmer thirty minutes. Remove the wool from the dye bath, rinse in warm water until the water is clear. Hang the wool in the sun to dry.

"As soon as you put your onion skins on to boil, wash your

wool in a good soap suds, rinse thoroughly and allow the wool to remain in water until ready to use."

The color you get will be shades of yellow.

From rhododendron leaves you get a beautiful gray with a brownish cast that is very unusual; I've never seen another color just like it. It's best to soak the leaves overnight before you begin. You use an iron kettle for rhododendron leaves, and they should be boiled two hours. Then strain and return the ooze to the same kettle and add enough water to make a generous dye bath. Next add copperas, which is a mordant or setting agent, and after it has dissolved, put in the wool and allow the mixture to simmer thirty minutes. Then take your wool out, rinse until the water is clear, then hang the wool in the sun to dry.

As long as there is dye in the water, you can add successive skeins of wool. Each time, however, the wool takes up a certain amount of the dye, so that each batch is lighter as it comes out.

From the wild coreopsis you get a beautiful color that may range from burnt orange to dark red. It's hardly red, either; it's more of a rust, I'd say, and if you keep adding successive batches of wool, the color gets lighter and lighter until it is a pale rose or coral pink.

So actually you can never entirely match colors. Each batch is unique. Each has its slightly individual color no matter how hard you work to make one batch like another. That's why we usually dye several pounds of wool at a time, in order to get enough wool to do something with, you see. But commercial dyes do not completely match either.

I was telling about using onion skins to procure yellow dyes. Broom sedge also gives a beautiful yellow—just plain old broom sedge grass. You put it all into the brass kettle, stalks and everything, and you use alum as mordant. The first dyeing is a strong yellow, and each batch takes some of the color out, so that the yellow gets lighter and lighter as more wool is put in.

Back in the old days it was sometimes difficult for the isolated mountain folk to get the necessary mordants, and occasionally, when they had no copperas or alum, they would use sumac leaves. These contain tannic acid, which serves as a mordant.

Smartweed gives a beautiful chartreuse. It grows out in the garden, has a little long flower with tiny red things on the stem. You put flower, stem, root, everything into your brass kettle and boil it.

Marigold blossoms make a deep yellow dye, and if you wish the yellow still darker, put a half-dozen black-walnut hulls in with the marigolds; the color will be about that of beech tree leaves in the fall.

Pokeberries make a red dye. It takes about half a bushel of berries for each pound of wool.

Students often ask us how we get a green dye. There is nothing we know about that makes green. We have to mix indigo, or blue, with yellow. Of course, blue and yellow, as any painter knows, makes green.

One day Mr. Owl, who lives at the Cherokee Indian reservation, was visiting us, and we discussed methods of dyeing. In fact, we were working in the Dye House that day. Mr. Owl is an educated man; he has two college degrees, one from Carlisle and the other from, I believe, Oklahoma University. He is greatly interested in preserving the history and traditions of the Indians in our state.

During our conversation he asked me about green, and I said that we had been unable to get green; did he know how?

Mr. Owl shook his head. "In the early days, Miss Lucy, the Cherokees did get a green, but nobody knows now what they got it from," he revealed. "Though we have experimented a great deal, we have never recovered the secret."

Walnut hulls make a beautiful brown, and butternut hulls—they call it the white walnut up here—make a medium brown. Sassafras makes a soft yellow-tan, goldenrod blossoms make yellow, acorns provide a tan if you use alum as a mordant and a darker grayish-tan if you use copperas. Doghobble, which is our Penland name for leucothea, gives a very dark brown with a greenish cast; cocklebur, using everything about the plant except the roots, provides a satisfactory chartreuse; pecan hulls make a tan; apple bark gives a dark yellow-tan if you use alum and a distinctly brass color if you use chrome as mordant.

But I believe my favorite color is procured from the little madder plant. It makes a red color, in varying shades. You can get successively lighter shades as long as there is color in the dye bath.

Madder is a weed, a little plant that grows in meadows and damp places. Its color is more of a rose, I suppose, though we can get it in a really deep red, too. It is a pleasure to experiment with madder; you get an amazing range of tints and shades.

We don't go in for dyeing with clay at Penland, although Aunt Manda Bailey told me that she used to get clay around here somewhere and use it for dyeing. But we have tried out any number of plants—tree bark, nuts, berries, flowers, roots, stems, grasses, burs, hulls—and we have made some interesting discoveries.

We have found that the sort of pot or kettle you use is of

94

considerable importance. We have three pots, iron, brass and copper, and we long ago learned that the pot you boil a plant in makes all the difference in the world in the kind of dye you get. For instance, the darkest dyes you do in the iron pot and the lightest colors in the brass. The metal actually affects the color.

We have discovered, for example, that sumac leaves or blossoms boiled in an iron kettle will make a dark gray dye. But boiled in the brass kettle, the color comes out a tan.

And here's something even more intriguing, I think: For some of the dyes, the kind of day you have when you are preparing the dye bath makes a material difference in the results obtained. For example, madder should always be dyed on a sunny day. As soon as the dyed wool is rinsed, we hang it out in the sunshine to dry. It must be the action of the temperature that brings out the colors. Maybe it's comparable to the coloring of the leaves in the fall. Scientists claim to have exploded the theory that it is frost that produces gorgeously colored fall leaves. They say that the colored leaves are a result of the extremes of temperature to which they are subjected. If you have a cold night—it doesn't have to be freezing—and a hot midday, the spread in temperature will assure gorgeous fall leaves.

There's much to learn about dyeing homespuns with dyes procured from our native plants. It's a fascinating subject, one about which we'll never know all the answers. And like working in handicrafts in general, you learn by doing. That, I think, is the way we grow.

CHAPTER 10

THAT FIRST YEAR Mr. Worst came to Penland—
in August 1928—he was with us three days.
He spent them busily, visiting with the neighboring weavers, showing us the products of his own hands and
looms, tying up and adjusting the multiple-harness loom he
had given us, and inspiring us generally.

When Mr. Paul Bernat, publisher of *The Handicrafter*,
learned that Mr. Worst was coming to Penland, he came down
to observe him in action, and the next issue of his magazine
carried an article about Mr. Worst's visit to our school. As a
result, letters began coming in from all parts of the country
asking if Mr. Worst planned to come again and, if so, might
the writers join us during the time he would be here?

We replied that we were sorry that could not be. We explained that Mr. Worst had come to Penland because of his

interest in what we were doing with weaving in our mountain community. He had charged us nothing, we revealed further, and we thought it would hardly be fair to him to have people waiting on our doorstep to be taught by him when he was actually coming to Penland on his vacation.

When we told Mr. Worst about the letters, however, he said: "Let anybody come who wants to." Mr. Bernat came every year as long as *The Handicrafter* was published, and he wrote more articles about Mr. Worst and Penland. After the article in 1929 there were again eager requests, and so we accepted the applications of seven women. We quoted them the exorbitant rate of a dollar a day for room, board and tuition! Since Mr. Worst charged nothing, we thought we should charge only what it actually cost us to feed and house the group.

It was in August 1929 then, that I consider the Penland School of Handicrafts was born. That was the year we had our first outside students.

All our activities were still carried on in Morgan Hall, the building that had served Rufus as the rectory. It did have six bedrooms that provided accommodations for officials such as Mr. and Mrs. Worst and members of their family, the bishop when he came for a visit, the lady who snored too loudly to be put with the group, and so forth. The rest of us were to sleep on the upstairs porch in the twelve cots that had been made of cot parts discarded by the Appalachian School and stored in the basement. Some of the heads did not match the feet, and sometimes neither head nor foot matched the body, but my brother Ralph and Mr. Wyatt wired the parts together securely so that they served satisfactorily.

As letters began to come in, we wondered just what people

expected. One mother wrote that she would have to bring her three daughters, but she would solve that situation very easily by taking a small apartment in Penland, she explained. One applicant asked for a private bath, and when I wrote that we had no private baths she replied: "It is very necessary that I have a bath."

How was I to answer that? Bonnie, Tony and I cogitated upon the matter, and Tony came up with the answer: "Write her to take it before she leaves home!"

Before these people arrived in Penland I got out all their letters and tried to read between the lines. I thought I'd try to give the best cots to the fussiest people and the worst ones to those with good dispositions. That would certainly not be a fair way of assigning cots, my conscience told me. But I didn't have to wrestle with it long, because when they came we found to our joy that they all had good dispositions.

We all used a common dressing room, the room that we went through to get to the sleeping porch. The first morning I sensed that the folk were feeling that they had no privacy. They hadn't said anything, but I definitely got that feeling. So quickly, at breakfast before they had time to begin complaining, I stood up and said: "If anybody feels she would like more privacy, she can take a piece of chalk, mark a circle around herself and say, 'Please do not look beyond this.' Her wishes will be respected." After that everybody felt relaxed and at ease, and I never again had the feeling that people were uncomfortable.

The following summer we had sixteen people attending what we called our "institute," and each year after that the numbers attending doubled those of the previous year as long as our facilities made this possible. Rooms were rented at the

Appalachian School, and the old farmhouse I had bought was made livable, although there was no running water there except for a faucet in the back yard.

So that we might have more room for looms, the school allowed us to use the lower porch of old Ridgeway, its academic building, which was 101 feet long and roomy enough. But the trouble with that porch was that the school was conducting a summer camp for young children and on rainy days they used the upper porch for roller-skating. Fancy learning how to weave with roller-skating going on over your head.

But this may have been a blessing in disguise, after all. That was the year the students decided that, if they wished to continue coming to Penland, it seemed to be up to them to provide a place where instruction could be given without too much interference.

So they began to inquire about costs. How much, they wanted to know, would it cost to build a log cabin to be used for just that purpose? We consulted our neighbors, Mr. Wyatt and Mr. Ellis, who said that a log, if bought and delivered on the grounds, would cost about $2.50.

Every student gave a log, some gave more than one. A great day had dawned. One of my friends wrote that Mr. Beeson, an architect in Johnson City, had heard of the way our new weaving cabin was being made possible, and would like to contribute his services in drawing the plans. Of course we thanked him, and gladly accepted his generous offer. When Mr. Beeson came to discuss the house and what it was planned to be used for, he suggested that we build it large enough to take care of our needs for many years ahead. Consequently, the more we planned, the larger that house on paper grew.

We foresaw a dining room and kitchen, sleeping quarters

and plenty of space for instruction. When it finally reached the blue-print stage, it was no longer a log cabin but the mansion in the sky that I had dreamed of for years. It would be eighty feet long and fifty feet wide and, since it would be constructed on the side of a hill, it would have a daylight basement on the lower side. On the main floor we would have the dining room and kitchen, two large rooms for looms, an office, a washroom and a recreation room. On the second floor would be sleeping quarters.

Very quickly we learned that building this mansion, as we considered it already, would be quite different from putting up a little log cabin. For one thing, this building would require a large and substantial basement.

To advise us on this project we called in three angels: Mr. B. C. Burgess, our constant friend and business adviser; Mr. Herbert Duncan of the Spruce Pine Lumber Company; and an expert in log construction, who was actually an Angel, Mr. Merrit Angel.

The immediate problem was how to get the basement finished in time for a log-raising the next spring. We had no money, and so we concluded that we would wait until spring before starting the work so that the bills wouldn't be too old by the time the students began arriving with—we devoutly hoped—enough money to help materially. But Mr. Duncan warned us that excavation and building of the basement would take time and good weather, and he said we would never be ready for a spring log-raising if we didn't start work that fall. But how could we do this without money?

Mr. Duncan made it all sound easy enough. He told us his company would let us have whatever we needed, and we could pay for it whenever we were able. When I demurred, telling him we could not pay for anything until summer, and that it would take two or even three summers to pay for that basement, he still insisted that we get on with the work. He declared that payments were no matter of concern with him.

Well, he made the thing sound so promising that we decided to do as he had suggested. But then the thought occurred to us: What of the labor that had to eat to live, and what of materials that we could not get from Mr. Duncan and would most likely have to come from outside the county?

I went to the bank and borrowed from it and from the Building and Loan all the money they would let me have. I had offered to put up the eight acres of land and the old farmhouse on it, which I owned, but the finance folk told me that the property was worth little as collateral, and so I had had to use my life insurance policies.

That was a scary time. I felt that I was skating on very thin ice. Everything we owned was at stake. What we had was a stack of donated logs and a faith that in the dark was shaky but before the public had to seem strong and bold or we were lost. We had started with plans for a small log cabin and in almost no time were in the midst of a program to build a tremendous, expensive building. But if my friends were demonstrating their faith, shouldn't I show faith too? What could we do but go ahead?

So Mr. Angel got his crew of workmen together and they went to work. That was long before the day of bulldozers, and every shovelful of dirt was moved by hand or wheelbarrow, or pan and mule team. But the men and mules worked, and by springtime the basement walls and foundation were finished, the subflooring was down, and all was ready for the logs to be put in place.

The next thing was to raise the logs.

We remembered that beautiful and happy day when we had raised the logs for the Weaving Cabin, that May fifth with the apple orchards in bloom. So we set this log-raising for the fifth of May and hoped again for apple blossoms.

It was an early spring that year and apprehensively we watched the apple trees bloom before their usual time, and we saw the blooms shattered and blown away before our great day arrived. We wished that we could spray those blooms with glue to hold them on the trees a little longer, but we could do nothing but watch them go, and sigh resignedly. But just then, in time for the arrival of our guests and in time for the log-raising, the wild crabs burst into bloom, with their delightful and very special fragrance which is, I think, the most all-pervading and heavenly fragrance there is. Of course, I think the same thing of the wild honeysuckle when it is in bloom.

So after all, nature was most co-operative. Besides the wild crabs blooming all over the hilltops, the woods, paths and fields abounded with the dainty little wild iris; lush, long-stemmed blue violets, here and there white or yellow ones, peeped modestly forth; everywhere were the white spikes of the mountain galax, and all the tender greens of returning spring.

We asked our new bishop, Bishop Gribbin, to plan a special service with which we might begin the day, and we marveled at how aptly he found passages in the Bible perfectly fitted for a log-raising day. Although we had thought tentatively of having this service at sunrise, we finally decided that the day would be full enough without so early a start, and we had it at eight o'clock, just after breakfast, on the subflooring of what would be our Edward F. Worst Craft House. Mr. Lambert, the new clergyman and the future director of the Appalachian School, brought a little portable organ and played the hymns. Neighbors, workmen and guests gathered for the impressive little service. When it was finished, the work of the day began.

The four notchers took their places, one at each corner of the building. Neighbors hitched their teams to "swingle" trees or doubletrees and snaked the logs to the places from which other men with cant hooks would roll and heave them into position. Notchers measured and notched, mules strained and pulled, men with axes and saws worked and sweated. It was a busy time.

Meanwhile at the old Pines a quilt was in a frame, and any of the women who tired of the log-raising activities took up their thimbles and needles and put in a few stitches on what would be a gift for the next community bride.

But at noon all these activities ceased. The mules were fed and watered; and the men, women, children and babies gathered under the trees at The Pines, where there was spread out such a dinner as only a rural community can provide. For miles around the women had come in with hams baked to a delicious tenderness, fried chicken, sausages, vegetables of every sort, jellies, jams, pies, pickles and cakes, all of sufficient appeal to make today's vainest women, were they to fasten their eyes upon such food, cheerfully abandon, at least for that meal, their dieting schedules.

And after the busy morning in the open air, certainly no food ever tasted better. When everybody had had his fill and after we had talked about what an important role the new Craft House would play in the life of the community, the men, the mules, the axes and saws and cant hooks all went back to work. By nightfall the four walls of the Edward F. Worst

Craft House were standing, waiting for their roof. Through the summer the work on the building continued; the day before Mr. Worst returned in August the last nail went into the roof.

It was a joyful occasion when the returning students saw the new structure and each conjectured which log in the wall was his, and everybody marveled at the miracles wrought through concerted and joyful effort. We had profited by adding a much-needed building to our plant, but we had profited even more in having worked together as a community in attaining the answer to our need. And we had enjoyed doing it.

That summer the Craft House was used thoroughly and effectively. To be sure, it had an unfinished basement, walls with no chinking, a subflooring of green lumber that in drying left cracks wider by the day and knots that dropped out. But it was a happy house. "Let's never put chinking between the logs," students would say, "because the way it is now we can sit anywhere in the building and enjoy the views in every direction."

The knots and wide cracks in the subflooring, however, were at times disturbing, because bobbins, reed hooks, shuttles and other small treasures when dropped would sometimes fall through. But when enough such items had been lost through the floor to threaten the crippling of weaving activities, some brave soul would venture below and return as popular as an old-time peddler with a pack on his back.

Two black snakes lived in the basement, but we did not disturb them. They were as good as cats at keeping the mice away, and I have always understood that black snakes keep away the venomous kind. Nor did students who slept in the

Craft House that summer fear our pet snakes, even though the snakes could easily have entered their rooms through doorways, between the logs or through the knotholes. To create rooms in the house, in fact, the students hung up blankets and coverlets or fashioned walls out of scraps of building paper left over, or of cement tow sacks. And they saw no need of having doors; doors might shut out something interesting.

Nor was there any lack of social events. It may have been the perpetual Turnbulls, as we called them, who started serving tea in the amen corner of the second floor dormitory or it may have been that Wild Irish Rose Baldwin; at any rate, the first tea service was nicked cups discarded from the kitchen, with the wrong end of a toothbrush used for stirring sugar, or a spoon brought from home. Eventually, though it was after the passage of a few years, the perpetual Turnbulls perpetuated the tea habit by donating a tea set of real cups, saucers and plates.

People that summer, not to be outdone by the log-givers of the year before, gave windows. And it happened that a window sash cost the same as a log, two dollars and a half. Everybody gave at least one window sash; some gave whole windows, some gave doors, and two students from St. Louis, Lucy Elliott and Lonnie Baird, gave the fireplace and chimney.

Our mansion in the sky was rapidly becoming earthbound, solid, substantial. And it was an inspiration, a challenge. No playhouse built by a group of children anywhere could have created more interest than did ours, in which the concerted efforts of students and teachers had created this combined recreation hall, social center, workshop.

So by the time the students and staff began returning the next summer, we had windows and doors in and some of the

105

bedrooms furnished. And before that summer was over, other people expressed their eagerness to give bedrooms, so many, in fact, that there were more people wanting to give than there were bedrooms. Interest was contagious, growing, glowing, satisfying.

That summer before the students began returning, I recall, as I would walk through the building, planning and trying to get ready for the summer's activities, I seemed to get the feeling that the walls themselves reflected the love and the joy that had gone into the creating of that house. Bonnie Ford once said that Penland was a composite of all the friends that throughout the years have come to be a part of it. It may be my imagination or it may be something even more ephemeral, but to me it seems that the Craft House is a composite of all the love and joy and togetherness that have gone into its building, and whether or not newcomers are conscious of it, I feel quite sure that they are affected by it.

I am at a loss to express just what I feel. But an early student at Penland, Edna Kleinmeyer of Lakewood, Ohio, wrote me a letter in which she told of the part played by nature in giving depth and strength to the meaning I seek to express. Edna said I might quote from it:

"Figuratively, as well as literally, it has been a mountain-top experience," she said of her time at Penland. "Not knowing the Penland tradition, I had expected to find only a school where one might learn a skill; I did not dream that it was the expression of a way of life. The distinctive spirit of the place . . . was a subtle thing, found in the fragrance of unvarnished wood in the morning dampness; at Bailey's Peak swathed in mists or printed blue-gray above the pink mimosa blossoms; in the comfortable clopping of the looms. It was in

106

Auntie Freas' cheery good humor and in Mr. Peters' twinkle and unruffled patience; in the plaintive music of the shepherd's pipes; in the voices singing 'Auld Lang Syne' softly in front of the glowing embers of the great stone fireplace while Mr. Worst examined the lovely St. Francis he had just received; in Mr. Worst's serenity of voice, and his fine tact, kindliness and respect for the dignity of men and women; in Mrs. Conley, motherly and competent, carding wool or stirring yarns in the steaming iron pot in the dye shed; in Professor Lear's barbed jests deflating little sham balloons; in the glitter of mica in red clay roads; in Mrs. McElwain's brook laving forget-me-nots and peppermint; in velvety, myriad-colored moths fluttering into the dormitory out of the darkness where the whip-poor-will called and the moon rose over the corn; in Mrs. Ellis ladling out cider in the fresh coolness of her spring house; in a woman in the fold of the hills, washing clothes in a brook and in an iron kettle over an outdoor fire. . . . I've never known a place where one experiences such a feeling of liberation, of taking for granted that mistakes are a normal part of the learning process; of tolerant acceptance of people as they are, yet faith in their desire and ability to grow. . . ."

CHAPTER 11

B Y THE SECOND summer the windows and doors and the chimney and fireplace had been built in the Craft House, so that life assumed a degree of graciousness. The huge fireplace itself, I thought, made the difference between a house and a home, for what is a home without a fireplace? And this fireplace, I felt, was a very special one, for our friend and neighbor Bascom Hoyle built it with the utmost feeling. For the chimney he chose stones with moss, to be laid where they would be enjoyed from the terrace. And for the hearth he had searched Mr. Henry Willis' place until he found one huge flat stone three feet by nine feet; it made the entire hearth. The five-foot fireplace he lined with soapstone which Doc Hoppes gave us from his quarry.

But that year the most outstanding, conspicuous, pressing need in the Craft House was for bathrooms. We had a bathroom, of course. With the exception of a few bedrooms, there were no finished rooms in the entire three-story, fifty-by-eighty-foot building; there was only the studding to show where the partitions would be. But at the corner of the second floor, just at the head of the stairs, we tacked up building paper around the studding to enclose the solitary lavatory and toilet. Thus we had a bathroom. And this bathroom was supposed to provide for the needs of the large and growing family on the three floors of that big craft building. People who have never lived in a house with a paper bathroom just don't know what they have missed, for I have never known a more entertaining room.

For example, when the school opened that summer, carpenters were still working on the house; as they would carry lumber upstairs on their shoulders they would have to turn the corner where the bathroom was, and in doing so they were likely to rub themselves or the lumber against that paper and maybe even punch a hole in it. And right there is where I discovered an interesting phenomenon. If there was a man in that bathroom when this occurred, nothing whatsoever would happen. But just let a woman be in there when the carpenter lumbered against the paper wall, or worse, when he stuck the end of his timber through the building paper! In that very instant he would be assailed by squeals, ejaculations, vituperations! Some people were even saying that modesty no longer existed, at Penland, I mean. But it made stories to tell, and after the worst was over, I'm confident that even the principal characters in some of these situations enjoyed their roles.

So the students who came that year agreed that the greatest contribution they could make to Penland—and themselves while they were here—would be to provide additional bathrooms. The gifts the year before, they remembered, had been in amounts of two dollars and a half, the cost of one log, and although no one could think of any piece of plumbing that would cost as little as two-fifty, there was much joking about it, and planning and giving too.

But we were hardly ready to accept with equanimity the good fortune that came to us one evening—it was while that same group was with us—when an interesting-looking foreign car drove up the hill—the first foreign car ever to have been driven up our hill as far as I had seen or heard about. We were still living in Morgan Hall, and as we watched the car being driven around the house to the front, we were all consumed with interest and downright curiosity. A gentleman and two ladies alighted and I went out to greet them and make them at home.

"We are about to sit down to supper," I said. "Won't you join us?"

They said they would be glad to, and they did. And after supper we all went over to the Craft House, for that is where we took all our guests, since it was really the showplace of the county. We showed them over the house and I happened to have the gentleman along with me. With much pride I showed him the prize room of the house, which was the little paper-partitioned bathroom. But he seemed rather bored. I thought that the poor man simply had no sense of humor, and I shrugged off his lack of appreciation of our bathroom.

After we had looked over the house, we gathered around the big fireplace as we customarily did, and chatted. In our group was Professor Lear of the electrical engineering department of the University of North Carolina, who came every summer as long as he lived, who liked Penland so well, in fact, that he built a home and retired here.

110

The first chance "Pop" Lear had to get my ear he said, "Do you know who that man is?"

"He told me his name was Mr. Crane," I replied. "That's all I know about him."

"Yes, he's Mr. Crane, all right," said Pop, a wry grin on his face. "*The* Mr. Crane—one of the Cranes of the Crane Plumbing Company."

"The Lord sent him up this hill," I said, and I meant it.

I was glad I hadn't known who he was when I showed him the bathroom, because I would have felt very self-conscious. But I was happy that he had seen it.

Afterward I asked Mr. Crane how he had heard about Penland, and he revealed that he had been to the White Top Folk Festival and someone—he did not remember who—told him not to go home until he had been to Penland. So he had come over.

Well, it happened. After he returned home his company sent us fixtures for three bathrooms.

Soon after these had arrived I received a letter from Professor Lear, now back at Chapel Hill. He asked permission to write other plumbing companies. He would write, he said, to tell them what Crane had done; he would not ask for anything. Then we would just wait and see what happened. The professor well knew that it was against my principles to ask for money for the Craft House. I regarded it as my firstborn child, and one does not beg for one's children if there is any other way to manage. According to my sister, I won't beg for it but I don't mind exposing its needs. Clearly, Professor Lear's suggestion involved only "exposing its needs." I gave permission.

Dr. Lear wrote to both Standard Manufacturing Company and to Kohler of Kohler, Wisconsin. And they replied that they would be happy to furnish the plumbing for the entire building! When the fixtures arrived that winter we displayed them on the stage of the Spruce Pine Room, where they were admired and discussed by us, of course, but also by all our many visitors. By summer, all had been installed. Now there is on the door of each bathroom a copper plate, etched in our own metal shop with the words: "Plumbing given by Crane" or "by Standard" or "from Kohler of Kohler."

But having a school grow up around us involved more than building buildings and begging plumbing. We would soon have to have water, and, of course, we required a septic tank. The first water supply was comparatively simple and inexpensive, because our good friend Tim Wyatt had been digging ditches and laying pipes down from springs up on Art'urs' Knob, and we had been getting our water by gravity. Then, too, there was an old abandoned well near the Craft House, and temporarily—until we could get some money and ascertain how to arrange a better disposal system—we dumped the sewage into it.

Generous and far-seeing Pop Lear, wise in the ways of the world and more particularly of state boards of health, knew that there would have to be a more dignified sewage-disposal system. So from Chapel Hill he lured his brother Merritt Lear, a fellow professor at the University, and the two sat around our living-dining room table by the hour, making plans, studying specifications and writing letters. They sent for blueprints, got the state board of health to send experts to advise, got special permission to act as planners and supervisors, and they and Mr. Wyatt went to work.

It literally required weeks to do the job. Difficulties were met and discussed, dispositions wore threadbare, vocabularies were taxed. When a teacher or pupil, seeing Pop and Mr.

Wyatt sitting on a log in heated argument, would draw near to see if all the tales they had heard could be true, they retreated hastily and in pale wonderment that the half had not been told! But looking back a moment later they might discover Mr. Wyatt lending a helping hand to exhausted Dr. Lear. And the two would take up their picks and start digging again.

That septic tank and draining field must have been scientifically designed and built, for now that Mitchell County has graduated into the status of having a health officer of its own, with a supervisor who inspects us regularly, we consistently display proudly a Grade-A rating for sanitation.

But as more and more students came to enroll at Penland, more and more water was used. Mr. Wyatt played around up on Art'ur's Knob, coaxed all the little trickling springs into a central pool and with concrete was able to form a reservoir of sorts. But in order to make use of all the springs he could bring together, Mr. Wyatt had to spread out his reservoir so much that he could not put a cover over it, and without a cover it did not meet state requirements. And there wasn't enough water anyway, even with that reservoir, for our ever-growing summer family. And to make bad matters considerable worse, the following summer was extremely dry.

What a summer we had! There were days and even weeks when no tub baths were possible. There was one day when there was *no* water, and we had to haul in some from a neighbor. That day I called the staff and students together, told them that enough water would be brought in for face-washing and tooth-brushing, but for other needs each person would have to go to the woods. It was primitive! Why that group of students stayed I don't know, but nobody gave up. Perhaps it was the challenge of the situation. I spent days and nights of wondering, scheming, praying for rain, and debating with myself whether or not to close the school, until one night I knew within my soul that if there was no rain within the remaining days of that particular three-week term, the school would have to be closed. And then, the decision made, the rains came!

But I knew that we were at the end of our improvising for water. Before summer came again we would have to have a well drilled. Soon we began to receive gifts earmarked for a water supply for the school, and when we had received enough to dare negotiate with well-drillers, we sought prices. Once more that mystical two dollars and a half was presented to us: it would cost two dollars and fifty cents a foot for well-drilling. And cash when the job was completed. There could be no waiting; it wouldn't be like our dealing with the Spruce Pine Lumber Company, or any of the other business concerns in the county who had been so patient with us.

I took a chance; I told the men to start drilling. The depth of the well would determine whether we had enough money to pay for it. And they kept going down. It seemed to me that as that drilling machine banged deeper and deeper into the earth it was saying with every drop of the hammer, "two dollars and a half, two dollars and a half, two dollars and a half."

Water was finally reached in sufficient quantity at a depth of 315 feet. And 315 times two dollars and a half was a lot of money, considerably more than all our gifts for the well had amounted to. But by robbing every account we had, and by devious twists and turns of one kind and another, we found the money and the men were paid—and blessing of all blessings, the water flowed!

The Edward F. Worst Craft House still lacked a great deal.

Having to turn our best energies to getting water, of course, delayed the job of finishing work elsewhere. But it was taking shape, surely if not very rapidly, as various individuals and groups were inspired to give entire rooms on the main floor. The largest of these was the recreation room, with ample space for folk dancing and a stage for use in the presenting of plays. This room was given by the civic organizations of Spruce Pine, which were in the main made up of men representing companies who were "carrying" us. That, I thought, was all the more indicative of the generosity and good will of these businessmen who did and continue to do so much for our school. On the wall of that room a small copper plate says "Spruce Pine Room" and by that name the room is known. Another room was given by a women's auxiliary of an Episcopal church in Pittsburgh that had sold our community products over a period of many years. Now the library and exhibit room, it has a copper plate reading: "Pittsburgh Room, Woman's Auxiliary, Diocese of Pittsburgh."

Perhaps the most conspicuous room in the house, however, is the one entered from the east terrace, which might well be called the front room. In the early years this large hall was used for looms, but later became the lounge, given by former students of Mr. Worst and called the "Chicago Room." Even before it was finished, the Worsts began to use their hangings, coverlets, draperies and such on the walls, giving it a very gracious and welcoming appearance. Throughout the years this handsome room has received much attention from various friends who have woven for it curtains in lengthwise stripes of woods green, blue, red, a little yellow and a little black, and "settin'" cushions of a matching green. Earning money by giving afternoon teas and such, they have chosen with loving care appropriate chairs, a writing desk, coffee tables and other furnishings. We consider the Chicago Room one of the most gracious on our campus.

The second-floor dormitory occupies almost half of the floor and the students one summer combined to pay for the finishing of it. Strolling through the room one day, one of our Penland boys, Ralph Conley, noticed signs reading "Ohio" or "New York" or perhaps "Michigan." The signs meant that students from these various states were responsible for certain projects. Ralph was depressed by the fact that nowhere had he seen even a small sign referring to Penland. He came to me, considerably disturbed, and told me about it.

"Miss Lucy," he said, "that's bad. And I'm going to do something to remedy the situation."

So he began to collect money from Penland neighbors, and this little community, which isn't even a village, contributed enough to finance the stage in the "Spruce Pine Room."

During these years of growth Mr. Worst brought down during their spring vacation a group of his nephews and several other Chicago teachers to put up sheet rock for the walls of the second and third floors. It was a satisfying and exhilarating experience to watch that group of earnest young men going to work with saws and hammers, and it was amazing how quickly they performed that task of loving service.

The architect originally had not planned a third floor for the building, but when we found how much room there was in the attic, we asked Mr. Beeson to come back and alter his plans to provide the third floor. He did; he added dormer windows, and we had another floor for sleeping quarters!

While Mr. Beeson planned the dormer windows, Tony Ford designed closets, cupboards and drawers to be built into the eaves, so that the spaces between the dormers were utilized. When the work was done, the third floor became one of the most popular residences, especially for the younger crowd.

But there was one thing lacking. On that third floor we had built two bathrooms, but only one of them had a bathtub! The rest of the fixtures were in, but as it was continually doing at Penland, the money had run out with one bathtub short.

There were seventeen beds up there and they were full. So those third-floorers decided they needed that second bathtub, just had to have it. But how?

They decided to raise money with which to purchase one. And after much thought and planning they agreed that for one of the money-raising schemes they would sell tickets at a quarter apiece for the first bath; they would draw the winning ticket from those sold. But if you bought a ticket and didn't win the first bath, it was also agreed, you would be entitled to *watch* the winner take the first bath. So the tickets sold quite well.

Then they had auctions. If you went upstairs you couldn't get down again without buying something. I remember one of the girls had to pay thirty-five cents for an old green peach before they would let her come downstairs. And they polished shoes and did all sorts of other things to raise money for that bathtub. One day they reported to me, beaming, "Miss Lucy, we've got the money for the tub!"

The tub was duly purchased and quickly installed. Then they held the drawing for the first bath.

And would you know, the best-looking girl won it! She was tall, had beautiful red hair, and was just a beautiful girl every way.

So the night came for the bath, and there was great excitement. Everybody gathered upstairs to see the performance. The press was there, and the photographers were there with their cameras ready, and everything was lined up to see this good-looking girl take the first bath in the new tub. The third floor was crowded and everybody was trying to push into the bathroom to get a peep as she got into the bathtub.

And so, when the assemblage is all set and everybody is ready for the performance to begin, the girl comes up. She is wearing a shower cap and a raincoat, and as far as anybody can see, nothing else. She stands beside the tub, and it is announced that she is now ready to strip off the raincoat and step into the tub. And the proverbial eyes are proverbially glued.

Well, she took off the raincoat, and of course she had on a bathing suit, though it was a rather scant one. And the first bath in the new tub began.

The photographers aimed their cameras and flash bulbs popped, and the girl promptly disappeared, except for head and shoulders, into a bubble bath that would have made even Hollywood envious.

So the evening ended hilariously, and we had bought and paid for our new bathtub. Once more it had been shown that the ingenuity of our Penland folk is immeasurable, boundless, unpredictable.

Another time on the third floor of the Craft House we had a circus, a carnival. On that floor Tony had built cubbies, as I said, one cubby for two people, with ample drawer space and places for shoes and to hang clothes, and a little dressing table. Well, we used those cubbies for our carnival. One was a fortune-telling booth, one sold cookies and cakes and candies, another one had a grab bag in it, another had a bingo game going—each cubby had something to raise money. One bathroom was a chamber of horrors. I don't know what they were doing in there—I never went in—but everybody came out screaming.

CHAPTER 12

E WERE BEGINNING to move now. We were getting along toward the materialization, in part at least, of our long-cherished dream. The ancient craft of hand-weaving was being revived in many a mountain home. Down in the coves and along the slopes of the Blue Ridge women toiled happily at looms and over boiling dyepots; they were fashioning materials of practical value and great aesthetic significance. For many the revival of weaving meant money with which to send their children off to college, or to provide needed medical or surgical care, or to take care of other pressing needs. At times the market for their products had been slow, of course, but over the years they had been working, it had been generally good, and having something to sell from time to time for many women in our region had been a veritable godsend.

To me the joy of knowing that the wonderful craft of

hand-weaving was not to die, but instead would be nurtured and perhaps even improved upon as eager and imaginative and responsive souls became interested in it, outweighed even the happiness I had in seeing our project becoming financially successful.

But one thing was beginning to give me concern. As the gradually completed Craft House grew in value, I became more and more uncomfortable. Since the property on which it was built belonged to me personally, the Craft House was actually my personal property. I knew that wasn't right; it wasn't the way I wanted it. All the donations of logs, windows, doors, plumbing, wiring and labor had not been given to me, but for the development of a school.

It so weighed on my conscience that I was driven to consult two of the cleverest lawyers I have known, Mr. John McBee, Sr., of Spruce Pine and Mr. Haywood Parker of Asheville. I told them my problem. I wished to deed the property to a self-perpetuating board of trustees, and I wanted as trustees local people who would know and appreciate the community and its needs and level-headed businessmen who could advise me and help me to make important decisions properly. I explained that almost without my realizing it we had grown into an important and imposing craft school; we had done it too without my knowing that we were going to, and I told them I was afraid it was getting to be too much for me.

They listened carefully to my story, as good lawyers do, and then both advised me against deeding to a board of trustees. They gave a number of sound reasons. In the first place the school would never have attained the position it had reached if it had been under the government of a board of level-headed businessmen. "They wouldn't have allowed you to undertake the things you have undertaken and done," they explained. "It's a good thing you weren't hampered by having such a board."

Their advice was not to deed but to make a will leaving the property to a board of trustees.

I allowed myself to be persuaded, and all three of us worked on the will to make it fit the needs of the school's future and at the same time be foolproof. One lawyer would do what he could with it, and then I would take it to the other to see if he could shoot any legal holes in it. And finally it was finished. We all thought it a good will. I liked it.

For a year or two we went along under this arrangement, but still I was not comfortable about that will. Suppose I should live to be really old—old enough not to think too clearly—and should make other plans for that property. Legally, it was still mine to do with it as I wished, but morally it wasn't.

I went back to the lawyers. "You'll have to make that will into a deed," I told them. And it was done.

To the board of trustees I appointed Bonnie Willis Ford, whose family had been a pillar of strength in the community as she had been a pillar of strength to me in the school; Clementine Douglas, with whom I had worked hand in hand in the Southern Highlands Handicraft Guild; Mr. B. C. Burgess, who had been a staunch friend and a wise counselor throughout the years; Mr. Jason Deyton, the first superintendent of Mitchell County schools to possess a college degree; and Edward Fortner, cashier of the Bank of Spruce Pine. Bonnie had helped me select the board members, and looking back upon it, I think we could not have made better choices.

Mr. Burgess' duties were unchanged now that he was a board member, but his name was listed on the school stationery. The same was true of Bonnie, except that in her new role she kept the minutes of the meetings. Clementine Douglas came over from Asheville to bring spice, zest and a world of wisdom and foresight to the board sessions. Jason Deyton's life from the time of his graduation from the University of North Carolina practically parallels the history of the Mitchell County public school system. He is an educator, an idealist and, I insist, an artist and a poet, whether or not he has ever painted a picture or written a poem. As for Ed Fortner, I can truthfully say that he always believed in us more than we believed in ourselves, and that fact challenged us to stay on our toes. And he was cashier of the bank, and heaven knows we needed friends in that bank.

The agreement we had made with Bishop Horner concerning the status of the Appalachian School and community weaving, incidentally, held good until after the beloved bishop was gone and a new bishop had taken his place. That was during the Depression. The Appalachian School was in the red, and the weaving project, which had lived gloriously during the boom years and then had been laid low by lack of sales for that long lean period, was sadly in the red indeed. The bishop and others concerned got their heads together, and we all decided it would be best for the school to go its way without responsibility for the weaving, and for the weaving to go its separate way on whatever resources it might be able to achieve and command. So when I made the deed of the property over to the board of trustees, it embraced the community weaving program as well as the school for students from out in the world.

The deed was properly recorded, and the Penland School of Handicrafts was incorporated under the laws of North Carolina as a nonprofit educational institution.

122

Approaching Penland School

Log raising, Crafts House

The Chicago Room, The Edward F. Worst Crafts House

Community weavers at Penland about 1924

Community weavers in the Weaving Cabin

The Pittsburgh Room, The Edward F. Worst Crafts House

The Crafts House in 1960

The Weaving Cabin

Spinning on the low wheel

Spinning on the high wheel

Displaying coverlet to foreign students

Entertaining Penland guests at Hoot Owl Holler

Bottoming chairs with hickory bark

The first instructor of lapidary

The Reverend Rufus Morgan dedicates the outdoor shrine

Coverlet of handspun, vegetable-dyed wool

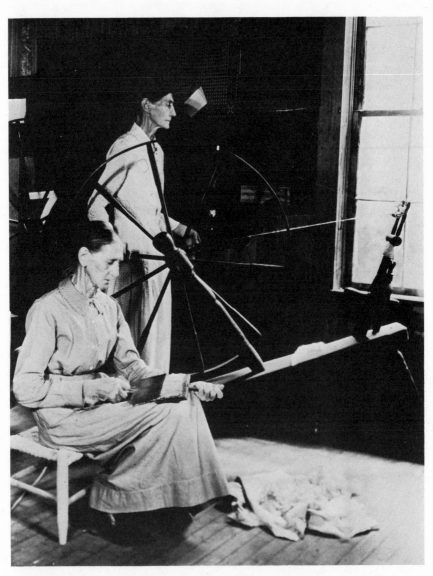

Veteran carders, spinners, and weavers

Making pottery

Instructor in glass blowing

Making jewelry

Penland "rock hounds" at the Emerald Mines

Gem stones collected by "rock hounds" at Penland

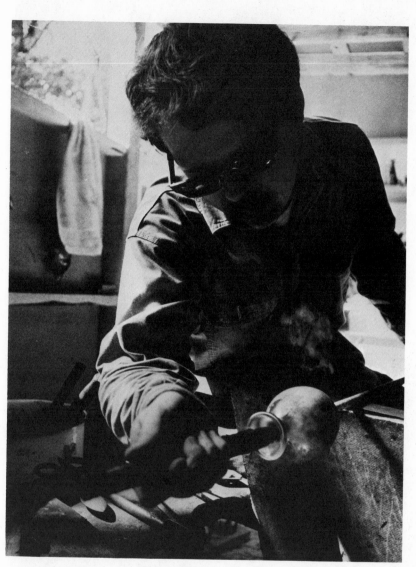

Metal working

Weaving Independence Hall baize

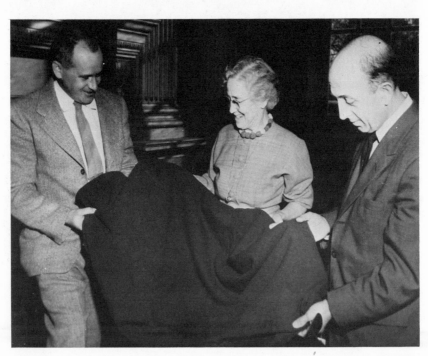

Miss Lucy presents the green baize

Threading a loom

Photography instructor and students on field trip

Vegetable dyeing

Penland pottery display

Miss Lucy Morgan

"MISS LUCY," someone will often say to me, "operating this school up here at Penland, you must meet a lot of interesting people." I do. That has been one of the joys of living and working in such a place. And you don't have to run all over the world to do it; they come to you. Already persons interested in handicrafts have come to Penland from some fifty-five different nations in almost every part of the world.

And many have come year after year, or have come and then decided to stay for good, as members of our faculty. We have been fortunate in being able to obtain persons highly proficient in their crafts and peculiarly fitted for teaching them, even though always we have had little money for salaries.

Such a man is Mr. Peters.

The first summer we were in the Craft House one of our

students was Mr. Rupert Peters, director of visual education in the Kansas City public schools. When he came to Penland,' Mr. Peters had been weaving less than a year; for instruction he had been using Mr. Worst's book, *Foot-Power Hand-Weaving*.

We soon discovered that he was a perfectionist, and at the end of his stay he had become such an excellent craftsman that we asked him to return the next summer as Mr. Worst's assistant. He agreed, and he did. He has been teaching at Penland every summer since, and when he was retired in Kansas City he built his home here and now teaches the year round.

I really don't know how many years we conducted a summer school before we paid any teacher a salary. Mr. Worst, of course, charged us nothing, and everybody must have known that we had nothing to pay.

But after years of no salaries, we did begin to pay some teachers a very small salary, just a little bit, because I was ashamed not to. One summer, I recall, we were paying Mr. Peters the handsome sum of a hundred fifty dollars for teaching twelve weeks; another teacher, also from Kansas City, said he happened to know that Mr. Peters had been offered a hundred dollars a week for twelve weeks to teach in another school.

That disturbed me. It was just too much to let pass. So I sought out Mr. Peters, told him what I had heard. "Mr. Peters," I said, "I appreciate your loyalty, but I just can't allow you to turn down a salary of a hundred dollars a week. You just can't afford to be that loyal."

"Miss Lucy," he replied, "it's worth the difference just to be in a place like this where there are no requirements, grades, papers to correct, or rules, and where students don't have to be urged but are here because they want what we have to

offer. It's an interesting place to be, with interesting and congenial people to be with. I'm staying here."

If Penland and $150 was worth as much to him as some
other place and $1,200—well, what else could I say? And I
had to confess that I felt the same way about it.

We think that Mr. Peters' training in visual education is an
excellent background for a teacher of weaving, and we think
nobody could give a better course in basic weaving than he
does. He knows his field, that's for sure; but there's something else that helps, too. The twinkle in his eyes, and his
quiet, kindly humor provide the key that reveals a personality perfectly suited to a teaching role at Penland.

There's Martha Pollock, too. She came to us as a student
under the GI Bill and specialized in hand-weaving. We never
had a more apt pupil, and when she had been here a year she
was designing her own weaving patterns in multiple-harness
techniques.

Even before Martha left Penland, a linen tablecloth that she
had designed and woven was accepted at an international textile exhibition and was awarded first prize in napery.

Martha Pollock now has her own studio in Beverly Hills,
California, and designs and creates fabrics for interior decora-
tors, among them Bill Haines, one-time movie star and now
an interior decorator. Her creations have been pictured and
described in *House Beautiful* and in various craft publications.
The name Martha Pollock is well known in the world of
craftsmen.

We are proud of Martha as designer and weaver, and just as
proud of her and her gracious mother as people. The only
possible criticism we could make of the two is that they have
put too much distance between themselves and Penland.

I could go on for a long time, in fact, naming persons of

whom we are proud, persons who came to Penland and very distinctly left their imprint upon us. I am thinking at the moment of two such women, one Swedish, the other Danish.

One summer the Lears had as their guest Mr. Kendall Wisegar, who had gone to college with Pop Lear. Mr. Wisegar brought with him an exhibit of unusual and very beautiful weaving done by Mrs. Margaret Bergman of Poulsbo, Washington.

Mrs. Bergman had designed her own patterns in multiple-harness techniques, and we were all so greatly impressed with her work that I wrote Mrs. Bergman and asked her if she would consider coming to Penland for the next summer, even though all we could pay her were transportation and living expenses.

She replied that she would be glad to come. And for three summers she was with us; she brought looms of her own design and taught us her very special methods and techniques.

Mrs. Bergman was Swedish and spoke English with enough difficulty that it was easier for her to demonstrate than to explain by speaking. But that year we had as a student Irene Beaudin of Canada, who was able to put into words Mrs. Bergman's instructions. Irene worked closely with Mrs. Bergman and was an apt interpreter.

It was a great experience to know this wonderful Swedish woman. She was kind and gentle and eager to pass on her craft skills. Her hands and fingers knew weaving as none other I have ever known. They seemed to know what to do without being directed by her mind. And besides this great skill, Mrs. Bergman had a delicious and twinkling sense of humor.

Although she was perhaps seventy-five when she came to us,

Mrs. Bergman joined in the folk-dancing with agility and grace. She even taught us the Swedish Weavers' Dance, which has become a Penland favorite.

It was while Mrs. Bergman was here that another weaver of ability and accomplishment came to Penland. She was the Danish lady, Mrs. Emmy Sommer of Copenhagen. She was teaching weaving as occupational therapy at Walter Reed Army Hospital in Washington.

Mrs. Sommer's specialty was tapestry weaving, and she had done some of the restoring of tapestries for the famous Gobelin Art Gallery. She taught us about tapestry, including much that is not in books and not done on looms. Mrs. Sommer was one of the great souls it has been my happy privilege to know.

CHAPTER 14

THE RESCUE FROM oblivion of the wonderful craft of hand-weaving which had begun to disappear with the passing of the elderly women who had learned it from their mothers and grandmothers in mountain homes, had been for years my driving passion. This was Mr. Worst's craft, and his interest in it and his pre-eminence among those who taught it naturally heightened my concern for its preservation. So during the first years of our school we taught only weaving.

But as the school's fame spread, we began to receive letters from experts in other crafts who told us they would like to have the experience of a summer at Penland, in exchange for which they would be glad to teach their respective specialties. So that's how we got started in other handicrafts.

Pottery was the first addition, and we began teaching it in

the little log stable, which was actually the only place available at the time. I remember going one day to Charlie Tipton, our man of all work.

"Charlie, some friend of Bishop Horner's is giving us a pottery kiln," I told him. "The friend doesn't want his name to be known; maybe he thinks we would ask for other gifts. Anyway, he heard I had done some work in pottery when I was up with Mr. Worst last winter, and he's giving us a big, heavy metal kiln that is too heavy to put on any floor we have. The only thing I know to do is to clean out that old log stable and use it as a pottery."

So they took out the mangers and some of the stalls and scraped up all the loose dirt, leaving the hard-packed earth for the floor. Then the freight train brought our kiln and we had it hauled up the slope to its home.

After the kiln was in place, Bascom Hoyle built a flue for it. To assure the flue's having a proper draft, we got a long metal drainpipe, a corrugated thing that certainly gave our old stable a strange modern touch, and set it into the flue.

When summer came, Mr. Worst brought down a potter who was working with him, a Mr. Fowler, and our pottery department was on its way.

Two of our young neighbors, John Morgan and Rufus Wyatt, were among the first to become interested in this craft. They were constant companions of Tony Ford, who had the charm of perpetual youth. Tony had learned a great deal about wild flowers, particularly the unusual and lovely ones to be found on the mountain tops. While off superintending crafts over the state, Tony would spend his Sundays and holidays with the flowers. If someone chided him for not going to church, he would declare that God did a good job

129

with His flowers and shrubs, but He really needed someone to help Him.

And so the three could usually be found puttering around the old stable, working not only with the kiln but with flowers and plants too. They made such a beauty spot of the grounds around the stable that visitors would stop to look, explore and revel. Many of the plants brought down from the mountains were quite rare and guests would ask about them. Tony could answer any of their questions, but the boys seldom knew which name belonged to what plant. Tony had cautioned them to avoid saying, "I don't know," even to make up a name if they had to. One day when a lady asked Rufus the name of a certain flower she was admiring, Rufus compromised: "I don't know, lady," he said, "but I think it's an anthem."

Rufus quickly learned the art of making pottery, though, and he was soon making things to sell as a part of our community activities.

During the time we were establishing the pottery I got involved in another project. Mary Clark invited me to visit her in Bronxville where she was taking evening classes in metalwork. One night she took me along with her. With the others I learned how to hammer pewter disks into plates. After hammering out three plates in different sizes, I told myself that next to weaving this was the most fun I'd ever had. And so I inveigled the instructor into selling me three molds and three leather-covered hammers, which I happily took home with me.

As soon as Mary arrived at Penland that summer, we ordered pewter; then she and John Morgan and Rufus Wyatt hammered out plates that sold almost as fast as they could could make them. They were working in Morgan Hall, but

130

the hammering was so noisy that we decided another place would have to be found. So we moved the equipment down to the old stable, which was roomy enough to serve as both metal shop and pottery.

Now, with so much going on in the stable, we began to notice that it was really showing its age. It had been serving in many capacities over the years, and it was getting in bad shape. The logs next to the ground were badly rotted, much of the chinking had dropped out from between others, and one corner of the building was settling down. The poor old thing looked worn and discouraged.

One day I spoke to Charlie Tipton about it. "The pottery is our most picturesque building, Charlie," I said. "It would break my heart if it should tumble down. Can't you do something to make it a little more stable? Couldn't you prop it up at the corners, or fix a frame inside for it to sort of lean on?"

He shook his head doubtfully, but he went down to the stable and looked it over thoroughly. When he came back to report he was still shaking his head. "Miss Lucy," he declared solemnly, "if I go in there and commence hammerin' around, that buildin's going to fall on me."

"Well, Charlie," I assured him, "you are more valuable than any building. I reckon we'll just have to let it go."

But I still wasn't reconciled to seeing the stable deteriorate. A little later Mr. Angel was up at the school, the man who had had charge of building the Craft House. Mr. Angel was a contractor and builder and an expert with logs, as he had already demonstrated to us. I told him about the old log stable and asked him if he thought anything could be done to save it.

He went down and investigated. He stuck his knife into some of the logs, hit others with a hammer and listened to the sound, inspected the structure from ground to loft. Then he figured, and he gave me a price for which he would rejuvenate the building.

Then I began to get cautious. "Mr. Angel," I said, "I don't want you to get hurt working for us. We need you around here. Do you think there's any danger of that pottery falling on you?"

He looked at me and his eyes twinkled, and in the characteristic understatement of the man of the mountains he replied, "Miss Lucy, I ain't never yet had a building fall on me."

Mr. Angel went to work. He propped up the sunken corner and replaced bad logs, poured a concrete floor that extended under the walls and put new chinking between the logs. When he had finished, the old stable had renewed youth but had not lost its old charm.

That old log stable is still in use. In it we teach how to make lamp shades, and non-fired pottery which is related to kiln pottery but is quite a different craft. It serves too as the darkroom for our photography department and has all the equipment necessary for that work.

The little stable has been added to, propped up and rejuvenated, but it remains unspoiled and is actually one of the most picturesque buildings on our campus. We are happy that it did not go the way of many other old log buildings that once dotted our mountain slopes and valleys.

Before I leave pottery for a discussion of other crafts that we began teaching, I want to mention one of our teachers who gave life and vigor to the course in pottery. Peggy Jamieson, like so many of our Penland folk, made a profession of her craft; she now has her own pottery on Merritt Island, Florida. Peggy always enjoyed the charm of the place and its people, but particularly engaging for her was the saucy little Carolina wren that built a nest right above the potter's wheel and raised a family there with constant scoldings for those who invaded its neighborhood.

Our interest in metal work led us to establish a department to teach metal work and jewelry making. This was taught by Mr. Clyde Miller, whose wife had registered with us for weaving. He wrote that he would like to spend the summer at Penland with her if he could pay his expenses by teaching his craft. We welcomed him. He taught his classes in the old stable along with the pottery classes, and he was a very good teacher. Soon we began to see that we would have to find some other place for the metalcraft classes. There just wasn't enough room in the stable.

So now I can tell about Radcliffe House.

During those early days of the school a friend had given us $1,500 toward the building of a structure to be named for our community nurse. Carrie Radcliffe was an obstetrical nurse and midwife; one year she delivered fifty-one babies in fifty-two weeks. A natural-born missionary, she gave her services in exchange for whatever the patients might be able and willing to pay.

We decided to build Radcliffe House as a place where mothers could go to have their babies under Carrie's watchful care and direction. But before it was finished, our county established a central health office with public health service, and we felt that it would not be necessary to use Radcliffe House for the purpose it had been planned to serve. But we had other needs. We always do! So in the main Radcliffe House became, and continues to be today, a dormitory.

We started using it, as we have all our buildings, long be-

133

fore it was finished. Students and teachers slept upstairs when there was nothing but rough studding between the rooms and there were no doors and windows.

And we moved the metalcraft classes a hundred yards up the hill to Radcliffe House and gave them a home on the first floor.

Then came the summer when all the rooms in that building had been enclosed, and our summer family had so grown that we desperately needed every room for sleeping quarters. Jealously we began to eye the space being used by the metalcrafters. But if we threw them out of Radcliffe as we had thrown them out of the old stable, where would they go? And we didn't want to withdraw those courses; they were becoming increasingly popular and excellent work was done. But registrations were pouring in, and where would we put the overflow students?

Well, our men got busy and in three days they built, at the enormous expense of $75, an outdoor metal shop. It was ready when the students began to arrive. This shop, which we still use, has a floor, a roof, and walls just a few feet high. The rest is screened. In the summer time it is a pleasant place in which to work, because the soft breezes blow through it unhampered. There's no problem of ventilation! But we cannot use it in the cold winter months, of course, and what metalcraft is done during that part of the year is done in the basement of Radcliffe. Right now we are yearning for a year-round metal shop. And I'm of the opinion we'll get it. Providence seems to look with special kindness upon orphans, widows and old maids running mountain schools.

Our general pottery course was growing in popularity too and soon it began to outgrow the log stable. So we transferred it to a building made of rough lumber and originally used for

134

a wood shop where looms were built before shortage of labor and materials made this impractical. The upper floor of this hillside building is the ground floor from the pottery shop entrance, and the wood shop, now the school's maintenance shop, is on the floor below, which is the ground floor on its level. The structure served very well its dual purpose, but we realized it was only a shell of a building and hardly suited for year-round use. If we could only make of it a more permanent, all-weather building, we thought, how much more efficiently it would serve us. But how?

Once more, an answer came. Five young men and five young women were sent to us in 1948 by the American Friends Service Committee for what they called a work camp. Such groups are sent to localities where projects of special interest to these young people are in operation, and they get college credits for living in the community and working on the project chosen.

These ten young persons came from Yale, Wellesley, Pennsylvania State, University of Chicago, Antioch and several other universities and colleges. As interesting and co-operative a group as one could wish to have, they certainly gave as much to our community as we could ever expect them to learn from us. They were mature beyond their years; and they entered into the social life of the school and the neighborhood, took part in church services in our rural areas, and enriched us generally. They added zest to our folk dances and made permanent friends throughout the community. With the ten was their director, the Reverend Walter Kring, plus Mrs. Kring and their two children. Mr. Kring, whose hobby was pottery, was pastor of the Unitarian Church in Worcester, Massachusetts.

And what do you think this group had been assigned to do?

135

You guessed it: build stone walls for our pottery and maintenance building.

We had arranged with Mart Grindstaff to supervise the work of the students, which had been planned for a year before their arrival. But Mart was not enthusiastic and, when they arrived at Penland and he had taken a look at them, he shook his head sadly. Those college boys and girls? What did they know about rock work?

"Miss Lucy," said Mart to me one day, "it'll be a sight cheaper just to hire two or three good men and get this job done, even if them boys and girls do work for nothin'. They'll just mess up a lot o' good rock, and all they do'll have to be done over."

But I told him that the students were on a work-camp project and we'd have to let them see what they could do. Maybe he'd be surprised anyway, I suggested.

Well, when those boys and girls came to Mart and literally sat at his feet to glean his words of wisdom on rock-setting, and continued to do so all summer, you could actually see Mart growing in stature and self-esteem. And those youngsters worked! The girls put on their blue jeans and worked as hard as the boys, and as successfully. They lugged stones, made mortar, laid the stones in place. And as the work went on, Mart and the ten became fast friends.

Once Mart invited the group to a Sunday dinner at his home. He told them, however, that they wouldn't have anything but cornbread and beans. They, believing him, assured him that they would love to come, that they were particularly fond of cornbread and beans.

When they got to Mart's house that Sunday, of course, Mart had everything you could think of on his table—fried chicken, country ham, all the vegetables of the season, pies, cakes, jellies, jams. And how those college youngsters did stuff themselves! Mart appreciated them and they adored Mart. He still hears from them all. A few years later one of them brought his bride to Penland and spent a part of his honeymoon with the Grindstaffs.

CHAPTER 15

I N THE EVENING when the busy day's work was
finished, we would gather about the open fire.
Even here Mr. Worst's hands were never idle.
He delighted in making things. And he seemed just as happy
to show others how to make things. He demonstrated how to
make dolls, woolly animals, and handbags from rug roving.
Children's caps he made from looper clips. With materials
near at hand he fashioned beautiful and fragrant bayberry
candles, floating candles and other unusual things.

Mr. Worst's fireside industry was contagious. Other teachers and students had pet projects, and soon both watching and
participating groups grew beyond the limit of the fireplace
circle. Gathered around one table could be found a group
making papier-mâché objects; at another table puppets might
be the main interest; at still another one could watch character dolls being made of corn shucks.

We usually had some occupational therapists at Penland. In addition, there were often a number of 4-H Club workers, Girl Scout leaders, rehabilitation workers or others in related fields who were always on the alert for projects requiring little financial outlay, projects that could be completed in a comparatively short time. Thus every time a new project of this kind was introduced it had an immediate hearing, and the simple crafts quickly grew in popularity and significance.

One summer we had two students who were particularly adept at these crafts. Ruth Harris and Floride Stoddard taught us how to make so many things that we asked them to come back to Penland the following summer and teach for half of every day in exchange for their room, board and tuition.

Thus was born a new department which we called Related Crafts. One can now learn from sixty to seventy different techniques, among them stenciling, block printing, spatter-work, finger painting, crayon resist, papier-mâché work, chip carving, guimpe work, chair-seating, and making bobbin lace, felt articles, puppets and masks, rug-roving dolls and animals. Most of these are comparatively simple, though some very professional work is being done in silk-screen printing and in leather work.

The first chair-seating we did was taught by two of our good neighbors, Mr. Arthur Woody and his daughter Miss Decie, who have given instruction to numberless persons in the art of seating chairs with hickory bark, as their forebears did before them. Many a twinkle have I seen in their eyes as they marveled at the number of thumbs people can have on two hands.

Mr. Woody had been seating chairs a long time; he was no amateur at that task. One morning when Mr. Woody came up to the school a city student greeted him cordially. "Good morning, Mr. Woody. How are you?" he asked.

"Tol'able, just tol'able," the old gentleman replied. And his eyes sparkled. "But I can do more than most boys of ninety-three."

And that was the solemn truth.

Mr. Woody died a few years ago, only a little short of his century mark. It rejoices my heart that three of the stalwart, honest, worthy grandsons of Mr. Woody are carrying on in the footsteps of their father and grandfather in a much larger way as proprietors of Woody's Chair Shop on Grassy Creek just out of Spruce Pine.

The younger Woodys are remarkable craftsmen. Their exhibit at the Craftsman's Fair at Asheville in the summer of 1957 included scale models of their Betsy Ross and Colonial American chairs. And I want to tell what happened as a result of that exhibit. It happened that a lady from Norfolk, Virginia, saw it. She told Walter and Arval Woody that she collected rare and unusual dolls from all over the world; she had paid as much as $600 for one particular doll. She told them that she had looked for years for good-quality furniture small enough to display her dolls, but until she saw the Woody exhibit she had been unsuccessful in her search. She wanted a complete set of the Betsy Ross chairs and various other pieces of furniture in miniature.

Arval and Walter talked it over and decided they could make the furniture. They told her, however, that because of the difficulty of the work they would have to charge her the same price for the doll furniture that they would have charged for full-size furniture of the same models. She readily agreed, and the Woodys went to work. The complete order consisted

140

of six Betsy Ross side chairs, a Betsy Ross rocker, a Betsy Ross arm rocker, a Gout rocker, a sixteen-by-thirty-two-inch doll table fifteen inches high, and a mammy bench. They were all made of solid walnut and beautifully done.

We have craftsmen in our mountains!

The Woodys have adapted their work to the tastes of their own generation and are making beautiful chairs and tables and other handsome pieces of furniture to order, using black walnut, butternut, wild cherry, maple and other indigenous hardwoods.

The beauty and comfort of my own living room is enriched by pieces they have made for me. But their beautiful furniture goes far afield from Penland. Our student Maria Halva from Helsinki, Finland, was so intrigued with the Woody rocking chairs that she actually took one with her when she returned to Finland by freighter, and rocked as she sailed!

Before I get away from Mr. Arthur, Miss Decie and Mr. Arthur's grandsons, I want to tell of a remarkable work of handicraft produced by another Woody. She is Mrs. Leila Woody, widow of Barney Woody, and I think Arthur and Barney were not related. Mrs. Woody is one of our community weavers, but recently she had to give up weaving because of ill health. She lives with one of her daughters.

I wish to relate the story of Mrs. Woody's famous coverlet, not because of the beauty of the coverlet—and it is an amazingly beautiful piece of work—but because of her ability to make something of such beauty with things at hand. Mrs. Woody, I think, illustrates the ability of our people to improvise, to adapt themselves to their circumstances, to do, and do with great success, with what they have or are able to procure.

Who couldn't make something beautiful and useful if she

had the appropriate materials, the necessary tools, and the ability and will to create? But I wonder how many of us, given a bag of looper clips, a waste product of hosiery mills, could produce a coverlet as beautiful as the one Mrs. Woody made.

Mrs. Woody's niece worked in a hosiery mill, and one day she brought her aunt a bag of looper clips. Mrs. Woody raveled out several of the loopers and discovered that each had not less than eighteen yards of raveled thread. So she planned an eighteen-yard warp.

She warps with ten ends, so she drove ten nails in a board and fastened this board to the wall. She put a looper on each nail and on her warping bar warped eighteen yards. Then she cut off the ends, put up ten more loopers, tied the ten threads to the ends she had just warped, and continued with her warping until she had the necessary 1,080 threads, each eighteen yards long, which are required for a thirty-six-inch warp for a coverlet.

A honeycomb weave was what Mrs. Woody wanted, and for such a weave a fine thread is used for the background and a heavy thread for the honeycomb. The ravelings were all right for the fine thread and she used the loopers and filled the bobbins with these. For the heavy thread she doubled and twisted the ravelings several times to produce a thread of the size she wanted!

The fringe she made of doubled and twisted looper ravelings.

That coverlet has been a great inspiration to me. But even more so has Mrs. Woody, not only to me, but to many others.

After her husband had an operation and was having a long, slow convalescence, she knew that she could not keep him from doing things that would be harmful to him unless she

142

could find some way to keep him busily occupied. So she persuaded him to weave, which he did well and happily.

Among those who have been inspired by our Mrs. Woody are many foreign students. We had a picture made one day of her and her gorgeous coverlet, and standing by admiring it were Mr. Guillermo Mendoza, director of vocational education in the Philippines; Maria Halva, supervisor of needlecraft schools in Helsinki, Finland; Michito Sato of Japan, Bobg Wha Kim and Huun Ja Kim of Korea, the last three of whom were sent to Penland by the foreign division of the national YWCA.

Once when we were having a Guild workshop at Penland, someone suggested that it was so very sad to think that those who do the weaving cannot afford to own the beautiful products of their own handicraft. I made no comment, but hopped into my little car and went out to Mrs. Woody's.

"Mrs. Woody, I want you to come with me and disprove that idea they have," I said, after I had explained the situation. "I want you to show them not only how weaving is done but how our woven material is used in our own community." She readily agreed.

We took a coverlet off her bed and woven place mats and napkins off her dining table; we picked up a bureau scarf from the bureau. Then Mrs. Woody and her daughter put on their own hand-woven dresses, and back we went to Penland and our commiserating friends.

I was just as proud to introduce Mrs. Woody as I would have been to introduce the First Lady of the United States. Then I asked her to show them her hand-woven things, especially the coverlet, and I suggested that she tell them how she made it. She did. Speaking with great graciousness and poise, she gave one of the best, most interesting talks of that conference.

But let me get on with my story of the development of the Related Crafts Department. After it had evolved from Mr. Worst's busy fingers in front of an open fireplace, with interested admirers intently watching him, the students were taught in a narrow daylight basement room of the Craft House, which was not heated and could be used only in the summertime.

In the summer of 1947 we had an outstanding student in that department, Mrs. Eulalia Burns. She was such a good student, in fact, that I asked her if she would remain as a teacher the year around.

Well, Mrs. Burns accepted my offer. But she couldn't stay in that cold basement room of the Craft House, because winter was coming on and nobody would be able to learn anything in that place with teeth chattering and breath making white mist patterns.

That year for the first time we had the use of the new building that I will tell of later, The Pines, which had furnace heat. We had now accepted students under the GI Bill to study with us during the full-year period. Proudly we had evolved from a short summer-period school to full-term status, with the only difference that our vacation period comes in mid-winter.

Brave and resourceful Mrs. Burns moved her equipment into the basement of The Pines and there functioned efficiently, along with the furnace and all sorts of stored materials, and with little ventilation and only artificial light. But somehow she managed to keep her students busy and happy.

Then, when summer came, she moved into Radcliffe House, where the welcome rays of the sun stream through many windows and the air is fresh and bracing. And after two years of such moving back and forth, we managed to get heat into Radcliffe and Mrs. Burns and Related Crafts stayed put. But not for too long, because our student body was growing to such proportions that more room was needed and the Related Crafts room became a five-bed men's dormitory during the summer. But by that time the Lily Loom House was being built—a project which I shall happily tell about later—and Mrs. Burns and I fairly purred with satisfaction as we planned roomy, functional quarters to serve as the permanent home of an expanded Related Crafts Department.

The fact that Mrs. Burns had never complained—and who does complain at Penland?—made my elation all the more understandable.

CHAPTER 16

But in my eagerness to relate the story of Penland's extension of its curriculum in handicraft studies—and it is always a temptation for me to get ahead of the chronology in my enthusiasm for the handicrafts themselves—I have failed to record the effect upon our little community of a happening in New York that quickly had momentous repercussions throughout America and the world.

I am referring, of course, to the stock market crash in 1929, when billions in securities tumbled. We consider that the Penland School was founded that year, if indeed we can actually put down a definite date. Strange to relate, the crash of the stock market meant nothing more to us folk back in the mountains of North Carolina than black headlines in the newspapers—so we thought. But not for long.

Soon the great Depression was withering the land and in not

many months Penland too was feeling the effects of world conditions. We had managed to get our community weaving program well under way and in many homes back in the coves the women were working into the night to produce hand-woven products that we were selling for them at good prices. The revenue was sending their children to school, improving their homes and doing other good things of tremendous importance to them.

But with the coming of the Depression the bottom dropped out of our market. We had a Weaving Cabin stocked with beautiful articles and no way of disposing of them. What would we do? We studied and we figured and we sought suggestions. Sometimes we almost despaired. But we refused to surrender to doubt and hopelessness, and as I look back now, I feel that our greatest successes and achievements came as direct results of the struggling we had to do to overcome what seemed at times insurmountable difficulties.

We knew that a World's Fair was to be held in 1933 in Chicago, and we knew that we had friends in that great city, including Mr. Worst. People began to ask us if by any chance Penland would have an exhibit at the Fair, and of course we said we would not. How could we get to Chicago with an exhibit when we could hardly make ends meet at Penland?

But as we thought about it and remembered the Weaving Cabin filled with wonderful hand-woven articles for which Penland had no market, we began to get ideas. Maybe, just maybe, if we could have an exhibit in Chicago we might be able to sell some of those products.

I called the weavers together—I always did that when there was much at stake, so that we could cogitate in unison—and told them what I had been considering. If we could get our weaving and our hand-hammered pewter to Chicago, I said, we might be able to sell it.

"But even if we can get a concession at the fair, we'll be taking a tremendous risk," I warned them, "because it will cost a lot of money, which we don't have."

"Then how do you aim to manage it?" one of them asked me. I had foreseen, of course, that such a question would be asked; it invariably happens that way.

"First of all, I need the help of you weavers," I told her. "If we sell anything, we will probably sell a lot, even more than we have on hand now. So if we decide to go into this thing, I'd want every weaver who is willing to run the risk to weave all this winter. And understand this: there won't be any money to pay you with until we make sales. And the risk is so great that we may lose everything we have, and you may never get paid.

"But this I do know," I went on. "As things are now, we can't pay you, and we know that we're already lost unless something happens. This is a gamble. We may lose, but we may win. This is the way I look at it: I'd rather put every ounce of energy I have into this, and then go down with a bang, than to die by inches. I'd know that I'd done everything I knew how to do."

I could see that the weavers were inclined to go along with my view.

"But even so," I hastened to tell them, "I don't want you to be too much influenced by me; I want you to use your own judgment on weaving all winter. If any of you would rather not take that risk, and then we should succeed, I'll never hold it against you for being cautious."

Do you know, every weaver without hesitation said that of

148

course she would weave, that she had nothing to lose but her time. And since it would be during the winter when there were no gardening and canning to be done, there would be plenty of time for weaving.

So it was agreed. Then I wrote Mr. Paul Bernat of Emile Bernat & Sons Company, from whom we were buying all our weaving supplies. I explained the situation to Mr. Bernat as I had explained it to the weavers; I told him that if his company would be willing to supply us with yarns until our Chicago venture had succeeded or failed, I would be pleased, but that if he thought the risk too great, I would understand.

That courageous and noble man wrote me to order what we needed and pay for it when we could. His letter was almost in the same words of the Spruce Pine Lumber Company people when we discussed with them the building of the Craft House.

Next we invited businessmen of Spruce Pine and Bakersville, people of the various churches in the community, representatives of civic organizations, and other friends to a dinner at the school. It was really a mass meeting to discuss the merits of having a Mitchell County exhibit at the World's Fair. North Carolina as a state was not exhibiting, we had been informed, and it seemed all the more important that our county provide an exhibit. That was the feeling of the group, too, and quickly it pledged $500 toward promotion of the venture.

So off to Chicago I trekked to see what I could find out.

We had no money for a concession, and very quickly and plainly, I felt, the World's Fair people showed they had little or no interest in us. But there were several influential persons supporting us, including Mr. Worst, Dr. Howard W. Odum of the University of North Carolina sociology department, and Miss Helen Bennett, who headed the Women's Division of the Fair, and I had the feeling that the Fair folk didn't want to say no abruptly but hoped that if we were put off we would give up and go home.

But I was not willing to give up. I was staying with my good friend Mrs. Evans in Berwyn at no expense to me or the school and I spent nine weeks pleading, figuring, arguing, urging and being put off. I was getting mighty discouraged. One day as I boarded a suburban train for Berwyn after another dreary and unproductive session with those Fair folk, I had had about enough. They hadn't quite said no, but I felt they would the next time I confronted them, and I was almost defeated. I thought of the letters I had been getting from those back in Mitchell County recounting their doings to raise money toward that $500. They believed in us implicitly, I knew, and yet I was about to fail them. I was sitting by a friend, and I turned to her.

"Tell me a funny story quick," I said. "I think I'm going to cry."

But I held onto my hopes nevertheless, and the very next day one of the officials at the Fair telephoned me to come in. When I got there he told me that we could have a small portion of land—which was really nothing but a breakwater—between Ann Rutledge Tavern and the Lincoln group. The charge for it, he said, would be a certain percentage of the sales made, and he warned me that it would be so difficult to make use of those few feet of land, which was covered with large boulders, that it would be prohibitively expensive and we could not hope even to make expenses on such a concession.

I told him we would take it. And with great relief that we

150

had a place on which to exhibit, even if it seemed to be a very poor place, I wired Tony Ford, who was at that time teaching in Stillwater, Oklahoma. Tony got in touch with the boys at Penland, and they came out to Chicago. There they lifted and heaved and shoved those boulders about until they had leveled off a place large enough to accommodate the two little seven-by-twelve cabins that Tony and the boys had built some months before. One had been constructed as a trailer and we had used it as a traveling gift shop; the other was made of lumber hewn to look like logs, with each piece fitted into place so that it could be taken down and hauled to the Fair and then reassembled.

Tony had supervised and helped in making the ground ready for the cabins. By this time we were beginning to feel that we were putting on the World's Fair ourselves. The boys had returned to Penland to get the knocked-down cabin, and Tony and the boys began putting it up—and found themselves embroiled with the labor-union people. That little cabin was so small that they hadn't discovered it until our boys started nailing on the hand-riven shingles, and then they had insisted on taking over. We got it settled, however, and we were thankful that they hadn't discovered us sooner.

We didn't take the little trailer cabin to Chicago until just before the opening of the Fair. Then my nephew Ralph Morgan, Holmes Wyatt, Ernest Morton and I departed Penland in the midst of great excitement. It was fun all along the way, too, for when we stopped for gas, groups gathered and asked questions. At some of the stops persons even offered to buy the cabin.

We got it safely to Chicago and parked it in Mrs. Evans' back yard for a day or two, to the great delight of the neighborhood children, while we waited the day when we were supposed to take it into the fairgrounds and set it in place, so that it would be in readiness well before the opening date. Tony laid out the route over which we would take it from Berwyn to be sure that all the underpasses were high enough to permit its passage. Then the day came for us to move to the fairgrounds.

I hoped that simple little log cabin would not feel embarrassed and inferior among all the ultramodern buildings there. But as we drove through those great gates I got the feeling that the little cabin arched its roof a bit and felt a modest pride in being just as good and important for its own purposes as those skyscrapers and great glass palaces were for theirs. So we took our places with a feeling of achievement and dignity.

Before the opening of the Fair I had spoken in and around Chicago before women's auxiliaries of various Episcopal churches and they had generously offered to assist in making sales at our cabins. Incidentally, it was while she was helping with our sales that I met Mrs. McElwain, who subsequently came to Penland to spend three days and is still here more than twenty years later.

Since I wouldn't be able to spend much time in Chicago during the Fair, because the weavers and I would be busy at home, I asked a former Penland teacher, Mrs. Hensley, to take charge of all details of organization and selling, and when the stage was all set and the opening had been recorded as a success, I returned to Penland.

That first day at the Fair sales were so good that I knew it was not going to take many days to pay Emile Bernat all we owed, which was approximately a thousand dollars. I had never even seen a check for as much as that, much less written one. And in a few days there really was enough money to warrant our writing a check for the entire amount we owed.

Bonnie and I talked about it and glowed over it, and she wrote the check, because she not only writes a better hand than I do but she keeps the books and does the figuring. We both kissed that check and sent it on its way, and I wrote Mr. Bernat that I hoped he enjoyed getting it as much as we enjoyed sending it.

And at Penland there was great rejoicing too; the weavers all got paid.

So the Chicago World's Fair, from Penland's standpoint at any rate, was a marvelous success. But our rewards were not entirely pecuniary. And that brings me to recall our good friend Mr. Hoppes, the banjo-picking, fiddle-playing storyteller-philosopher, and his trip to the Fair.

We seldom had friends come to Penland that we did not take them to visit the Hoppes family if time permitted. We would sit on the porch or, on winter evenings, around the open fire and bask in the genial and witty atmosphere of that home, listening to Mr. Hoppes' delightful stories, interspersed with banjo music and song. Mr. Hoppes was so good at storytelling that actually I have recognized people on the streets of Spruce Pine just from his impersonations.

I delighted in taking people out to the Hoppes house, and he seemed to enjoy their coming. "I reckon you have brought a thousand people out here," he said to me one day, and I agreed. I suppose I have taken more than a thousand. I remember that on one particular evening we took a Greyhound busload of visitors out there—though not in the bus, because it could never have made it over those roads. They were from Ball State Teachers College, and they had a most wonderful evening being entertained by the genial host.

I could never think of anything we could do for Mr.

Hoppes as a sort of token of what he meant to us. We did try to keep him in banjo strings, but, after all, what is a banjo string when he and his family meant so much to us and to literally thousands of our friends? It was wonderful just to be in his home. As we sat on the Hoppes front porch on summer evenings, watching the glimmer of glowworms in the yard and listening to the whip-poor-wills, peace and contentment would permeate our beings and we would be held spellbound by the spirit of things beautiful and good.

One such evening during the months we were preparing to "assist in putting on the World's Fair" and I was telling Mr. Hoppes of our plans for Chicago, he said to me, "If I could travel around as much as you do, I could make some awful pretty songs."

Right there the answer came. "That's what we'll do," I said to myself. "We'll take Mr. Hoppes to the Chicago Fair." Then I turned to him. "Mr. Hoppes," I said, "would you be willing to go to the Fair with me and pick the banjo to draw a crowd so that we can sell more weaving?"

"Yes," he answered without hesitation, "I'd be glad to accommodate you like that."

To be sure, at that time I didn't know how we were going to buy gas to take ourselves to Chicago, but I knew that all his neighbors and all the visitors we should take to see him on his return would enjoy his stories about the Fair as long as he lived to tell them. What better investment could we make? And I had an idea that Mr. Hoppes would really enjoy it.

So we worked it out. On one of our several treks to the Fair that summer, Brother Ralph and I took Mr. Hoppes, and as we drove along in this little period of intermission between our busy days at Penland and the exciting ones we were an-

154

ticipating in Chicago we discussed various philosophical problems of living with our fellow men. Mr. Hoppes was a gentle
but sustaining power in his own church and in his community
generally and I always got as much good from his discussions
as I would from a sermon. So I remember that one day as we
were driving to Chicago I asked him if he had ever thought of
being a preacher.

"Yes, I did," he replied. "I thought a lot about it when I
was young. But I decided that the Lord gave me a talent, a
talent for music, and that He meant for me to use it. That's
what I've tried to do, to use my talent to help keep people
happy and friendly."

Mr. Hoppes was one of my favorite philosophers.

So we arrived in Chicago, and we took Mr. Hoppes out to
the Fair. We set a chair by the rail fence in front of the
cabins, and he took up his banjo and began picking. The first
thing we knew, crowds had gathered to listen and watch. I
went back into the cabin to help with the sales and presently
Mr. Hoppes came in.

"Look here," he said, "if you want me to pick that banjo,
you'll have to get somebody out here to do the handshaking.
Some of those people out there have been right down home on
my front porch, and they all want to shake hands, and I
can't pick the banjo and shake hands at the same time, that's
a sure thing!"

"Mr. Hoppes," I told him, "you'll make just as many friends
for Penland and help make just as many sales by shaking hands
as you will by picking the banjo. So just take as much time for
shaking hands as you need."

He did, and it worked out fine. As he said, many persons at
the Fair had been his guests on his own front porch and they

were amazed and delighted to encounter again their jovial mountain philosopher and musicianer.

I wanted Mr. Hoppes to do and see everything that would mean most to himself and his neighbors after he had returned home, and I remember that the thing I had enjoyed most when I first went to Chicago was a boat trip to Milwaukee. I hadn't been used to a big body of water, and that trip had meant a lot to me. I was confident Mr. Hoppes would enjoy such a trip, too; so I asked Ralph to go with Mr. Hoppes to Milwaukee and back. On their return I asked our friend how he liked it.

"I enjoyed the trip going over all right," he said. "I didn't enjoy it so much coming back though, because there wasn't nothing to see but water, and I saw that going over."

The first time we sat on the Hoppes porch after returning from the Fair, we had with us several Chicago people, and of course they wanted to hear from Mr. Hoppes about his experiences there and what he enjoyed most.

"I enjoyed everything so much I don't hardly know what I enjoyed most," he replied. Then Mrs. Hoppes spoke up.

"Tell 'em about that taxi ride, Dock," she suggested.

So he told us that when they returned that day from Milwaukee Ralph asked a taxicab driver if he could get them over to Union Station in time for the ten-thirty train for Berwyn, where they were staying with our friend Mrs. Evans.

" 'No, I don't think I can,' the taxi man told me and Ralph," Mr. Hoppes related. " 'That there's a fifteen-minute ride and we ain't got but twelve minutes. But get in and I'll try.'

"Well, sir," Mr. Hoppes continued, "we hadn't no sooner got in that-there taxi before that taxi man shot out o' there like a bolt o' lightning. He went in and out of them postes and I don't know how we kept from lamming agin one of 'em. But he didn't hit one of 'em once.

"He run so close to all the other taxis and streetcars and everything that was a-passin' us that if you had poked your finger down 'tween the fender of our taxi and all them other things that was a-passin' us hit would a-mashed it!" Mr. Hoppes was warming to his story.

"By that time I said to Ralph, 'Ralph, ain't he a-runnin' over ever' red light in town?'

" 'No, I don't think so,' Ralph said. 'I think them's caution lights.'

" 'Well,' I said, 'if that's what they are, he ain't bein' a bit cautious!'

"When we got to the Union Station, the taxi man said, 'Here we are!' and stopped so sudden that it pulled us all right up on our feet, and all we had to do was just step out o' the taxi."

He said they made their train.

I saw and enjoyed more of the Chicago Fair on Mr. Hoppes' porch, through his eyes and ears, than I saw in Chicago. He didn't miss a trick, and what he saw and heard was pleasurably enhanced by his delightful wit.

CHAPTER 17

URING THESE EARLY years when the school was beginning to see its course ahead and look forward confidently to continuing growth, the Fords and I were living at Morgan Hall. Tony's work was taking him away from Penland much of the time, but as often as he could he got home.

Then in 1935 their son William Howard was born; Bill he would be to us. That was an event we had been looking forward to, and I prayed for a real boy, rough and tough—not bad, of course, but all boy—and that's what we got.

I'll never forget that day the telegram came from Tony over at Banner Elk's hospital. "William Howard expected about noon today," he wired. "Come on over."

Mr. Meacham read the telegram to me over the telephone. I was all excited and fluttery, of course, and I began telling Mr. Meacham what it was all about, when I heard the click of the receiver as he hung up. It wasn't like him not to discuss news, and I felt a little let down. But I jumped in my little car, went over and picked up Mrs. Willis, Bonnie's mother, and we set out for the hospital. "Now, Mrs. Willis," I said to her, "you pray and I'll drive."

"I've been doing that ever since I left home," she said. "Haven't you?"

Bill was everything we had asked for. But he was hungry and howling for food. They wouldn't feed him, though, until he was a certain number of hours old, which made me a little sad and a little mad too, and when I went to sleep that night I thought of that poor little hungry baby who couldn't have any food.

Tony asked me to send telegrams to his family, for he had never sent any like that before, he explained. So next morning I called up Mr. Meacham and proudly gave him the wires to send. "And tell Mrs. Meacham, Mr. Meacham," I said, when I had finished with the telegrams.

"I done told her yesterday," he said. And then I understood why he had hung up on me.

When Bill Ford was about two years old we had a year of very disconcerting experiences. As I look back now, I realize that it was a year of great significance for our school, a year of decisions, and what seemed then to be thorns in the flesh actually were goads urging us forward to larger horizons and greater achievements.

The Appalachian School by this time had grown to the place where Morgan Hall was needed as a dormitory, and so we would have to make other plans not only for ourselves but also for dining room and kitchen facilities for the students and teachers of the summer sessions.

We had planned for the Craft House to serve eventually as dining room and kitchen, as well as for teaching and sleeping; but already we had set up looms all over the first floor and were using every foot of space in that building.

What would we do?

We talked about the farmhouse on the property I had bought and which we used as overflow quarters. We talked about taking out partitions and making the first floor into a dining room and kitchen and screening the side porch to provide additional dining space. But Tony and the other men agreed it would cost more to do this than it would ever be worth, and they counseled that it would be better business to start from scratch and build a new dining room and kitchen.

But the old bugaboo arose to taunt us again. We didn't have any money. The Pines, the name the old farmhouse was known by, was at least a start toward what we needed, and Bonnie and I decided that we couldn't possibly face the gigantic problem of borrowing enough money to build a new structure; we felt that we might possibly undertake the task of getting The Pines done over.

We solved the problem of where we should live ourselves by moving into the little log cabin to which Rufus had brought his bride when he came to establish the school. The bishop had deeded it to me. It was one room and a lean-to downstairs, with a loft upstairs and a shelf for a sleeping porch.

Our plan was to add two rooms to this cabin. Tony drew the plans and was ready to start work when I had to go to the hospital for an emergency major operation. Clementine Douglas invited me to go to her house in Asheville when I was ready to leave the hospital and remain there until I could go home, and I very happily did. The Fords would come over to see me and bring reports, and send them by others, concerning progress being made on the addition to our cabin. And then, a few days before I was to leave for home, that little cabin burned to the ground!

It had been a zero morning and they'd had a larger fire in the stove than usual, it was explained to me later, and we supposed the added heat cracked the terra cotta flue, for it was in the flue that the fire had started.

The family considered waiting a few days before telling me about the fire. But then they thought I might see it in the paper, or if it had been cut out of the paper I was given to read that I would wonder why and demand to know. So they consulted the doctor on what to do if when they did tell me the news was too disturbing, and he gave them directions.

So they told me. My first comment was: "I hope they let little Bill see the fire. He is the only one who could enjoy it." And I survived without having to undergo any of the emergency treatments that had been prescribed.

The various descriptions of that fire were interesting. My nieces Helen and Esther Warner were with us for the winter, doing metal work for sale. After the fire had finished the cabin, they went over to the Wyatts for the day and had lunch there. Esther said that everybody was crying and she thought that she should cry too, but she couldn't.

Georgie had brought milk from home for Bill the morning of the fire, as she did each morning, and she rushed over and poured the milk on the fire, that being the only fire extinguisher she had. Afterwards they took Bill over to the Weaving Cabin across the road from the smouldering remains of our little cabin, and the baby would look out the window toward the barn and observe wisely and calmly, "Cow say moo." And for us there was little else to say.

The Fords went up to The Pines, where Brother Ralph was batching, for his children were away at school and his wife away for the winter. Ralph welcomed the homeless and disconsolate warmly and comfortingly, and after a few days when I was ready to go home I joined them there.

Friends everywhere seemed to get news of the fire, and gifts began pouring in, especially clothes. Every time a "fire box" would arrive we would all gather around eagerly and divide the loot. We were all different sizes and shapes, so there was little argument about who should have what.

Until after that fire I never knew how many colors I could wear happily. Nor had I ever known just how simple it was, I might describe the feeling as relieving, to have nothing. I determined that never again would I exert myself to collect "things," since living can be so much simpler and less weighing upon one without them.

We had decided before the fire to postpone doing over The Pines until spring so that the bills would not be too old before the summer guests should come in and make it possible for us to pay some of these bills. And now we had not only a dining room and kitchen to provide, but also a home for the Fords and me.

Soon a letter came from Mr. Allen Eaton saying something like this: "You have done rather well by having three calamities—the loss of Morgan Hall, the operation, the fire. If there had been only one, your friends might hardly have noticed it; if two, they might still have done nothing about it. But since you have had three, they really want to put their shoulders to the plough and do something. But don't ever try staging a series of three again without consulting me first."

162

Mr. Eaton, Miss Ann Morgan (whom Bonnie and I had met through mutual friends), Mr. Lear at the University, and friends generally began exchanging letters, telegrams and telephone calls. With the financial assistance of everybody concerned, including the active interest of the businessmen of Spruce Pine, we were able to get to work on The Pines and our own little home as soon as spring broke and weather would permit.

When time came for students and teachers to arrive, The Pines really looked attractive with the two front rooms and passage made into a dining room finished in knotty pine. Opening off the dining room was the screened dining porch.

We had also put a new roof on the main part of the house, but the roof over the porch was the old one, and there were times that summer when we held umbrellas as we dined. This really embarrassed me a little, but our guests seemed to think they were having a lark.

One thing the making over of The Pines did, we quickly discovered, was to disconcert whatever it was that had been making noises for which we could not account. Whether it was rats, mice, flying squirrels, bats, ghosts—who knows? I never saw them, but I certainly heard the noises many times.

The old Pines had no running water in the house, only a faucet in the back yard just beyond the kitchen door. When bedtime came, any of us who happened to be living in the house were likely to go out to that faucet to brush our teeth the last thing before going to bed.

Now this house, like many old farmhouses of our region, throughout the country in fact, had a front porch with a door opening into a hall or passage. On each side of this hall was a room—on the right a bedroom, on the left the living room. Back of the living room was the dining room and behind the dining room was the kitchen. A door joined the living room and dining room and another the dining room and kitchen.

One by one most of us had heard, always about midnight, the front door open and footsteps going along the hall into the living room, then the dining room, then the kitchen, and out through the kitchen door to the back porch. We took it for granted that it was a member of the family going out to the faucet to get a drink of water or to brush his teeth.

But little by little we learned that nobody had been up and about at midnight when we had heard the footsteps. This was interesting, and quickly it became exciting. Every time we would hear our "ghost" we would report it the next morning and check to see if anyone had been up at the time we heard the noises. And almost invariably no such midnight prowlers had been reported.

Brother Ralph pooh-poohed what he termed such flights of our imagination, but his skepticism didn't decrease our interest and excitement, nor did it dull our hearing.

And then one night when Ralph and his family were living in the house they had company and sat up visiting rather late. It happened that the only place Ralph had to sleep after taking care of the guests was on the couch in the dining room. As he tucked himself into his covers he looked at his watch and saw that it was midnight. He leaned over and blew out the lamp, stretched his long legs and settled down into his pillow.

Then, very distinctly, he heard the front door open and footsteps coming along the hallway, then into the living room, and in a moment into the dining room within a few feet of where he was lying! His first thought was that somebody was trying to play a trick on him. He jumped from the couch, lighted the lamp as quickly as he could, and rushed toward the kitchen in pursuit of the footsteps. But just as he got to the kitchen he heard the door to the back porch slam, and as he sprang to open it before the intruder could get away he discovered that the door was securely locked from inside!

Ralph declared even then he wasn't convinced that The Pines had a ghost. But he couldn't explain it.

CHAPTER 18

URING ALL THE years that we were engaged in building Radcliffe and the outdoor metal shop and re-doing The Pines and building our little house, we were working also on the Edward F. Worst Craft House. It was continuing to grow; in fact, it is not yet entirely finished in every nook and corner.

Strange as it may sound, I was becoming sorry for future students who would not have the thrill of helping build the Craft House; for each person who had given a log, a window, a room, or even a batch of shingles had become an integral part of the school, had felt himself actually built into its physical plant. For those of the future who would not experience that great joy, I had sympathy. I believe at Penland we truly appreciate the utter truthfulness of that divine admonition that it is more blessed to give than to receive; in our small but sincere giving, we have received bountifully.

So we were getting along, making progress, slowly but surely going ahead.

And then it happened. On December 1, which by coincidence was the one zero-temperature day of the year 1944, The Pines burned to the ground.

That morning Charlie Tipton, who took care of us, was attempting to thaw out frozen pipes, when there was an explosion in the pipeline that brought oil into the house to be generated into gas. In a moment the oil had flooded over the old Pines, which was dry and thin and excellent kindling, and the electric motor in some manner caused the oil to be ignited; a strong wind fanned the blaze, and in forty-five minutes there was no house left.

The three of us who lived there were fortunate to escape unhurt, for none of us realized how fast the building was going. I remember that I rushed to the telephone to call for help and by the time I had finished the frenzied call the smoke was so dense that I could not see the steps. I grabbed a handful of clothes and stumbled down with them, and then I realized that Mrs. Hendricks was still in her room upstairs. We all kept yelling to her, and Charlie was on the point of attempting to get up to her at the risk of losing his own life, when she emerged through the smoke. She had managed to find her way out, she told us, by coming toward us as we shouted and screamed to her; our frantic voices had directed her.

We all spent that night and many future ones with Tony and Bonnie Ford. Bill by then was nine years old and had had a birthday only a few days before; for his birthday present he had been given five one-dollar bills. That night when I was getting ready for bed the little fellow brought those bills to me with his own little scrawled note: "This is for Lucy and the new Pines."

Martha Ford was only three, and although she had heard

167

discussions of the fire it had meant nothing in her experience until she went with her mother for the mail on Sunday and saw the forlorn chimneys of the old Pines standing alone and bleak.

She came back to the house wailing, "I didn't want the Pines to burn!" I went out and carried her in. "We'll build a new Pines out of stone," I told the disconsolate little girl, "and stone won't burn." And she could help build it, I assured her, by hauling stones for it in the little red wheelbarrow her daddy had made for her. After that whenever we started discussing plans for our new building, Martha would run for her little wheelbarrow, ready to go to work.

It was our custom to send out a Christmas or New Year's letter, and this time we wondered what we would say about the fire. We didn't want such a letter to be a begging one, but we were sure our friends everywhere would want to know what had happened and what our greatest needs were now that the old Pines was gone. We finally compromised by deciding to add a postscript declaring that "Any gifts to the new Pines can be deducted from income tax."

About that time, too, Mrs. S. T. Henry, who with her husband published our *Tri-County News,* telephoned and said they were making a front-page article of the fire and that if we would send down a few hundred names of those likely to be most interested, they would send papers to them. I thanked her and asked her to let us have the postage bill, and she said they would prefer doing the whole thing.

They did do a very fine story about the fire and sent out copies of that issue to our friends throughout the country. And in response to it and to our letters, gifts began coming in, most of them five dollar bills, until we had received a total of about $2,000. We had insurance of $3,500, and this with the gifts we had just received encouraged us to plan a new building. We hoped to be able to get a subfloor down and a roof in place in time for the expected summer crowd. So we set to work.

We barely got the building in shape for use when the first group arrived; in fact, it was hardly usable, but we used it nevertheless. We did have the subflooring and the roof, but there were no stone walls and no inside finish, only tar paper to keep out the weather. And the roof wasn't permanent, only tar paper there too, but it served to keep out sunshine and rain.

Hardly had that first group got here, though, before they pitched in to help with the new Pines project. And that year students did more toward financing our growth than had ever been done at Penland before in a year's time. That building was a real challenge. We all knew that for the first time we were to have GI Bill students and that we could not take care of them unless and until the new Pines could be made livable for winter. So students and staff put on all kinds of projects for making money. The young ones polished shoes, some taking white shoes, some brown, some black; they charged twenty-five cents a polish and frequently they had an announcement made at the tables that shoes around Penland were looking mighty shabby.

Each floor of each building would have some sort of project. I recall that one group gave a party for which admission was charged. But there was a trick to it; you also had to pay to get out again! Colonel Fishback, an army officer who had been wounded in the service, did his bit by writing to every company with which we dealt. In his letter to each company he told what a summer at Penland had meant to him. He declared he felt that he was not asking for charity but was rather giving them the privilege of sharing in a most worth-while undertaking.

And do you know, every company he wrote to responded with a check, some for $25, most as much as $100. And one day when the mail came up I heard him making a strange noise, a sort of groaning, and I went by his door to see what was the matter. There was the colonel, draped over his bureau, with a check in one hand, and he was shaking his head and moaning, "I can't take it, I just can't take it!" He saw me then and showed me the check, and I understoood why it had almost overcome the colonel. The check was for $500!

But the letter with it was as inspiring as that check. It was from the president of one of the cotton mills; he said he had known of the work at Penland for many years and that the woods up here were full of his relatives, and that he felt privileged to send the check in memory of two of his employes who had given their lives in the service of their country.

That check paid for two of the larger bedrooms in the new Pines and the names of those two men are on the doors of the rooms that memorialize them.

We had many auction sales. Usually the articles sold were things students and staff members had made in the shops. But sometimes they brought in things from the outside. This was the year that nylons, chewing gum, cigarettes and chocolate bars were all but unobtainable. Now and then somebody would bring some of these things in and add them to the articles being auctioned. And what prices they brought! I remember once a Hershey bar brought $1.76. The funds obtained in these various ways during the summer, we were happy to discover, supplemented the money we were able to borrow on our collateral to the extent that we took bids on the finishing of the entire structure and went to work.

In the fire, of course, all dining room and kitchen equipment had been destroyed completely, so in our catalogue we had suggested that each who could conveniently do so bring a plate, cup, saucer, knife, fork and spoon. Every student did, and I had never enjoyed any variety of dishes more than that summer's array. Every plate I looked at reminded me of the person who brought it, and each piece, I became firmly convinced, had personality.

The building of The Pines was done during war shortages and there were complications of many kinds. One shortage was labor, and even if we'd had money, we could have got very little domestic help. That summer we had no paid help in the kitchen and dining room except Henry the cook. Everybody waited on tables, everybody took turns washing dishes. We had a paper on the wall where people signed up for days when they'd wash dishes.

Two teachers of art in a western college wrote applying for positions as art teachers for the summer. I wrote that we taught only crafts, nothing in the fine arts. I did tell them though that if they really wanted an interesting summer and one that would be different from anything they had ever known, I could provide them jobs if they were willing to accept them. The jobs, I said, were dish-washing; they could have them, though they carried no salaries, I wrote. I explained that when they were not over the tubs they would have their time free for doing anything in the crafts they liked, at no charge. They accepted. And as they were leaving they told me they had never had a more enjoyable summer.

That was the summer that Mattie—Mrs. B. G. Mattson of

Michigan—instituted what came to be known as the "jumping" system in our dining room. In this plan one person at each table volunteers for one day a week to jump up and get what's needed and also to remove plates and food and bring on the dessert, and afterwards to clear the table.

At one table there were a college president, an M.D. who was a scientist at Oak Ridge working on the atomic bomb, a teacher of art, and a real estate man from Florida. I was somewhat embarrassed at the thought of those men jumping table; I felt that very probably they had never done any domestic work and would be awkward and cumbersome.

But the four men said to the women at their table: "You women stay seated; we are going to take over this table." And I would watch intrigued as they would go to the kitchen; they would look so important, as if they had finally found out what made the wheels go round; they had achieved, they had arrived. And when those men left, the college president and the doctor told me that they hoped that when things became normal again we'd never go back to having waitresses. "We would never have known people as we have come to know them by rubbing elbows while doing that sort of work together," they explained, beaming.

When the doctor and his wife signed up to do their dishwashing turn, they discovered that their sixteen-year-old daughter had signed up for the same day. They thought that she probably would rather wash dishes with the young folks and they said, "Peggy, did you know that we're going to wash dishes the day you have signed up to wash them?" And she said, "Yes, I know it." Then they asked her why she had signed for the same day. "Because," she replied, grinning, "I wanted to see Daddy washing dishes."

"Miss Lucy," this atomic scientist said to me one day, "until I came to Penland I had never found a place where I could forget my worries." And I didn't know until that first atomic bomb went off just what he meant. I knew then that he had really had worries. The men at Oak Ridge had a serious job. It must have been a terrific mental and moral strain.

Dean Knapp of the School of Mechanical Engineering at Purdue University once told me that he had two looms in his basement at home. He would go down there and lock his door and weave. "It's the only time, Miss Lucy," he said, "that I can forget my troubles." That was his idea of relaxing recreation.

Working with your hands has a definite therapeutic value; in fact, that is what occupational therapy is. Professor Kessler of the Department of Electrical Engineering at the University of Illinois came down here with his wife one summer. He announced that he wasn't going to do one thing except rest; he was weary, worn out, he didn't want to do a thing but sit back and take it easy. Well, before they had been here long he was changing all the lights over in the weaving room of the Craft House; he put up fluorescent lights. He went around with his little bundle of tools just having the best time, and he was busier than anybody else on the hill. When he went away, after working like a Trojan, he told us he had never before felt so rested.

Two years ago we had two of the nation's topflight tree pathologists here from Washington. They were not interested in crafts, but their wives were; and their wives had persuaded them against their wishes to come here to spend their vacations.

So they came down. The husbands said they would just sit

around and rest; they didn't know what to do with themselves; they had only come because their wives had insisted, and they would just sit it out.

Well, they got so interested in crafts—they were doing metal enameling, and they did some beautiful pieces that we hadn't done, including transparencies such as lavalieres—and their wives were so overcome with amazement at what their husbands were doing that they practically spent all their time watching and gloating over their husbands' accomplishments.

There was a lady from Alabama who had never worked at any crafts. She came in on a Sunday night, and she was very weary. She had with her only one large crate; she told us she had shipped all her clothes. "I brought this," she said; "it's my sewing machine. I have never done any crafts and I just know I can't learn, but I know I can sew. So I brought my sewing machine."

Do you know she never unpacked that sewing machine! She got started on crafts, and she just did everything—working from daylight until dark, and in the evenings. She worked in a number of crafts and did them well. She just took to it naturally, and she almost worked herself to death having fun. And she took that sewing machine back to Alabama still crated.

The young teacher who had to go away to summer school to get her certificate renewed is another example of how people who have had no experience in handicrafts and view such experience with skepticism often become avid crafters. This girl had sent for catalogues to several schools and she chose this one, she frankly told us, because it had the shortest course of them all—three weeks—and announced that the people who came could do as much or as little as they liked. She was coming to do as little as she could get by with.

She came for the first summer session, and she stayed all through the summer. And how she did work! She told us, laughing, that nobody could have made her work like that.

We don't give college credit here, although some colleges have required certain of their students to take courses here. But teachers have to take refresher courses in the summers, and they can take such courses at Penland. They do not get college credits, but they are credited with having done required summer work.

So they come here not only to take this required refresher work but also to enjoy a constructive vacation in a beautiful locality. It's more than a change of climate, it's virtually a different way of life for everyone who comes. And almost without exception, I'm confident, they love it.

But I'm about to get away from that summer when we were living in the shell of the new Pines and domestic help was scarce and money was scarcer. Had it not been for this volunteer service, I don't see how we could have operated. And we had such an enjoyable summer, too. We got along happily enough, and the dollars saved could go into the further building of the new Pines; we were looking forward with more hope and confidence to a building completed to the extent that it could be used by the following winter. But it still lacked a lot of being completed.

One industrious student was helping one day by sweeping the second floor of The Pines; she had started at the west end and was sweeping along the hall toward the stairway, and her purpose was to sweep the accumulated dirt down the stairway and out the front door. But though she had swept dirt and swept dirt, when she got to the stairs, there was no dirt; it had simply dropped through the cracks in the floor. Housekeeping in a shell of a house may have its advantages, after all.

CHAPTER 19

THE ONLY PAID worker in the kitchen and
dining room, I have pointed out, was Henry,
the Negro cook. But Henry deserves more
than a casual mention in any story of Penland School. Henry
is himself an institution.

Henry enjoyed the Penland family that summer, more particularly, I thought, because there was no partition between
the kitchen and dining room, only the studding, and he could
stand in the kitchen and count the number of rolls each person ate. The more each ate, the broader was the grin on
Henry's face.

When we were planning the new Pines we arranged for a
bedroom and bath on the sunny side of the basement. We
thought Henry would like the new and comfortable quarters.
But he didn't; he wanted to continue living in the little cabin
we had built in the back yard of the old Pines, which had been

constructed of the wrecks of all the old houses that had been on the place when I had bought that property. So we put up a sign over his door: HENRY'S HOTEL. And there Henry reigned happily.

Henry is a philosopher. He neither reads nor writes, but what has that to do with wisdom and native wit? In the summers I always went down for an early breakfast, and while Henry did my egg, tossing it and turning it in the air for my entertainment, we philosophized on the problems of yesterday and the predictions for today. He would tell me of those who had asked him for recipes for some of his dishes, which he had given them. "But it won't taste like mine when they makes it," he would say, and I have a very decided opinion that Henry was right.

Sometimes I'd ask Henry how he made some particular dish. His answer would be about like this: "Well, you takes your flour and you siftes it." (Henry's *sifts*, like so many words in our mountain region, goes back to Chaucer's day.)

"Yes, Henry," I'd say, "but how much flour?"

"Well, now that depends on how many folks you is cookin' for."

"Let's say we're cooking for six. How much would you use for six?"

"Well, that depends on just how hongry they is. So you takes jest about enough flour for six and you siftes it, and then you puts in it a little salt, and you puts in about enough baking powders to make it light."

"But how much, Henry?"

"Jest enough to go wid that much flour."

And on and on. I agree with Henry. It won't taste like Henry's when I make it—if I ever do—from Henry's recipe.

Only once, as far as I can remember, did Henry make a mistake in his cooking. Although he couldn't read, he could tell by the pictures on the cans what was in them, and he arranged them on his shelves so that each thing was easy to find. It happened one day that somebody had cleaned his shelves and rearranged his cans of spices and seasonings. The ginger and the red pepper were in cans of identical size, shape and appearance, and they had swapped positions on Henry's shelf.

So the next day when Henry made gingerbread, which was one of his specialties, he used red pepper instead of ginger.

I believe that Mr. Greenwall was the first to take a bite of what we supposed was gingerbread. And he took a big bite. Without saying a word, he put his hand to his mouth, reached for his water, and hastily explained that he had just thought of an excruciatingly funny story. It worked. Nobody suspected what had happened, and one by one each person in the dining room tasted that red-pepper bread, until there was not one innocent left to be watched by the knowing. Nobody that day could say that Henry's dessert wasn't so hot. And needless to say, though it wasn't a culinary work of art, it was a tremendous social success. But Henry was chagrined. Not to be outdone, he made gingerbread again that afternoon and we had it for supper. This time Henry made sure it was ginger he used. And it was delicious!

The year of the gasoline shortage we had had more applications for the summer session than we had ever had before. With the announcement that gasoline was being rationed, cancellations poured in until we didn't know whether we would have summer school or not. Suppose we had a full house of teachers and no students! And Henry engaged, and everything!

The time came for Henry to arrive; and I went to Marion to meet him. Henry didn't like to ride from Marion on the bus. When we reached The Pines, Henry got out of the car, looked around at familiar sights, and observed comfortingly: "Now, Miss Lucy, you ain't got nothin' to worry 'bout. I'se here!"

I was as nearly in a state of worriment as I would allow myself to be, and Henry's calm words and presence were strangely helpful. I had long since learned that I could not afford to worry, that, after all, worry was only a waste of energy and already there was more to do than I had energy for. But nevertheless I was beginning to get on edge, I suppose. Henry boosted my morale and his genial philosophy helped me carry the day.

During those war years Henry was employed by the Navy to cook in one of the mess halls taken over by the Navy at the University of North Carolina. The Navy's operations at the University were year round, and as late spring approached I wondered if they would release Henry for our summer term at Penland. I was in Chapel Hill about that time, however, and Henry assured me that, come summer, he would be in Penland.

When the time came, sure enough, Henry's wife wrote me as usual to meet Henry at Marion, and I gladly did. I asked him how he had managed to get the Navy to release him. He said that when he had told them he was coming up to cook for the summer, as he had been doing for years, they told him they couldn't let him go.

"I'se got to go," he told them. "Miss Lucy's runnin' that big school up there and she jes' can't run it without me; and anyway, she come all the way down here from the mountains to ask me was I goin' and I'se done promised her I was."

"Well," said the Navy man, "if you go, you won't have any job when you get back."

"I knows that," Henry replied. "But I'se goin' and I'se jes' bein' polite and tellin' you beforehand."

Then the Navy man went off, Henry said, but after a while he came back. "Henry," he said, "when you come back from the mountains in the fall, come on back here and go to work as usual."

Henry had told the man the truth, I agreed. I have thought many a time that I couldn't run this school without Henry's help.

Henry cooks during the regular school sessions at a fraternity house in Chapel Hill, where he is quite a favorite with the members and alumni. His children are all college graduates. For years his wife cooked for Dr. Frank P. Graham and his family. Dr. Graham was then president of the university; afterward he was United States Senator and now he is one of the American officials in the United Nations. Henry knows well and appreciates—and is appreciated by—many distinguished men and women. But certainly no one appreciates him more than I.

CHAPTER 20

ANDICRAFTS, OF COURSE, make Penland, but almost without exception those interested in handicrafts are wonderful personalities. At Penland, I have made the trite observation again and again, one really does meet such interesting people! I could name them by the dozens.

There's Ruby Burkheimer, for instance. I'll tell about Ruby for several reasons, one of which is that she gets me back to our building problem. In fact, we have never long been away from problems related to building. And Ruby, beyond being an interesting member of our Penland family, was an angel with a checkbook.

The fall and winter group living at The Pines while it was being built knew what it was to go about their work to the raucous sounds of hammers and saws and to eat larger or smaller portions of sawdust with their meals. They did it cheerfully, too, for people at Penland generally do not complain, and so we got through that period without losing our minds or even our hearing. And the work on the building moved along.

One morning at the breakfast table I made the remark that even though the building was not yet finished, we already had applications from more people than we could care for comfortably. Ruby Burkheimer was sitting at my table, and she turned to me. "I notice there is a lot of room on the third floor, and I can't see why you don't finish that for a dormitory," she said.

"Money, Ruby," I said, "or rather the lack of it. I'm sure I have borrowed the last dollar the bank will let me have on the collateral I put up, which was all my life insurance. I doubt if they'd lend me another dollar."

Ruby said in a matter-of-fact way, "Well, if that's your trouble, I could lend you the money."

"But, Ruby," I protested, "I'm personally responsible for every dollar we've borrowed. I've got a heavy load on my shoulders now, and I'm getting older every year, and I don't want another dollar's worth of debt to worry over."

"We don't have to call it debt," Ruby countered. "I'll tell you what I'll do. If you'll find out from your contractor how much it will cost to finish the third floor, I'll make out a check for that amount. And I'll agree to stay at Penland until my room, board and tuition amount to the sum I've advanced."

I was delighted, of course, and readily agreed. I made arrangements with the contractor and we finished the third floor.

I would say that no one at Penland has been a more glowingly enthusiastic devotee of handicrafts than Ruby Burkheimer. She borrowed my own Bergman loom, put it up in her room and wove by day and night. She was original, daring, venturesome. Students, teachers and guests just naturally gravitated to her room, and each came away fired with new enthusiasm.

Ruby wove every conceivable type of material: upholstery for chairs in my living room, suitings, dress material, stoles, special and very handsome handbags, table linens, draperies. She was one of the busiest persons on the hill.

After she had been here about a year, she came to me and said, "I really must go out to Seattle to see my family. I do have one, you know. I don't want my grandchildren to grow up without my knowing them, so I'm going out to visit them. I'll be gone two months—it's such a long trip that I'd like to stay awhile."

So she went—with her trunks full of treasures she had made herself.

We were sitting around the fireplace one evening a month later when all of a sudden Ruby blew in, looking as though she were an adventurer back from the moon and fairly bursting with eagerness to tell of wonders she had experienced.

She saw that we were astonished at her untimely reappearance.

"I just couldn't stay away any longer," she hastened to explain. "I bought my plane ticket back to Asheville before even telling my children I was leaving," she said. "I couldn't run the risk of being begged off."

The visit had been delightful, though, she assured us. "But, oh, it was wonderful! You know, I had never been anybody to my family before, except just mother. I never had an identity of my own, and I wasn't expected to have. My children loved me, I know, but they just took me as their mother, someone they were expected to love. They are all happily married, and they don't really need me, you see. To them I was just mother.

"But now!" Ruby beamed and her eyes showed her excitement. "Now I am somebody. I am a celebrity. I can really do something. When they saw all the things I had made, they were stunned out of their normal way of thinking about me. 'Why, Mother,' they raved, 'did *you* make all these? Did you actually make these beautiful things *yourself?*'

"I'm a personality with them now. Not just mother, but somebody. They had me get out all my things for special exhibits; they called in their friends to see them. They introduced me to friends, clubs, art groups, and with the pride of discoverers declared, 'This is my mother. She did this.' Suddenly the word *mother* had a new meaning for them. It was wonderful, and I loved it. I just soaked it in. But then I realized I had been there long enough, and I had to come back."

"My, Mrs. B, but it's wonderful to have you back. We've missed you, and we've missed your showroom," I told her. "Now why can't you just stay with us always?"

There was suddenly a faraway look in her eyes. She answered, "It would be wonderful, but I can't. I know now that I must do something really worth while with my crafts rather than follow them just as a hobby. Why, if I had been willing to, I could have sold everything I had with me. I know I can produce for sale, and I know that I can teach. I'll tell you what I'm going to do: I'm going to stay at Penland until I have used up the money I spent on the third floor, and in the meantime I'll be deciding on just how to use best what I have learned here."

184

A few years later Mrs. Burkheimer, a successful and recognized weaver of special textiles, was back at Penland on a visit. As we sat and reminisced, she told of the reaction of several of her friends to her years spent on that faraway mountain top down in the North Carolina Blue Ridge country. They just couldn't understand why she had done it, couldn't grasp it at all. "How could you stay out of things so long?" they asked her. "What did you find down there, anyway?"

"What did I find?" she repeated their question. "Well, I think I found—yes, I know I found—my soul."

Perhaps Colonel John Fishback could give a similar answer truthfully were he asked such a question.

He came to us first as a student. And this is the story his occupational therapist told me. Mrs. Perry had learned handicrafts at Penland. One of her assistants at Lawson General Army Hospital came to her one day and announced: "There's a wounded colonel here whom I'm working with. He's a nice man, but he's cranky, and I just haven't been able to interest him in a thing. I wish you would come down and see if you can do something with him. He has a young wife he's crazy about, and if you could interest him in making something for her, I believe you might get somewhere with him."

Mrs. Perry picked up her little eight-inch Structo loom and took it to him and asked him if he wouldn't like to weave something—perhaps a handbag for his wife. He took the little loom, looked it over carefully and said, "Do you mind if I take this apart?"

She told him to go ahead, and he did. He tore the loom down, put it back in perfect order, and went to work. He became so interested that she told him one day about Penland. "There's a little school in the North Carolina mountains where

I learned how to weave," she said. "You're doing so well that I thought maybe you might like to go to Penland for a while."

The idea intrigued him. The result was that he telephoned Penland from the hospital and applied for the summer course for himself and his wife.

They came. He soon proved himself a perfectionist. In fact, he did such good work and seemed to be enjoying it so that I asked him if he would return the following summer and assist Mr. Worst and Mr. Peters as an instructor in weaving.

"I appreciate the compliment," he told me, "but I'm retiring. We're going out to California and build a home there."

So they left Penland for California and they did build their house. They lived in it two years. Then the Colonel wrote to ask me if my offer was still good to teach at Penland—no salary, no charge for board. I wrote that the job was still open, and that I would welcome them back. So they sold the California home, came east, and he has taught at Penland every summer since. At the end of each summer session when I am re-engaging our teachers for the following summer, the Colonel and I enjoy this little exchange: "Colonel, will you teach for us again next summer for the same salary you had this year?"

He would answer, "Yes. The job and the salary are quite satisfactory for another year."

Sometimes we even discuss what a ten-per-cent salary raise would mean, but we haven't yet figured out just what such a raise would mean for either of us.

The Colonel's wife Ellen works on the same salary schedule as do many persons at Penland. She serves afternoon tea to the school every day except Saturdays and Sundays when people are apt to be off on mountain trips. She arranges the social calendar—and surprisingly perhaps, the social life at Penland is no simple matter, because there is so much to be seen and enjoyed near by, in so short a time.

For instance, Ellen makes arrangements for such things as one real mountain trip during each three-week session, and picnics in various places in our section of the mountains. One of these picnics is likely to be at Wiseman's View, one of the most majestic lookouts in all the Blue Ridge, from which one may see the mysterious Brown Mountain lights, a phenomenon that, despite the efforts of many persons, including government scientists, has never been satisfactorily explained. On one evening at the school there will be an auction sale, of things students and teachers have made or otherwise acquired and then donated, the funds obtained going to whatever happens to be the acute need at the time—and there are always acute needs. On another evening we show the pictures taken on our European craft tours; on still another day and evening we have an exhibit of the work done by the students. And throughout the sessions there are special evenings of talks or pictures given by extra-special guests, and there are invariably such guests with us. At least once a week, too, we have folk-dancing. So social life at Penland is indisputably varied.

While I'm thinking of characters that have helped to make life interesting and colorful at Penland, I'd do well to include Uncle Charlie. That's what he is called by Penland folk, young and old.

Mr. Charles Bennett came to us in his seventies, retired and crippled with rheumatism. He walked with a cane, or sometimes one crutch, sometimes two. But wherever Uncle Charlie happened to be, he was the life of the party. No one took his ills more lightly than he himself. He even attended our folk dances and put aside his cane or crutch when a waltz came up and did at least a turn or two.

Uncle Charlie took up simple jewelry making at Penland and quickly became fascinated with it. His rheumatism bothered him so that he could not sit too long on the benches in the metal shop, but he bought a few jeweler's tools and the necessary silver and kept these in his room. From time to time he would hobble down to the metal shop and get enough instruction to carry him along awhile longer in his room.

Uncle Charlie's eyes were none too good, and so he bought himself a special lamp with a hundred-watt bulb and reflectors. We gave him a simple desk that a guest had made for our lounge, and Uncle Charlie's room became his studio.

His room was at the head of the stairs and he worked with his door open, so that people coming up the steps and along the hallway at mealtime or at the end of the day could see him at his work bench. Since Uncle Charlie was indeed a social soul, they would stop in to see what he was making, and his room quickly became one of the school's social centers.

Uncle Charlie gave away much of the jewelry he made—as birthday presents, wedding gifts, for auctioning in behalf of any fund that was being raised, or on almost any other provocation. He was a generous soul. When a person insisted on buying one of his productions as a special gift for a friend, he would sometimes sell, but it made him happier to give.

I had been invited out to dinner one evening, and as I went through the lounge on my way out, Uncle Charlie saw me. I was wearing a dark blue dress, no jewelry, no rouge, no lipstick, no highlight of any kind. I noticed him eying me. "Wait, Miss Lucy," he commanded, "you are not quite right. Come up to my room."

188

We went up, and he tried one piece of jewelry after another until he found just the necklace and bracelet he thought would give an inconspicuous individual in an inconspicuous outfit the necessary fillip.

It worked, too. I'm sure I had a much better time at the party for having worn Uncle Charlie's jewelry. It is strange what zest a little unusual jewelry can add to a dinner party, or to any other occasion. And even now when I wear these tokens of his thoughtfulness I feel that Uncle Charlie goes with me.

Recently my brother Rufus, Auntie Freas and I stopped in to see Uncle Charlie in his Florida home. The minute he heard our voices he boomed his welcome. We found him in a wheelchair, with a tray arrangement accommodating the equipment and materials for making jewelry.

"How are you, Uncle Charlie?" we inquired, after we had greeted him.

"Pretty good! Pretty good!" he said cheerfully. "I can't get about much, but I've got a wheelchair. I can't see much, but I've got good glasses and a strong magnifying glass, and I can feel. I can't hear very well, but I've got a hearing aid." He grinned broadly. "And I can still make jewelry. I'm not doing any big business—I don't have to—but I make gifts for my friends, and that pleases them. And I sell a little, enough to pay for my materials, and that's just what I want to do. So I'm getting along fine."

Our visit to him was a tonic for us. He made us feel that he was sitting fairly on top of the world, radiating happiness and good will, and we left with our youth renewed and our spirits aglow. Soon afterwards we got cards from him wishing us cheer and happiness on his eightieth birthday anniversary. I have often thought, a little fearfully, I confess, of what

189

might have happened to Uncle Charlie had there been no Penland at which he could learn his hobby of jewelry making, or had he failed to find out about us. Perhaps a man of his philosophic nature would have found another way to overcome his difficulties and achieve happiness and a sense of usefulness; but maybe he wouldn't have. At any rate, it makes me proud to realize that our little mountain school of handicrafts has been of much significance to quite a number of people like Uncle Charlie, and, we hope fervently, will continue to be.

CHAPTER 21

A VISITOR DRIVING up our hill and rounding the curve at the Appalachian School to leave behind and below the peaceful little valley will see off in the dim blue distance the upthrust and irregular line of the Black Mountain Range. Then he will marvel at the almost perfect cone of Bailey's Peak that stands near by, a rounded and symmetrical Fujiyama, bluish-green rather than white-capped. He will find straight ahead of him, rearing skyward, the huge mass of Art'ur's Knob.

And ringing the lower slope of the Knob and fronting the circling road, a group of buildings of varying types and sizes will reveal to him that he is almost on the campus of the Penland School of Handicrafts. Dominating these buildings will be the newest one, the Lily Loom House.

I'd like to tell about it.

Since the Penland School was started, to quote a friend, "on

191

a shoestring and it frayed," we had dreamed and hoped that someday we'd have such a building. But how could we ever expect to have one as handsome and impressive as the Lily Loom House?

It happened like this: Sometime during each of the sessions of our summer school, the weaving students and instructors go down to visit the Lily Mills at Shelby, North Carolina, where we buy most of our cotton yarns used in hand-weaving. We have bought from them ever since they started manufacturing yarns for hand-weavers, and even before they began such manufacturing they had studied carefully our needs, so that over the years a feeling of mutual interests, friendliness and comradeship had grown up.

It was during the summer of 1944 that Tony Ford, who had taken a group to the Lily Mills, was talking with the president of the company, Mr. Jean Schenck.

"I understand that every day you folk are turning people away," Mr. Schenck said to Tony.

"Well, that's probably true," Tony agreed. "It would probably average out to one person turned down every day."

"I'll tell you, Tony, that just won't do," said the mill president, smiling. "Every student you have is a potential weaver, and every weaver is a potential user of Lily yarns. We just can't have you turning away persons who want to learn how to weave."

"We hate to do it the worst in the world, too, Mr. Schenck," Tony told him. "But we just can't take them, we don't have the facilities. We're terribly congested at Penland. We've got weaving going on all over the main floor of the Craft House. The Pittsburgh room, which was originally planned for looms, is filled with them, and so is the recreation room, including even the stage. The Chicago room is so crowded with looms that it is impossible for us to enjoy that room fully in its capacity as a lounge. And even the long porch is so cluttered that guests dropping in to observe have to weave their way between looms to get into and out of the building."

Mr. Schenck shook his head, and then he looked straight at Tony, his countenance serious. "Tony," he asked, "is there anything we can do about it?"

Tony suggested that Lily Mills might like to help make possible a new building that would be used only for weaving, a yarn shop and weaving instruction.

The mill president was interested. He assured Tony he would try to get up to Penland before the summer was over and discuss the problem with us. Tony came home and told me, of course, what had happened.

So when the next three-week termers went down to the Lily Mills, I went along. Soon after our arrival I saw Mr. Schenck and immediately he said to me, "Miss Lucy, I understand you are interested in having us help you with a new building."

I assured him at once that he had not been misinformed. We discussed in more detail our needs and the probable costs, and in the course of the talk Tony suggested that we might call the projected structure the Lily Loom House. That seemed to please Mr. Schenck and he asked me what I thought the structure might be built for, one that would serve our needs adequately.

"About twenty thousand dollars, I believe," I told him, "would put up the kind of building we would need."

"Our company wouldn't consider giving that much, I'm sure, Miss Lucy," he replied. "We had thought of providing possibly ten thousand dollars. If we should give that much, do you have any idea where you'd get the other ten thousand?"

"No, I don't, Mr. Schenck," I replied quite truthfully. "We might go to the other cotton mills in the state and we could then name it the Carolina Loom House. But that name wouldn't be too good perhaps, because I believe there is a Carolina Mills Company."

Mr. Schenck agreed that name would hardly be appropriate. After a little further talk they announced that the lunch hour had arrived, and Mr. Schenck accompanied us to the community house, where we were all guests of the Lily Mills at a delicious luncheon. When we had eaten, he asked me to return with him to the office for a further discussion. He declared he really liked the suggested name of Lily Loom House, but that he was not at all sure that his board would approve of a contribution of $20,000. He would bring it up for their consideration, however, he promised. But before they could make any decision, he added, they would want more information about the school. They would want to know to whom it belonged, how much it was worth, the amount of its indebtedness and to whom it owed money.

I promised Mr. Schenck I'd try to get him a statement giving as accurately as I could the facts and figures he sought.

At Penland we went into action to acquire this information. It proved an interesting project. We had lived through the birth pangs of the school and all its growing pains, but we had never seen a statement in black and white of the facts we were now assembling. All those presents of logs and windows, those squares of roofing, all that donated plumbing, the value of the huge septic tank and drainage field engineered and supervised without cost by professors in our university, and countless other contributions of one sort and another had never been set down and tabulated. There was real zest and excitement in finding out for ourselves all this information.

The insurance company sent men to appraise our buildings, and our board members figured as best they could the value of our entire property. The more we learned about ourselves the more amazed we were. When we had done the appraising and the estimating and the figuring and the compiling, we found that on paper we looked about like this:

Edward F. Worst Craft House and contents . . .	$45,000
The Pines (dining hall, kitchen, dormitory and contents)	50,000
Radcliffe House and contents	12,500
Metal Shop and contents	6,000
Summer Metal Shop	75
Wood Shop and contents	3,000
Pottery Shop and contents	2,500
Henry's Hotel (cook's cottage)	500
Water system, including two deep drilled wells, a reservoir, three septic tanks and drainage . . .	10,000
Thirty acres of land	3,000

We sent this report to Mr. Schenck promptly, and his company soon decided to contribute $20,000 for a new building to be called the Lily Loom House! But Mr. Schenck made it clear to us that if they put that much money into a building they would want their architect at least to approve the plans before a contract should be let. I remembered very vividly the throes of building The Pines without benefit of architect or contractor. Hopefully and, I suspect, breathlessly, I asked Mr. Schenck: "Will the architect's fee have to come out of the twenty thousand dollars?"

He looked at me a moment without saying anything, and I saw a twinkle in his eyes. Then he said, "No. Miss Lucy, you are cute."

I was flattered by what he said, but I was even more thrilled, I'm sure, at having saved the architect's fee.

This was in 1944, as I have said, and during the war, when prices of material and labor varied and fluctuated and sometimes money and materials almost reached the vanishing point. Lily Mills advised us not to attempt building until things became more stable, so we bided our time. Finally—it was two years later—Mr. Schenck told us we might as well start building; there were no indications that more favorable prices would soon prevail. He told us that he would send his architect up to Penland to look over the situation and make plans for the structure.

As we awaited the coming of the architect, some of our friends offered the rather alarming suggestion that if the Lily Mills planned the building it would be a streamlined structure after the fashion of a modern cotton mill, and we knew that streamlining just would not go with rustic, natural, unsophisticated little Penland. But I had worked harmoniously with Lily Mills over the past years, and I wasn't too alarmed, just enough to be careful.

But with the arrival of two architects, Mr. Van Wageningen and Mr. Cothran, our fears evaporated like the mountain morning mists. They tramped over the entire property, asked detailed questions about each building and its uses, even asked about the paths and the traffic on each before deciding on a site for the new loom house. We had already picked out what we thought was the only spot for the building, but the site

196

chosen by the architects was obviously so perfect that it seemed the one and only place to build it.

We had already asked Bascom Hoyle, our rock mason neighbor, to be here with samples of local rock, and the architects had him lay up samples of masonry for us all to choose from. So carefully was everything planned and carried out that we all felt assured of having exactly the right building in exactly the right spot for exactly the right uses.

Then the architects went home to draw the plans.

When those plans came, we could hardly wait to unroll and examine them. And the building was handsome, so handsome, in fact, that it frightened me. Mr. Schenck and I both asked Mr. Van Wageningen if $20,000 was enough to build such a house, and he said he would not even hazard a guess, since prices of labor and material were too unpredictable. We both urged him to give us an idea, but he refused to commit himself.

But we went ahead; we knew that Mr. Schenck and his architect knew what we were building on. We bought materials and hired labor and started work. The building grew, week by week, month by month, both in size and impressiveness, until finally it reached the roof level.

Then the money ran out. We had used it all up!

I wrote Mr. Schenck and told him how we stood, and I asked him to come up, look the building over and help us make further plans. He wrote back that there was no need of his coming, that what we needed was money, and that Lily Mills was not in a position to put any more money into our building.

So I up and went to Mr. Schenck in Shelby. He was friendly, reasonable and understanding, but reiterated that

197

Lily Mills could do nothing more for us financially at the time.

I yearned, hoped and prayed that Lily Mills would help us finish that building. Hadn't their own architects, knowing that only a certain amount was available for its construction, drawn the ambitious plans?

On the other hand, Lily Mills had already given twice the amount they had originally planned to give, and that in itself was far more than any other contributor had given our school.

All the same, however one might figure it, there on the side of the hill was that handsome house all built up to the roof and with no protection from the weather. Unless we could get it covered it would not only be utterly useless but would quickly begin to deteriorate. I told Mr. Schenck that I had spent my Penland life borrowing for the school, that I was growing older every day but could reasonably expect to be active another ten years, and that I expected to spend those ten years paying off debts, not contracting more. I suggested that if he would promise to pay any certain amount each year until the Lily Loom House was paid for, I would go back home and arrange to borrow enough money at least to put the roof on; I was confident I could do that much. But that didn't work, either. Mr. Schenck wasn't able to make any further promises.

So, baffled, thwarted and, I'll confess now, a bit discouraged, I went back to Penland and borrowed enough money—$14,400 in all!—to finish the outside walls and put the roof on.

I wondered if Mr. Schenck may have thought that we hadn't managed his money well. I invited him to come up and look over the building and for his sake and ours see what he thought of the way we had spent his money. He couldn't come himself at that time, but he did send Bob Forney, his general manager, and the architect's assistant. I asked them to inspect the building very carefully and let us know their opinion. I wanted them to be completely frank.

They spent much of the day going over every detail of the building, and when they had finished they declared unreservedly that it was a very superior piece of rock work, and that we had got much more for the money here at Penland than we would have got in Shelby. That, at least, was comforting. But still our structure was far from finished.

Since that time, I hasten to point out, the Lily Mills have given us contributions amounting to close to $4,000. These gifts have not been applied to the debt, but have been used toward completing building details, such as work around the windows and doors and under the eaves, which has kept out wind and weather and made the structure fairly comfortable for summer use.

In fact, we folk at Penland have been fortunate in our friendships. We have had much encouragement and support in our efforts to preserve and extend interest in our native handicrafts. And we have been particularly fortunate in the type of students and faculty persons we have enjoyed having at Penland through the years. They have been interested, of course, in learning and in sharing the knowledge and skills they had. But they have also been interested in building the school, sometimes actually with their hands, always with their encouragement and ingenuity.

And their money, too. As I have already pointed out, they have been ingenious in their methods of raising money for our various projects.

The first year we used the Lily Loom House, for instance, it had no permanent floors and no partitions. It happened that we had that year a large delegation of students from Michigan, larger than from any other state, in fact, and this group undertook to finish the entire main floor of this structure, which is the floor that houses all the looms.

One of these students was Mrs. Mattson, or Mattie, as she is affectionately known at Penland. Mattie came from Michigan in 1941 as a student. She returned to do library work or fill in wherever needed. The year we were laboring to finish The Pines she had woven a skirt for one of the auction sales. She announced that if the skirt sold and anyone else should want one, she would weave it and fill the order. The skirt did sell, and Mattie began getting orders for others. She got more and more orders until she was spending practically all her time weaving skirts for Penland needs.

Mattie told us that she would do her bit by "weaving the floor" of the Michigan Room in the Lily Loom House. And within a year's time Mattie had done it! She had woven enough skirts to pay for the materials and labor required for an oak floor in the Michigan Room.

The Michigan Room—floor, walls, ceiling, windows—cost just about $3,000. Windows were sold at their actual cost of thirty-five dollars each and people or groups bought them, usually in memory of some loved one or in honor of a living friend. One student even gave one in appreciation of the Penland staff, which made us all bask and purr. And within three years the Michigan Room was paid for.

During the summer of 1949 a winsome, generous and gracious student gave us $1,000. The school always has so many needs that a gift of that size offers all sorts of possibilities. We have made it a rule to try never to use gifts for the paying off of debts, for debts are not romantic, while gifts are.

When we got this gift, our minds turned at once to

200

thoughts of plumbing. It seems that always at Penland plumbing has been a major problem. We had had trouble with our water supply and our sewage system; we had not had sufficient plumbing in the Craft House. And we still lacked adequate plumbing in the Lily Loom House. We knew at once what to do with this money. Before the summer was over, we had installed two washrooms on each of two floors, the first and the third, and a drinking fountain outside the south door. And since the donor wishes to go nameless, we can put no copper plates on the door, but that doesn't mean that there is no gratitude in our hearts every time we are thirsty or tired and dirty or are otherwise in need of the ministrations of plumbing, and don't have to go to some other building to obtain it.

That fall we had a couple with us from Louisville, Kentucky—Mr. and Mrs. Philip Mulkey. After they had been here a while he asked if we would like to have an electric water heater for the shower baths in the two first-floor washrooms. Gleefully we said we would like very much to have it. So he gave us one.

The next year students, staff, everybody worked toward getting the third floor of the Loom House finished. Lectures were being held there, and it was difficult to hear every word of the instructor when, through the cracks in the floor and because of the absence of walls, there came almost unmuffled the sounds of looms running on the floor below, people going and coming, laughter and talk. So everybody was willing enough to make things for the auction sales and then bid on them and in other ways contribute to the third floor finishing fund. Now there is a lecture room with a floor, walls, blackboard, desk, chairs—everything a well-equipped lecture hall needs.

CHAPTER 22

URING THE SUMMER months when Tony Ford is at Penland he publishes *The Grapevine*, a daily sheet which we find at our places at the breakfast table every morning. He also publishes a more elaborate periodical, *Mountain Milestones*, which, as is stated on the cover, is published "every now and then."

Tony's literary efforts in the main are devoted, I would say, to reporting the sayings and doings of our Penland folk—students, staff, teachers, visitors. And in my opinion he very accurately mirrors life at our school. The other day I was turning through back copies of *Mountain Milestones* and I came upon this paragraph, which is quite descriptive of us, I think:

"Names make news, the reporters say, and we have found that our friends, when they think of Penland, think of people—the folks who by their united efforts have made things

202

click and kept things rocking along. You notice when folks who have been to the same place get together the first thing they say is, 'Well, where is so-and-so? Is she here yet?' or 'Do you remember Mary Blank? Where is she now?' Well, we want to tell you about the Penland people now, old and new, because after all, Penland *is* people, not just a collection of buildings, looms and other equipment. Penland is all the folks who have dreamed and worked for the accomplishment of that dream—friends, students, and personnel. This then is about the folks at Penland who make the wheels go round. Up there in the head office Miss Lucy and Bonnie steer the boat as usual and there has to be someone up in the fo'castle that knows where the ship is headed for. The Captain and the First Mate are V.I.P. but the stokers down in the hold are sort of useful too, on account of, to get to port, it is not alone necessary to know the course to steer by, but somebody has to keep steam in the boilers to push the old tug along."

I glanced down the page, turned it over, scanned that one, and another. They were filled with names of people working at play, playing at work, whatever you may wish to call it, but accomplishing, creating, adventuring and having wonderful fun doing it.

"Take the weaving department . . . Mr. Peters is always the moving spirit. . . . Colonel Fishback and Irene have worn the floor thin in the aisle between the looms. . . . Dorothy Weichel has held down the high stool in the yarn shop, dispensing knowledge of texture and color as well as yarns . . . instruction in tapestry weaving during the part of the season that Therese LaFrance was able to be with us, Therese our little perennial from Canada . . . since she first came she has graduated from the Ecole des Beaux Arts in Quebec . . . the shuttle pushers have their heads crammed full as well as their hands busy. . . . Pappy Sims has been the wheelhorse in the metal-crafts department . . . during the fall and winter months Rissie Sparks handles things. This past summer we have had the very excellent assistance of Lorna Manzler of Cleveland, Ohio. . . . The related enameling on copper was capably guided by Rissie Sparks and for part of the summer she was assisted by Harvey Chase, a newcomer of whom we are very proud. . . . There has been a steady stream of students traipsing down to the old pottery building to make non-fired pottery lamps and lamp shades in plastic and spun glass. Here Lester and Flossie Perisho have continued the fine work that Flossie inaugurated some years ago . . . Mollie Sternberg again drove from California to spend her time with the chisel sockers. . . . John Morgan spent the afternoons as usual on the porch of the Craft House with the shepherd's pipe makers; Tony made with the words in the design department. . . . Bill Sumner and his Julia took in the summer with us while Bill conducted the new photography course and took pictures for us to use in our publicity. . . ."

And on and on. Names, names, more names of folk having the time of their lives making things, beautiful things that a few months before they came to Penland few would have thought they could ever make, or would ever dare attempt to make.

And Tony's publication, minutely read at Penland, not only gives names but tells what goes on up here on our hillside and on our jaunts to interesting places in our area. I read on:

"There were auctions. They were with us all summer. At unpredictable intervals one would pop up. Some straight auctions, some Chinese style. On one memorable night that famous Chinese auctioneer, Hu Dun Bid, officiated. It was that night, if memory serves, that there were auctioned some especially nice articles, among these a beautiful screen-printed lunch cloth contributed by Professor Emmy—other original stencil designs too by Frau Emmy and daughter Nora. All through the summer various students had the urge to contribute something for sale and there were many original water colors, sketches and other art creations put on the block ... many craft articles, gem stones, and other things less arty but of practical value. . . . Chances were sold on two very lovely craft creations, one a coverlet from Canada and the other a beautiful purse made and contributed by Mrs. Hendryx. Through the summer the auctions and chances brought to The Pines construction fund some three or four hundred dollars. . . . There were a number of other schemes afoot to bring contributions into The Pines fund. Helen Juhas set up a 'sundries' department that sold everything from shoe laces to shuttles and shears. . . ."

I noticed a note that was a sad reminder. "We have all been saddened by the death this summer of Dock Hoppes, who in the words of his own song has 'ridden to the last roundup, out beyond the twinklin' stars.' Dock has sung songs and told stories for many, many of you, and thousands heard him when he went to the World's Fair and sang for us in front of our little log cabin exhibit there. We have lost a fine friend and one more of that fast thinning group of older mountain people, product of days now gone and who can never be replaced. . . ."

And Tony wrote of places visited:

"Many of you will remember with pleasure the field trips to the old Emerald Mines, or out into the hills in groups—maybe nature hikes of your own. Some of you saw Roan Mountain covered with acres and acres of rhododendron in bloom. This is a sight comparatively few have viewed and which can be duplicated at only a few spots in the world . . . Some of you climbed Grandfather Mountain, one of the oldest mountains in the world. For ninety-five million years the great igneous and metamorphic folds of the Southern Appalachians have risen above the bed of the sea. For that many million years on Grandfather Mountain roots have been thrusting into these rocks and leaves have been falling on last year's leaves to enrich the soil. You have seen the Old Man of the Mountains himself and have grabbed a hand-hold in his whiskers as you scrambled up the rocks."

And of Penland:

"LANDMARKS. The holly tree in front of the Craft House. The twin hound pups, always under foot. The Peak, veiled in swirling fog. Bascom. Faraway Cottage and Blue Haze. The Reverend Schu, looming two hundred pounds plus above a defenseless little spinning wheel. (But he could schu spin.) Eppie and her bottomless bag. Pop Lear talking to a pretty girl. A pretty girl talking to the Major. The old log pottery in the moonlight. Slacks parade down the road after every meal. (Not much slack in some of 'em.) Jumpers-uppers on the jump. They all identify Penland."

Of our plant life:

"Myriads of brightly colored fungi under the damp trees. Bright red cups of Caesar's mushrooms, and the vermillion cap of hygrophorus, orange boletus, coral mushrooms, and the blushing amnita. Lichens—pixie cups and British soldiers; bracket fungus and puff balls. Queer plants supported by other plant matter living and dead—ghostly Indian pipe, beechdrops and ground pines. A paradise for the student of fungus growth and related plants, a fairyland of color for the layman. Remember the centerpiece for the table with some twenty varieties of mushrooms in many colors set in deep green moss?"

How Tony, that versatile young man of the mountains, can write! And how he knows us—our people, our places, our pleasures, even our moods:

"Henry cooking steaks on a campfire, the Linville River gorge a thousand feet below; great Hawkbill, a granite mono-lith in the moonlight. Table Rock, a blue shadow in the mist. The music of the pipes intermingles with singing voices, and finally the phenomena of the Brown Mountain lights moving along the dark ridge. Mysterious lights seen by the Indians before the advent of the white man in these hills, unexplained even today, suddenly gleaming, rising, floating and disappear-ing as strangely as they came. The scientific expedition of the National Geographic Society came to no conclusion concern-ing them; you who went on the picnic to Wiseman's View have beheld one of the wonders of our universe.

"Evenings by the fireplace, do you remember? Old songs, centuries old: Barbara Allen, the Cherry Song, Down in the Valley, sung to the accompaniment of the dulcimer. The dulcimer, an ancient instrument with an ancestry running back three thousand years to Persia, now forgotten almost everywhere except in isolated spots in our mountains. Eve-nings by the fireplace, thoughts to conjure with. Just talking and singing, and shepherds' pipes playing old sweet tunes.

"Mountain moonlight! Like no other wherever you may go. Sitting on the porch of the Craft House looking out across the valley to the Peak. Walking down the road, maybe hand in hand and such like! Could be. Worth remembering or perhaps dreaming about.

"Do you remember the rain that came down 'most every day about noon. . . . But it was all over in a few minutes and the sun shone again and everything was fresh. And that, after all, is the secret of our cool green land.

"Thus we could go on and on, piling memory on memory. For each of you there are countless long to be remembered facets of your visit at Penland, reflecting happy hours that are peculiarly your own. So, we say, Remember Mountain Days.

> "Remember mountain days,
> Blue peaks, quiet nights.
> Cool green forests, dressed with laurel,
> And stars above the swaying trees.
> Soft music and old songs
> As tired day goes to rest among the hills.
> Remember friends and mountain neighbors
> And the joy of hands at work.
> Remember mountain days."

CHAPTER 23

As PENLAND SCHOOL grew and its purposes and program became better known among those who love the handicraft arts, it began to attract more and more students from a wider and wider area. And soon students were coming into our mountains from every part of the United States and even foreign countries. So many of these foreign students, we came to notice, were from countries of northern Europe. In Scandinavian lands and Finland the handicrafts are understood and appreciated and students from these nations not only learned from us practices employed in this country, and particularly in the southern Appalachians through the long years, but also brought us an insight, which we could never have gained so well from studying their books, into the methods by which their lands have produced some of the world's finest handicraft products.

They brought us something else too. They brought to us a desire, an impelling urge, to visit their countries and see at first hand their craftsmen at work.

We wanted to visit craft schools, see all we could of their finished products, and get a feel of the meaning of folk arts and crafts in the lives of the people of those countries where the practice of handicrafts has never ceased to be an essential part of their everyday living. We wanted also to rub elbows with the people of those countries, to exchange ideas, to greet friends who had been to Penland and to make new friends. We knew that in doing so we would be meeting people who had interests similar to our own, and we felt that if by visiting them we could do even a little bit toward promoting friendly relations, Penland would be doing that bit toward world peace.

And, I must confess, we wanted to go for the sheer joy of such a trip, with all the contacts and experiences it would bring.

But again there was that little business of money.

And again a kind Providence, in the guise this time of a noble and generous friend, provided the money.

I went. Not once, but twice. And I traveled with few prickings of conscience, because the trips were costing the school nothing. I even salved my conscience by assuring it that I would of necessity learn things that would be helpful to Penland and perhaps make contacts that would bring other Scandinavian students and teachers into our mountains.

I'd like to recount some of the things we saw and did on the second of these trips, the more interesting one from the standpoint of crafts, I believe, and it is from that standpoint only that I feel I should describe it. Few things are more boring, I think often, than a traveler's detailed account of his trip abroad; I shall try to avoid that.

Eleven of us made this trip. We sailed April 1, 1953, and landed at Rotterdam. After two days in Holland we left Amsterdam on the Linjebuss for Copenhagen. The first night we spent in Boekelo, a beautiful country inn on a lake—De Zee op de Heide—the Sea by the Moor. Soon after boarding the Linjebuss the next morning we crossed the border into Germany and by lunchtime were in Bremen, the home of the Brementown Musicians of Grimm's *Fairy Tales*, my favorite when we were children.

After we crossed the German-Danish border we noticed more evidences of prosperity. Germany had still not recovered from the bombings and the other ravages of war. In Denmark the farms were well tended and neat and buildings were substantial. We drove through Odense, home of Hans Christian Andersen, and I longed to linger and look, but the Linjebuss didn't pause.

At seven that evening we arrived in Copenhagen at the lovely new Hotel Richmond, where I found flowers in my room and a note from Helen Roby, who had been at Penland and who soon came in herself to discuss activities planned for our three days there. She had had her dinner but sat with us and had coffee and rolls. Those rolls! The waiter thrust a thin roll two feet long into my hand, twisted his hand, and left me with about eight inches. (I'm getting into travel details, but that roll was certainly a masterpiece of culinary handicraft!)

At 8:45 the next morning we started for George Jensen's shop, where Miss Roby met us. A guide showed us through the workrooms where various types of silver articles were being made by apprentices who must serve four years in that

211

capacity. In one room they were making table silver, and in the illustrated price list they gave us I noticed that each design was identified not only by a number but also by the name of the designer. In another room they were doing large pieces such as bowls, candelabra and tea services. One lady was working on a large, modern silver jug of elegant simplicity. In another part of the shop they were making jewelry and I saw what I had never happened to see before, Jensen jewelry with stone settings.

We noticed that the shops, like everything else in Scandinavia, it seems, were spotlessly clean, and the workers wore white coveralls. As we were leaving, a cart of bottled milk was rolled by and the craftsmen had their midmorning refreshment.

Miss Roby had arranged for two limousines to call for us, and we discovered that the driver of the one I was in was a Mr. Rasmussen who had lived in America fifteen years; he was a great help to us as he explained the significance of things and places we were seeing.

We were going to Elsinore and Frederiksborg Castles, and as Mr. Rasmussen drove us along what is called the Danish Riviera, we saw swans in the sound, drove through forests carpeted with blue anemones, and by castles and royal residences, finally reaching Elsinore Castle of Hamlet fame. It is a huge castle, with a spacious courtyard where Shakespeare's *Hamlet* is played for a month every summer. But what caught my eye especially was the castle's furnishings of its own era—old carved chests and interesting crude tables made of heavy boards.

Mr. Rasmussen took us to a place up the coast where we had a wonderful smorgasbord lunch. We served ourselves and sat

212

at tables in front of picture windows looking out over the Katagat, and across to Sweden where we could see the summer castle of Sweden's king.

I have no idea of what all we had. As I looked at that burdened board I wondered what our cook Henry would say if he could see it. One dish that intrigued me was a large silver platter with a mound of smoked herring at one end and at the other a bowl of raw eggs in the shell, garnished with capers and set in a tray of flaky salt. Someone told me that those raw eggs smeared over some of the fish dishes made them more appetizing and tasty. I couldn't say. I understood there were also smoked eels, snails and reindeer tongue, but I took only those dishes I thought I recognized. As we were driving away, Colonel Fishback was describing a very choice dish he had tried and especially enjoyed. Mr. Rasmussen told him it was eel. "It was so delicious I would have eaten it anyway, even if I'd known what it was," the Colonel declared.

At Frederiksborg Castle we went first into the church, where we saw carvings and paintings on pews, stalls and walls in soft blues, reds and golds; they told us they are just as they were when the edifice was built; they are not even washed for fear the colors might be dimmed. In the castle there is room after room of art treasures representing every period of its history, rooms furnished for every occasion and representing these different periods. We noticed particularly the upholstery done in beautiful silk damasks in golds, blues, scarlets, depending upon the color schemes of the surroundings. These must have been done, we thought, on draw looms such as they still use in all of Scandinavia.

But the room I enjoyed most was a ballroom that must have been twice as large as our Craft House. The walls were literally covered with reproductions of tapestries of ancient times. They had been woven in the Gobelin Art Gallery. But what thrilled me was that our own Mrs. Sommer had done some of the weaving. She had told us what pieces she had worked on, and that if we looked closely we could find her initials. The initials of the weaver were always done in the same color as the background, but in a little different tone, so as not to be conspicuous and detract from the picture portrayed but at the same time to be legible. And by looking closely we did discover Mrs. Sommer's initials, and it made me feel very proud that the person who had helped create these beautiful Gobelin tapestries had also taught weaving at our own little Penland.

As we drove back to Copenhagen we saw two interesting examples of handicraft, though not exactly of the type we do at Penland. The first was a stork's nest atop a house. A wagon wheel had been braced to the roof as a foundation and on it the stork had built a nest of huge twigs. The storks, said Mr. Rasmussen, spend their winters in Egypt and come back in spring or early summer. One had come back to get this nest in readiness for his wife's return, Mr. Rasmussen explained, but Mr. Stork was not at home when we went by his house.

The other work of art in construction was a church built as a memorial to Bishop Grundvig, who founded the Danish Folk School movement. The architecture is unique, and the view of it from the front makes one think immediately of a huge pipe organ. Inside and out, the church is constructed of cream-colored brick. No other color is seen and the impression is one of magnificent simplicity. The windows are small leaded panes of clear glass. There are no decorations. The baptismal font is a huge fluted bowl of handwrought brass, set in concrete. Eight masons built the church in twenty years, and when they finished, they were knighted. They deserved the honor; they were truly craftsmen.

As I stood and looked in awe at that masterpiece of the mason's art, I wished that Bascom Hoyle, our Penland stone-setter, might be there to pass his opinion. I'm sure Bascom of Penland would have felt an affinity with those master crafts-men who had lifted toward the heavens that soundless sym-phony in enduring brick.

The next day we spent shopping and looking. Of all the cities visited, we would agree at the end of our trip, Copen-hagen was our favorite. Every store we entered might have been an art gallery. First we went to the display rooms of the Royal Copenhagen ware and bought for ourselves and our friends. Most of my purchases were of tableware in the Dan-ish Blue Flower pattern, for though I strolled leisurely through the various display rooms, I would always end up before the displays of that pattern. The white of the porcelain seemed a little more than white and the blue just the blue that I like most. No matter how many pieces I would compare, I would find the blue flowers on no two pieces exactly alike; that meant that each flower had been put on by an artist, free hand. So each piece had its individuality; that is one of the joys of creating or wearing or owning handicrafts.

We went next to my favorite store of all, Illum Bolighus. Each room was an excellent example of what can be accom-plished when the artist, the craftsman and the manufacturer work together. One room was simply but beautifully ap-pointed as a dining room, with the table ready for guests. The silver, china, place mats, draperies and upholstery were all designed to be used together. Yet there was no feeling of sameness but rather one of harmony and fitness.

We were particularly impressed with all the house furnishings. The woodwork was simple, modern, beautifully designed and executed. Much of the furniture appeared to be upholstered in hand-woven material, but actually it had been done first by the artist and craftsman and then reproduced by the factories.

Much of the drapery material was silk-screen print, really done by hand, and later we saw this being done. In one room there was nothing but silk-screen prints, and they so fascinated me that I could hardly take myself out of the store. I so wanted to own at least a yard of each design. And I did get a meter or more of several of the prints to take back to Penland for our permanent exhibit.

One day we went out to the suburban town of Holte to see two of the most expert designers and weavers of damask, John and Kristin Becker, who used hand Jacquard and draw looms. They had a small studio next to their own home, which was itself a veritable gem. Everything in it seemed to have been made by their own loving hands, and each detail was in harmony with the others, and with themselves. In the studio, just as interesting, people were weaving damasks for sale. The looms themselves were so intriguing that we almost had to drag Colonel Fishback away.

One weaver was doing a Christmas table set that the Beckers had designed; it was very much like one they use on their own table at Christmastime. It was in a bright Scandinavian red with bands of figures woven in white, showing the Madonna and Child, wise men, shepherds, angels and animals. We bought a set of these table linens for our Penland exhibit. Someday we hope to have those delightful Beckers come to visit us.

That afternoon we visited Holga Foght, the silk-screen

216

artist I had met through Mrs. Emmy Sommer when our Penland group was over on the first trip four years before. She most graciously explained her methods, showed us examples of her designs and workmanship, and demonstrated printing on long tables.

In all of Scandinavia and Finland, in fact, we saw a great deal of very original and exceedingly beautiful silk-screen printing, much of it in use in upholstery, draperies, table linens and wearing apparel. It was seen in both hotels and private homes. We were interested to learn about their methods of mass production. They used one, two or three tables the length of a whole building, and in some instances rollers and gauges for moving and placing the screens; thus the printing was done by hand, with no machinery.

Between visiting craft schools and studios we took time to walk down to the harbor where there were benches in the sun. We sat and visited and I feasted my eyes on one of my favorite scenes in all Denmark, the little bronze mermaid seated on a giant boulder and looking out to sea as she awaits the return of her human lover. An extraordinarily handsome piece of handicraft in fine art! Then we walked back past the Gefion fountain, mighty and impressive, the legend fashioned in bronze of the goddess Gefion, who was told that she might have as much of Sweden as she could plow around in one day. So she turned her four sons into oxen and urged and goaded them until they had plowed around all of what is now Zealand, Denmark's largest island, on which Copenhagen is situated. The fountain's waters gush from the nostrils of the straining oxen laboring under the lash of their goddess mother. It is indeed a masterpiece, but I prefer the gentle little mermaid.

We would have enjoyed stopping the next day at Göteborg to study crafts and craftsmen at work there, but we didn't have the time, and we went on to Stockholm, where we were put up at the Hotel Malmen, the last word in modern architecture and furnishings. We saw with delight that the handwork used throughout the hotel fitted perfectly into the ultramodern setting. The screen between the main dining room and the breakfast room was a grill of hand-carved figures, including a strange but artistically interesting combination of fishes and violins and what must have been elongated pineapples or pineappled tenpins.

But what really caught my enthusiastic attention was a huge cock on one breakfast room wall most intricately and artistically done in small pieces of cloth appliqued on a beige background. The predominating colors were reds shading into orange, and black. He was a rather modernistic cock in his lines, too, as well as his colors; he wasn't the sort we see running about the grounds at Penland, but I'd dearly delight to have one like him on one of our walls.

Our bedrooms had simple maple furniture. There were hand-woven rugs and bedspreads; the draperies at the windows were of silk-screen prints carrying out the same motif as the rugs and bedspreads. This was not an expensive hotel, but it was filled with handicraft products. We were impressed with the fact that those people live with their crafts. In America it is something extra, something we as a nation have forgotten and are now reviving as a hobby or as occupational therapy, not as an essential part of everyday living. A modern hotel in our country would bear all the earmarks of the latest and most scientific mass production. There might be an original painting on the wall, but most likely it would be a clever reproduction. It might be a scene we could enjoy, or it could well be an abstraction to baffle our imagination or threaten our sanity. Anyway, I liked that rooster and his glowing cheerfulness, and I liked the idea that a great deal of thought had gone into the planning and making of him, and that even some big commercial architect had shared in the creative joy of designing him and his setting. Such touches made that hotel a living personality for us. I wonder why we can't have more of this sort of creativity in America.

CHAPTER 24

WE WENT DOWN the gangplank at Turku,
Finland, and into the customs, where an attractive gentleman in an officer's coat came
immediately to us and asked if we were the handicraft party
from America. He was from the Tourist Bureau and at once
he introduced us to a delegation of a dozen or more educators
of Finland, most of whom could not speak English but each of
whom said to us very plainly: "Well come to Finland."

I thought how much warmer a sound it had than our "welcome."

They pinned a bouquet of wild anemones on each of us. As
we walked through customs talking and answering questions,
a reporter was trying to get in her questions, too, and as we
got to the exit door a photographer took a picture of the
group, which appeared the next day on the front page of the
Finnish newspaper. Our baggage was put on top of a bus, we

were put inside and told that the bus and the driver were ours for the day. Then our hosts and hostesses, who had got in with us, handed us each an attractive multigraphed program with a picture of Turku Cathedral. The program read:

```
 9:00   The Castle of Turku
10:00   The Cathedral
11:00   Breakfast at the Trade School
12:00   The Chapel of the Resurrection
13:00   The Handicraft Museum
14:00   Naantali Kultaranta
14:30   Lunch at Housewives School of Finland Proper
16:00   Mead with Mrs. Grundstrom
17:00   Start from Turku
```

For the first time our travel agency had planned nothing for us. From the time we arrived in Turku until we should board ship to return to Stockholm, we would be in the hands of our friends, Raili Seraste and Maria Halva, both of whom had been students at Penland and had planned our activities in their country.

So we headed toward the Castle of Turku, said to be the oldest building in Finland. It was being rejuvenated and modernized, we found, even to having radiant heat installed in order to make it more comfortable as a museum and added tourist attraction. But I won't attempt to describe all our stops on the busy schedule. I remember, however, that what they listed as breakfast was rather a heavy luncheon. We had eggs, cheeses of various sorts, including cheese made of goats' milk, sardines and other fish dishes I didn't recognize, various dark breads that were firm and natural and not blown up with air like so much of our bakery breads, delicious fresh

221

butter, milk and coffee. It's a little strange to us how those northern Europeans go for strong fish at breakfast. But, you know, after a while you get to like it!

At this breakfast we met Dr. Toini-Inkeri Kaukonen, national supervisor of all handicrafts for Finland, including Finnish Lappland. Her office had planned with her so that she or some other teacher or teachers would be with us during our entire stay in Finland.

I shall never forget the experience at the Chapel of the Resurrection. A burial chapel, it is one of the loveliest and most meaningful examples of good architecture and planning that I have ever seen. Its planners brought nature into their designing; wide, shallow steps led up to the chapel, the steps of slatelike stone, extending at the sides off into the turf so that one hardly knows where they end and the grass begins.

As we stood there at the foot of the steps the guide called attention to the slender, plain black cross at the left of the entrance. Then he asked us to close our eyes and walk up the steps.

"Now," said he, as we reached the top, "turn around and open your eyes."

We did so. We were looking directly toward the cross. But no longer was it black. It had turned to an eye-dazzling gold!

On the inside long wooden benches made of birch sanded and perhaps waxed, with no paint or varnish, were held together with wooden pegs. And they were diagonally arranged so that the congregation faced not only the chancel but the great outdoors, for the wall on the right was entirely of glass, and it was difficult to tell where the forest floor ended and the chapel began. High above there were windows which, though invisible from where we were sitting, must have been of clear

222

and pastel-tinted glass, for the flood of light falling through them into the chancel seemed a rainbow of promise. The guide spoke reverently and feelingly of the symbolic significance of the chapel and its surroundings. Nature seemed actually to come up the slope into the chapel to meet there the light from above.

We went then to a handicraft museum housed in buildings that they told us dated to the dawn of Finland's history and were still on the sites where they were built. As we came out we were photographed again and the next day our pictures were in the newspaper.

Next we were loaded into the bus and taken to the small town of Naantali to see the summer home of the President and then to the Housewives School of Finland Proper, which in the United States would probably be called a school of home economics. After being shown through the school we were served a delectable luncheon. We sat at a long table laden with great silver trays of hors d'oeuvres and salads, and the wait-resses, who as students of the school had prepared the meal, brought in great steaming bowls of boiled potatoes.

I well remember one dish. It was of daintily rolled bits of meat thicker and darker than chipped beef and of a stronger flavor. They told us it was reindeer. The food was delicious and we ate heartily. Then those plates were removed and others placed before us, and waitresses brought in other huge silver platters, each containing a large fish—baked and hot and delicious. It was a white fish, not salmon, and though they told us the name, that meant nothing to us. Then more bowls of boiled potatoes. And after that course a dessert made of cooked yellow berries that look much like our raspberry, but taste like nothing but themselves. They were served with

223

mounds of whipped cream. How those Finnish folk do eat!

Then Finland and Penland complimented each other and we departed.

We were supposed to stop at the home of Mrs. Grundstrom for mead, but we were running late and had to start for Helsinki, accompanied by Dr. Kaukonen. But we did learn that the mead we missed was a May wine. This wine, they told us, had no alcohol in it. It is made of hops, raisins, lemons, sugar, yeast and a certain little May flower.

Two hours from Turku we were in Helsinki, and there to meet us was our beloved Raili Seraste, looking handsomer than ever with her glowing pink cheeks and beautiful brown eyes and broad smile welcoming her Penland friends. With her was a delegation of hostesses who had invited the Americans to be guests in their homes. Raili had a sheaf of typed programs, one for each of us and the hostesses, listing the activities planned for our week in Helsinki.

This program was partly in English, partly in Finnish. And those Finnish words! North Carolina mountaineer that I am, I wonder how those wonderful people of Finland ever learn to spell. I'm sure that for Americans, who generally do well to spell *cat* in this day of new methods in teaching, it would be an insurmountable task. I looked down my program. The first thing on our schedule for the next Thursday morning at nine o'clock was listed "Kasityoopettajaopisto, Kulmakatu 5." The last thing that day was from "19:30 to 21:00, Kansantanssin Ystavat," which meant absolutely nothing to me if there hadn't been in parentheses the explanation "Folk dancing." But I ran my eyes down the page. The date for Saturday at ten o'clock stopped me. It read "Kasityoopettajaopiston kutomo ja Ammattienedistamislaitos," and in parentheses, "Weaving School."

Our first date was to visit the Kasityon Ystavat, which is a craft shop that might be likened to our Guild's Allanstand, though there is little in it besides weaving. The weaving we saw there that morning is very similar to that which may be seen in any of our Guild shops, except that there was much more in the way of complicated weaves which many of us have done for our own satisfaction, but which involve so much time that we consider them unprofitable. Some of their weaves that have not been done for sale in this country, as far as I know, were the beautiful linen damask done on the draw looms, or hand Jacquards.

I was delighted to see that some of the simpler weaves were in the same traditional patterns that we use. For instance, there were most attractive aprons done in the Monk's Belt pattern. The ways in which they used their colors and arranged their patterns was quite interesting. One apron that I was tempted to buy for Penland was white with bands of design in shades of blue. But I wanted just as much one of the others done in the same Monk's Belt pattern with several strong colors in the lower part of the apron. The colors, though strong—blue, yellow, green, chartreuse, rose red—were soft and much like the colors obtained from our vegetable dyes.

I did buy for Penland's permanent exhibit a lace-weave linen tablecloth about fifty inches square in a very soft light yellow. I also bought a Finn weave wall hanging in a soft deep rose and a beige which might be the natural undyed sheep's wool. The Finn weave is a double weave, a technique which we teach, but it takes much time to make even a little progress in this technique.

Then after visiting various craft shops, we spent some time in the crafts section of Stockmann's department store. Next

225

Harriet Turner and I were conducted to a radio station's studio for a national broadcast. There we were interviewed by nice Mrs. Tmpi Haulio, who introduced us to her radio audience in Finnish, explaining where we were from, what school we represented, what special interests had brought us to Finland, and perhaps other things related to our visit. After questioning us in English, she interpreted our answers in Finnish to the radio listeners. It was another experience for us. The interview was likely only a taped one, because two days later we listened to ourselves on the radio.

At thirteen o'clock—we would call it one o'clock in the afternoon—we had lunch at the home of Miss Virkki, author, and editor of *Omin Kasin*, a craft magazine to which Penland subscribes. Miss Virkki's apartment is modern and beautiful, with woodwork and walls finished in white and with green vines growing up the walls and along the ceiling. Much is made of green growing things in these countries where winters are long and severe. From her picture windows we could look out over the sea. It was a sunny day and sky and water were a lovely blue.

Her table was set with hand-woven cloth and napkins, and soon the food was brought in for smorgasbord or buffet. As was universally true in those lands, each dish seemed to have been made and arranged by a master craftsman. When we had finished luncheon a photographer came in and made our pictures and in the October issue of *Omin Kasin* we saw the pictures and a two-page write-up in Finnish. We could read only the pictures.

I must tell about the Children's Castle that we visited that afternoon. It was actually a most modern children's hospital. Every detail of that building showed loving thought and an

226

understanding of children. The walls were of stucco, and as I looked at them it seemed to me that while the stucco was still wet, some clever artisan had come along and with his finger had drawn figures here and there as fantasy prompted. I saw good luck symbols such as horse shoes, new moons, four-leaf clovers, and I saw stars, birds, animals.

The entrance gate was of wrought-iron gingerbread boys and girls; it was amazing, wonderfully designed and executed. The entrance steps to the hospital were normal steps but on each side were shallow steps to fit a child's stride, and the railing was in different pastel colors. Inside there were no square pillars and no angles in the walls; they were all curved, and it's more difficult to bump into a curve than an angle. The supports for the stair railing certainly would have caught the fancy of the small child; they captivated mine. They were red, blue, yellow, white, gold. And the door to the elevator was of wrought-iron figures of children, beginning at the bottom with a baby being delivered by a stork. Intriguing! But the prize, I thought, was in the diet kitchen: the wall of one whole end of the room had etched in the concrete a huge mama bird feeding her wide-mouthed brood. What child looking at that bird and her hungry babies could refuse to eat?

They told us that this Children's Castle had been built and was supported by legalized black-market coffee—whatever that is. I didn't understand, but I loved that place.

This has nothing to do with handicrafts, I'll confess, but I must tell about the famed Finnish bath. The last thing before dinner we went into Sauna, the bath, in the Palace Hotel. All of us women were ushered into the ladies' bathing quarters, where we immediately got into our birthday suits, quite an experience in itself, and then went into the steam room, where there was one shelf after another along the walls. We shelved ourselves according to our tastes; the higher the shelf, the hotter it was. Near the center of the room was a stove that seemed to be made of hot stones. Every now and then the attendant would pour water on those stones, and the steam would boil up. I never did know how high the temperature rose, but the only reason we didn't blaze, I'm sure, is that we were wet.

Then they brought us a bucket of water with tied-up bunches of leafy birch twigs, and with these we switched ourselves and our neighbors. I'm not sure whether this made us hotter, because we couldn't have been any hotter surely; in fact, we couldn't tell whether the streamlets pouring from our bodies were perspiration or steam.

After we'd all but melted, an attendant gave us a scrub-down with something rough that I think was the inside of a gourd. At least, it was similar to a plastic "chore girl" we use in the kitchen at Penland.

We had no snow bank or cold lake to jump into after this rubbing had been finished, but they did give us a cold shower, which ended the bath. As we strolled along the corridor to where they had provided terrycloth robes for us and couches on which to recline, it was interesting—and quite novel, I must confess—to meet members of our party and suddenly realize "Why, that's our Ellen" or "our Julia." Have you ever tried meeting your friends dressed only in the costume that Mother Nature provided? It is really amazing what a difference clothes do make!

We rested and purred for half an hour or longer, and then, clothed and in our right minds, I trust, dined with our friends in the hotel. And never so long as I possess this body do I expect to have it feel cleaner or more relaxed.

228

But I haven't told about our only man in the group, Colonel Fishback, for whom it was also ordained that he must have a Finnish bath that evening. Two young men had been sent over by the Office of Education to give him moral support when he donned his birthday suit in the presence of those buxom lassies who led him through the labyrinthine processes of such an ablution. This was not one of the things the Army had prepared the Colonel for. But he survived, though none of us will ever be quite the same people we were before we landed in Finland.

Thursday afternoon our teacher-guides took us to Kasityo-opettajaopisto, which is a handicraft school for teachers. There they were doing most beautiful embroidery, drawn work, cross stitch, punch work—any kind of "stitchery" you might want to mention. These techniques were used on tea cozies, household linens, baby clothes, lingerie, aprons, blouses, dresses.

Some of the tea cozies were so colorful and attractive that only their bulkiness kept us from asking if any were for sale. The ones that particularly appealed to me were of a rich gold color, embroidered in other strong colors. That gold was used very generally in Finland and all the Scandinavian countries. It is not mustard, not yellow, not orange, not quite chartreuse, but to me more pleasing than any of these. I can only call it gold.

We were told that young women in Finland, especially those in rural areas, still take pride in making by hand their household linens and personal lingerie before considering themselves ready for marriage. So it is felt that young women should be taught how to make these things attractive.

We had luncheon that day at the home of Mr. and Mrs. Kuusamo at Palika, a short distance from Helsinki. Mr.

Kuusamo was at one time Finnish Consul in the United States and he and Mrs. Kuusamo lived for several years in New York. They now live in the beautiful old home in which Mr. Kuusamo was born. Though it is modernized enough to be comfortable and has central heating, it retains the old tile stoves and the beautiful furniture of early days.

In every room there were large and lovely tapestries done by Mrs. Kuusamo's sister, Martta Taipale, who was acting as joint hostess. Martta was the subject of an article by Dorothy Liebes in *Craft Horizons* for October the year before. She has come to be one of our beloved friends of Penland, and we consider her one of the top people in all the world of the crafts.

In the Kuusamo dining room they made a picture of Martta standing beside one of her tapestries done in warm rich colors, mostly gold and rose and beige. In that dining room, too, was smorgasbord with all the trimmings, and this time, because we were Americans or because the Kuusamos had lived in America, or both, there were also a number of American dishes. Mrs. Kuusamo herself had prepared all the food, and it was wonderful.

We spent so much time enjoying the good food, and in seeing Martta's tapestries and buying some of them, and in visiting with the Kuusamos and Martta, that there was no time left for Eduskuntatalo, and now I've even forgotten—if I ever knew!—what that word means. We left the Kuusamos just in time to get back to Helsinki and the American Legation for cocktails. (Just think of Penland and cocktails!)

Nor was the cocktail party at all stiff and forbiddingly formal. But everybody seemed greatly interested in why we had come to Finland, and what we were doing. They knew about Penland School and the Finnish students we had had.

We talked with tall, handsome Mr. McFall, American Minister to Finland, and Mrs. McFall. They and Colonel Fishback had much in common, for Mr. McFall and the Colonel are both Hoosiers. We talked also with Mr. Paul Taylor, the American Consul, and Mr. Wilson, cultural attaché and head of the information service, and his associate, Dr. Lester Ott. These people had had something to do with arrangements for the Finnish exchange students who had been sent to Penland.

Dr. Ott had been in Italy and had returned the day before we arrived; he had telephoned Raili Seraste at eleven o'clock that night to inquire about our group, and it was he who had arranged the cocktail party for us. All those Americans were friendly and interested, and they showed their devotion to Finland and the Finnish people. They seemed grateful that we too appreciated Finland. Dr. Ott knew the way to a woman's heart, too; he admired my madder dress that I had woven with my own hands and he pleaded for enough hand-woven material for a jacket for himself, which he planned after examining my hand-woven hat.

Once again we'd had such a good time that we overstayed our scheduled period at the Legation, and so we had to skip the planned visit to Miss Virkki's studio and shop.

At the folk dance that evening the dancers wore traditional costumes in our honor. I was delighted when a nice gentleman asked me to dance with him in one of the simpler Finnish dances—which I did, acceptably, I hope. At any rate, he seemed pleased. None of them spoke English, but Raili served as our interpreter and at the end of the dance, with Raili's help, Finland and Penland once again made nice speeches to each other.

The next day we took a train to Hameenlinna, two hours

north of Helsinki, to visit one of Finland's finest weaving schools, Ketitoollisuusopisto. As soon as we arrived they served us coffee and delicious pastries, and then we visited the various classes, including carding and spinning, weaving, dressmaking and tailoring. It was at this school that we met Finland's foremost weaving designer, Miss Laila Kartiunen. We had seen an exhibition of her work in Helsinki, and often we see it illustrated in the magazine *Omin Kasin*.

There they put on a fashion show for us, wearing costumes that had been designed and woven under the direction of Miss Kartiunen. They must have shown at least thirty costumes, and although they were all simple and most of them had full skirts, there was an amazing variety and originality displayed. We saw house dresses, street costumes, sports clothes, and even a sauna robe. There was an exquisite black evening dress woven of fine wool, soft and fairly sheer. The full skirt had at intervals a loop fringe about an inch wide.

Especially appealing to us were the simple hats, some made of the same material as the dress, others of contrasting material with matching pocketbooks and gloves.

Again we were served a banquet. In fact, any of those meals we had could well be termed a poem, a symphony, a work of art. And wonderful to eat was that food too! It was during this meal that the radio was brought in and we heard the broadcast of our interview the Wednesday before. The people listen to the radio over there, I was soon to discover. As we were returning to Helsinki, a Finnish lady came in and sat next to me on the train and began fingering my woven dress and asking questions.

"I'm sorry," I said, "but I speak only English."

But she chatted on amiably, just the same. Finally Dr.

232

Kaukonen came to our compartment and interpreted. The lady, we learned then, had heard our broadcast and was wanting to know if we were the group of Americans she had heard about over her radio.

The dress I was wearing at the time was one that I had woven of yarn that Mrs. Conley had dyed at Penland. It was rose madder with bands in the skirt of blue from indigo, deep rose from sumac berries, a yellow-tan from onion skins, and a soft gray from rhododendron leaves. The dress looks very homespun, and I suppose it and our speech led the Finnish lady to recognize us as the visiting American craftsmen.

The first thing the next morning, which was Saturday, we went out to Finland's finest pottery, which is called Arabia. I was happy to get a look at this craft. Though my first love is weaving and the revival and continuation of the old hand weaving of our Appalachians, I am likewise enthusiastic about the other crafts, and certainly pottery making is among the most important and challenging. The pottery at Arabia is really a big factory where they do everything from mass-production tableware of ordinary quality to the finest porcelain, designed, decorated and built by hand. They do exquisite, almost paper-thin rice china; they do adorable little figures of people and animals, some of them sweet and beautiful, such as the mother and baby fauns, and some showing such charm and humor that they were almost irresistible.

It was from Arabia that we were taken to the finest weaving school in Helsinki. It certainly should be, if merit is indicated by length of names. I have already given its name: Kasityoopettajaopiston kutomo ja Ammattienedistamislaitos. Its director was Miss Aino Ollila, who has been most gracious and kind to all who have gone from Penland to Finland. Here we watched them weaving damask tablecloths, and seeing this work going on made us all the more eager to own one of the draw looms on which such weaving can be done.

For luncheon they took us to Kestikartano. The interior of the place was of logs to represent the early days of Karelia, and our chief hostess was Mrs. Kuusamo. She was wearing a Karelian dress and jewelry of the type worn two thousand years ago; and the waitresses, who served us a meal very much like smorgasbord, were dressed in the traditional Karelian costume of black full skirt, white blouse, embroidered bodice and colorful kerchief. One dish, I recall, was reindeer meat and reindeer tongue. As I ate I suddenly had the disconcerting thought that with one reindeer short, Santa Claus might not be able to make it to Penland on Christmas Eve!

After the luncheon Dr. Kaukonen, who speaks English with difficulty, expressed her country's appreciation of our visiting Finland, and I did my best to express the appreciation of our group for what Finland was doing to make our visit so pleasant and profitable, for Finland's tremendous interest in handicraft, and for the wonderful students Finland was sending to Penland.

We were to attend a ballet that evening, but the chief dancer became ill and the performance had to be canceled. We were not distressed, for we had been going at such a pace that a restful evening, which we spent in Raili's apartment, was welcome.

When I got up the next morning who should be in Raili's breakfast room but Maria Halva, who had spent seven months as a student at Penland! Maria had planned to return to Finland to greet us on our arrival, but our itinerary had been changed and we were in Finland to greet her. We were happy to see each other, and until we left the next day for Turku, Maria was our devoted slave.

Although it was Sunday, we didn't go to church; we excused ourselves by saying that there were no services in English. At noon friends took us to the National Museum. What interested me most about it was the evidence of Finland's great love of beauty as shown in the artistry and creative skills of the people of Finland and the other northern European countries, including the Lapplanders, even back in the earliest days of their history. Maybe, I thought, it was the long winter nights spent by the fireside that led men to spend so much time decorating such things as harness and saddles, chests, headboards of beds, doughboards and bread trays, even the rolling-pin-shaped cylinders on which women rolled their household linens before the days of the sadirons.

Nor could the women's fingers have been idle, for there were costumes of the Lappland women as well as the Finnish women, woven of wool, with blouses of white linen. Colors, we saw with appreciation, were evidently from vegetable dyes. The reds, we supposed, were from cochineal, for we did not know a vegetable that would make so gay a red. Their blouses, bodices, kerchiefs and pocketbooks were intricately and colorfully embroidered, and there was lace which was probably bobbin lace. It was difficult to realize that such early people, living so rugged a life, could produce things of such beauty, delicacy and workmanship. Our folk in the southern Appalachians years ago, we knew, had far more resources.

In the afternoon the group went to Raili's for coffee and pastries and to see an oriental rug that her father had just completed after a year's work. He was a teacher and had retired the year before. But, as seems to be true of all Finns,

235

he had no thought of being idle, so he learned oriental rug-weaving. He told us that there were 200,000 knots in a square meter of his rug! The yarn had been vegetable dyed by a professional vegetable dyer of Helsinki. And on the floor of the coffee room was a Rya rug done by Raili's husband while she was spending her year in America. He too is a teacher.

We were charmed by Raili's two daughters, nine and eleven. Very Finnish, they spoke no English, though they would learn it later in school. As they shook hands they curtsied—not just a little bob either, for their knees must have gone halfway to the floor.

We were given wonderful presents there. A book on handicrafts written by Raili and Maria Halva came from the publisher the day before we arrived, in our honor, Raili said. The two autographed copies for us and wrote little messages in them. We very proudly carried away the precious treasures.

And now, after so many wonderful things had been done for us, we were most anxious to give a really special dinner to our hostesses and hosts. The only time in our schedule that we could get it in was this Sunday evening. So we had planned it all with Raili.

We had chosen the Fisherman's Cottage. We had been introduced to this charming place by Veikko Ijanko on our first trip to Finland. It is on a lake just outside Helsinki, and I think it is certainly one of the most beautiful places we saw on our entire trip. Not grand and imposing like the Grand Hotel in Stockholm, but beautiful. It is a round building and the walls are all windows, with the blue lake to be seen through them. On each side of the entrance there is a long wide stairway leading to the balcony. We were on the first floor, and it was a gala party around our two long tables decorated with

American flags. The orchestra played many Stephen Foster selections, and other airs that were familiar to us, and we could tell by the way the musicians were beaming at us that we were being honored. Maria Halva and Raili's husband both have beautiful singing voices and they would start a Finnish folk song, and the people on the balcony would join in. The whole place seemed filled with spontaneous music and good fellowship.

Colonel Fishback thought that the occasion and the fellowship and the situation generally called for something to drink, and he asked Raili to order something locally popular. When it came it was red, and in little glasses, and I said to Mr. Seraste, "I like wine, but I don't like strong drink. What is this like?"

"It's not strong, Miss Lucy," he sought to reassure me. "It's only about sixty per cent alcohol."

That sounded pretty strong for wine, but I wet my lips with it, and licked them.

The next afternoon we gathered at the railway station; we were leaving for Turku. With us were our hosts, hostesses and many other friends. They had brought flowers, candies, and gifts of various kinds. They all *thanked* us for having come and many of them, even the men, actually wiped tears from their eyes. What people!

Less than an hour out of Helsinki we came to the little strip of Russian zone we had been told about, where iron curtains really were put over the train windows from the outside, doors were locked and sealed, our Finnish engine was disengaged and a Russian engine was hooked to our train. It required about an hour to go through this Russian territory. Then the iron curtains clanged down, daylight streamed in, engines were changed, and on we went to Turku.

As we got off the train, there were our Turku friends again with welcome and flowers. Mr. and Mrs. Grundstrom were the only ones whose names I could pronounce. Mr. Grundstrom went into the customs ahead of us and although we don't know what he said, we do know that our baggage was sidetracked directly to the ship without even being halted for customs, and we were asked but one smiling question: "Are you taking more or less money out with you than you brought in?"

"Less," we answered, grinning. "Much less!"

And on we went, up the gangway. We had spent for crafts to bring back to Penland as much money as we dared spend.

Those precious friends stood there on the dock in the chill wind and in the little sprinkle that came up and for more than an hour waited for our ship to pull away. After the gangway was lifted they came up until we could almost touch them. "Give our love to Ike," they called out, "and, oh, to Mr. Hoover."

Our whole experience in Finland was touchingly unbelievable. It made me feel humble and unworthy. Clever, wonderful people, those Finns. America has a great deal to live up to if we are to warrant their faith in us and their affection for us.

Our ship sailed at seven o'clock, and after dinner when it was too cold to sit on deck and watch the beauty of the moonlight on the water, I found a quiet writing room and tried to jot down some notes that our busy social life had not allowed time for. After some moments there was music over the radio, which sounded to me like some of Maria's Finnish folk songs; then "Carry Me Back to Ol' Virginny," sung in Finnish but with our tune and our "Virginny." Next I heard what turned out to be a news broadcast, with a word here and there that sounded strangely familiar. I recognized "America," and several words which sounded like handicraft terms I had heard in Finland, and then, distinctly, the name "Lucy Morgan!" I was so elated I got the Fishbacks up to tell them, and the Colonel observed rather sardonically that "They must be broadcasting the fact that the Americans have left and now everybody can get some rest."

CHAPTER 25

WE WERE BACK in Stockholm April 28, and we spent most of that day washing our clothes, catching up on our notes and getting a bit of rest from our exciting and inspiring but nevertheless tiring visit to Finland.

That evening we had dinner in the Gondolen, high up in the air overlooking beautiful Stockholm with all its waterways reflecting the sunset colors and the many slender spires.

The next morning, refreshed and eager, we resumed our craft-looking. First we went to Johanna Brunsson's Vav-skola, where we were warmly welcomed. Little English was spoken, but a delightful young lady, Miss Brita Sjoman, took charge of us, and we felt quite at home. Different languages were hardly a barrier between persons bound by respect and admiration for each other and united in their love of the crafts, particularly weaving. This school, we had been told, was considered the best school of weaving in Sweden; after we had inspected it, and examples of its products, we were not disposed to challenge the statement.

We Penlanders were interested particularly in their looms. Among those used were the complicated damask looms such as are found all through Scandinavia and Finland. Students were weaving in a variety of techniques, but we got the most graphic idea of that school's weaving course from an exhibit that had been arranged for us. Displayed on the walls, floor and shelves of a special room were examples of every weaving technique we knew or had ever heard of.

In this room we saw work representing four years of the school's five-year course, including carding and spinning, dyeing, sewing and tailoring, making bobbin-lace and, of course, weaving. We saw table linens, draperies, glass curtains, rugs and yardage of various types for clothing. The student whose work this room represented was there, dressed in the traditional costume of her province, a costume she had woven and made entirely by herself.

On a table were four large notebooks that immediately caught our interest. Any page of these notebooks would have been a decoration worthy of framing on a wall. For instance, the notebook on vegetable dyeing was as beautiful as it was instructive. Each page had directions for the use of the particular dye, a sample of the yarn dyed with it and a mounted sample of the particular bit of nature from which the dye had been concocted.

It was an amazing exhibit. We immediately tried to arrange for this young lady to come to Penland to work with our students there for a summer, but we found that she was engaged to be married—lucky young man!—and we couldn't get her.

At another outstanding school, Handerbetets Vanner at Skansen, Miss Ann Beal Carlsan, the director, showed us excellent work being done, though perhaps the weaves were of not so great a variety as those we had seen at Vavskola. We did see there, however, a piece of damask that pleased us more than any other we had seen. It had been designed by Miss Carlsan, and she introduced us to the young lady who had woven it. We wanted to buy it, but it wasn't for sale; the young lady was pleased that we wanted it and took our order for one just like it to be sent to Penland for our permanent exhibit.

Looms and equipment used in the schools we had visited generally were very similar to ours at Penland, we had discovered. In fact, on Mr. Worst's seven pilgrimages to Sweden, and especially to Johanna Brunsson's Vavskola, he had brought back to America actual looms which he had duplicated in his own workshop.

Another thing we noticed. The traditional old coverlet patterns used in the colonial days of our own country are in many instances the same patterns as those that have been used for hundreds of years in Scandinavia, even though ours have such American names as Braddock's Defeat, Lee's Surrender, Tennessee Trouble, Freedom's Home, Whig Rose and Mount Vernon. As I studied these things in Scandinavian schools, in magnificent museums and in elegant homes and imposing public buildings, I was quickly transported across the Atlantic to a little cabin in the Blue Ridge mountains where in imagination I stood before a stack of Aunt Susan Phillips' gorgeous hand-dyed and hand-woven coverlets!

In fact, except for the damask weaves done on the draw looms, or hand Jacquard looms in Scandinavia, the weaving we saw in those countries was very similar to that done and taught by Mr. Worst at Penland. There is a similarity in the traditional patterns used, the softness of colors produced by vegetable dyes, and the quality of cotton, linen and wool yarns, although generally speaking, their cotton had more of the appearance of having been hand spun than ours, and their colors from commercial dyes generally were both softer and stronger than ours. Our commercial dyes are likely to be harsh, but theirs show a kinship to the softer tones obtained from vegetable dyes.

From Miss Carlsan's school we went to the Town Hall, which Clara Laughlin describes as "the most magnificent in the world, and probably the most beautiful building of modern times." I would be disposed to agree. Sweden seems to have ignored costs when it came to architectural planning, materials and craftsmanship. Reluctantly, I was forced to admit that the Stockholm Town Hall was a little more imposing even than our Penland's Craft House or even our Lily Loom House—though I wouldn't trade!

The Town Hall has a magnificent setting on one of the canals, with a sculpture-filled formal garden leading up to it. A veritable jewel, truly. But naturally I was most impressed by the furnishings. Every room was furnished perfectly to the smallest detail, and almost everything was made by hand! In one room the draperies were woven of gold, silver and silk. Handsome! There were murals depicting Scandinavian folklore, mythology and history. The craftsmanship was amazing.

We had our lunch there and then chartered a boat for a two-hour trip through the canals, which included going through the locks, for me a new experience. Much of the city I saw was new to me. I was particularly interested in the apartment buildings made up of narrow wings with much window space. The Swedes want to make the best possible use of the sunshine. On the sun balconies were awnings in many colors. The waterways, with their colorful boats and ships and the many-colored nets of the fishermen, add to the impression that color is everywhere in Stockholm.

Our party luckily was there for May Day, which in Stockholm is observed with the same exuberance as we give our Fourth of July. We all went to Skansen for the celebration and especially for the folk dancing. We figured we might learn something we could make use of at Penland, where folk dancing is one of our most enjoyable diversions. There was a huge wooden platform for dancing, far larger than our entire dining room in The Pines, with seats for the musicians. At Skansen the fiddlers came onto the platform fiddling as they came and marching to their own music. They were dressed in the traditional costume of tight-fitting yellow breeches and black coats piped in red.

It was a day and evening of folk dancing, and many of the dances, we were again delighted to discover, were familiar to us. We had even done them at Penland! The dancers from the various provinces were each dressed in their own traditional costumes, and it was all colorful and beautiful. Colonel Fishback could have shouted—and I suspect he did—when he found that the color slides he made that day had turned out well.

We had dinner that evening in the Winter Garden dining room of the Grand Hotel, an experience every Stockholm visitor should have, and the next day took the train for Rattvik in the province of Dalecarlia, where more of the traditional crafts are perpetuated and practiced than in any other part of Sweden. The Touristhotellet where we stayed was very Dalecarlian, with its dining room and halls decorated with gay-colored paintings such as we had found in Iona Plath's *Decorative Arts of Sweden*. And they had also in evidence much weaving, pottery and copper. The waitresses dressed in the traditional costume of that province.

I walked up the hill overlooking Rattvik to the Lerdalshajden Hotel, where I had stayed on my visit four years before, and immediately was greeted as a long lost friend by Mr. Hogberg, the proprietor. I hadn't been there but a moment before I noticed that they had redecorated the hotel. In the dining room I saw upholstery, draperies and lampshades of silk-screened material done by the Jobs family. These especially interested me, not only because of the quality of the workmanship but also because I had met Miss Lisbet Jobs at the Touristhotellet and had told her that we were planning to visit her family's home and studio. After seeing these Jobs materials so beautifully used by Mr. Hogberg, I was all the more determined to visit the Jobs.

So we chartered a bus for the day—which actually costs little if any more than ordinary busfare—and the necessary taxi to get us to Saterglantan School of Weaving in Insjon, out from Leksand, both of which are off the bus routes.

Saterglantan reminded us so much of Penland in that the women of that community weave in their homes and sell their products through the school. The school furnishes materials, instruction and designs, and the weaver is paid by the piece. And like Penland, they have boarding students—from Sweden and from other countries, including the United States.

When we arrived at the Jobs house, an adorable craft home almost like a doll house, there was a table set for us with the usual coffee and delicious pastries. And when we had been refreshed, we frankly began our serious looking, for we had been peeping about as we ate and drank. We quickly saw that every detail in their home had been planned with loving and artistic feeling. In one room the walls were of silk-screen print on heavy crash or burlap. Even the ceiling of the little hall leading from the dining nook to Mrs. Jobs's studio was of silk-screen print, the same blue and white as that of the studio couch cover seen from that hall.

After we had been over the house, of course we wanted to go at once to their shop, where there were things for sale. And we all bought. I got out as quickly as I could persuade myself to go, because I wanted to buy more than there was room, money or need for; but I did purchase two choice pieces to add to our exhibit at Penland, and some small ones for gifts.

From the shop we went with Mr. Jobs to his studio, where he did silk-screen printing, using his own, his sister's and his mother's designs. He also did silk-screen prints for many other people. He had two tables the length of the building, long enough really for mass production, though everything was done by hand.

It had been an inspiration to meet that family, all of them artists, master craftsmen, gracious, hospitable, interesting, entertaining.

CHAPTER 26

INGEBORG HUGO, who had been a student at Penland, and Betty Johansen, who had taught pottery there, met us the next day when we crossed from Sweden into Norway and arrived at Oslo.

The girls seemed as pleased to see us as we were to have a reunion with them, and Ingeborg announced that her mother was expecting us all for dinner and wanted me and one other to be the house guests of the Hugos during our stay in Oslo. So Mrs. Stebbins and I went directly home with Ingeborg and the others went to the hotel where she had arranged for them to stay. As soon as they had freshened up, they followed us to the Hugo home.

There smorgasbord was laid out for us. The china, silver, linen and furniture was all old and interesting as well as beautiful, and the Hugos welcomed us with glowing warmth. They seemed deeply grateful for all that had been done for Ingeborg in America.

We were charmed with the Hugos. Ingeborg's brother Carl and his wife were there, and his wife's parents. Their warmth of hospitality, their sincerity, their eagerness to make our visit pleasant and profitable delighted us all. All of them spoke English fluently with the exception of Ingeborg's parents, who had studied it in school but had had little opportunity for practicing it. After we had sat down to dinner, however, Mr. Hugo made a halting but touching little speech of welcome, and we voiced our appreciation, and then we all lifted our glasses and said, "Skoal!"

Next day we were welcomed and coffeed by the Statens Krindelige Industrie Skola, of which Ingeborg is a graduate, and I was presented an autographed copy of a book about the school. They even showed me a copy of our *Mountain Milestones* and assured us that they knew much about Penland through students like Ingeborg.

At the Bygdoy Folkemuseum, where we went in the afternoon, we saw buildings that dated from the dawn of Norwegian history and were furnished as they were in the periods they served. To me the most interesting exhibit was the Viking ships, dating from the ninth century, the first century of the Viking era. There was one in which Queen Asa was buried about the year 850. It was a graceful vessel, beautifully carved, and perhaps was her pleasure yacht.

We went into the Stav church, the oldest building in the outdoor museum, built in the early days of Christianity in Norway. It has no windows and all the light that entered came through holes in the walls.

The next morning we left Oslo with its spring flowers and took the scenic train to Voss. As we climbed we quickly left the flowers behind and soon green buds on the birch trees were the only signs of spring; then there was nothing but the evergreens; and after a while there was no vegetation, only bare boulders, and then snow everywhere. From Finse, the highest point on that railroad line, we saw the Hardanger glacier, as well as other spectacular scenery. At Finse the snow was up to the eaves of the station and the only way to reach it was through a passageway dug to the door. At Voss we left the train, took a little electric one, and descended quickly to Granvin, which is on an arm of the Hardanger Fjord. At the small Maelands Hotel that night we had feather beds for covering, and we needed them. The little waitress wore the Hardanger costume, embellished with what we know as Hardanger embroidery.

The next day we saw no Norwegian handicraft products, but what was far more wonderful and awe-inspiring and soul-satisfying was some of the most marvelous scenery in the world—the very perfection of the handicraft of Providence! We took a ship to Kinsarvik and had a most beautiful trip in the fjord with the snow-capped mountains on each side and the majestic rock cliffs and plunging waterfalls. Wherever there was enough dirt there would be vegetation, though the mountains seemed almost solid rock. At the water's edge on little handkerchief patches of land were tiny farms, with sheep and lambs and often goats. Once we saw a goat standing out on a sheer point of rock and one member of our party almost wept because she just knew the poor animal would never be able to get down alive.

The scenery was constantly changing. At one time we saw off in the distance banks of mist, and then as one vista opened, there were billows of mist or cloud looking like a geyser, and near it, what some of us thought was a mirage that looked like an island; the whole scene was so ethereal that we never did know whether what we had seen was in the fjord, in the sky, or in the mist. It was as inexplicable as our own Brown Mountain lights. If we could have explained what we saw, the scene would have lost much of its romance, just as would our mystery of the lights dancing for aeons along the crest of Brown Mountain.

We stopped for the night at Lofthus on the Sognefjord, in the Ullevang Hotel. Our rooms looked out over the fjord and upon a terrace that was built out to the water's edge. Before dinner we walked up the fjord, and back at the hotel we went out on the balcony to drink in the scenery. After we had come from the dining room, our group gathered in the lounge for coffee and conversation, and everybody was warm, relaxed and comfortable. The hotel, unlike most we had visited, had not turned off the heat. The talk embraced many topics: fishing and the ways of cooking fish, cocktails and Hollywood, California, the variety of religious cults and crackpots in that great state—even, I'm sure, handicrafts. But presently I slipped out and sat in the long twilight, at peace, fairly intoxicated with a beauty experienced, a beauty like nothing I had ever before come upon. The fjord was maybe a mile and a half or two miles wide just there, and abruptly rising above it across from us were snow-capped mountains. Where I was sitting, it was spring and flowers were blooming. Across the fjord, halfway up the mountains the snow began, and on the top and to the left was Norway's third largest glacier. Waterfalls fed by perpetual snows and ice raced down the sheer sides of the mountains. Nor did the mountains seem stark and forbidding, but the smooth whiteness of the peaks against the deep blue of the sky in the afterglow of the sunset made a veritable dream world. In three different spots I saw a glow as if the moon were about to rise there. Actually they were reflections of the sun, which had long since disappeared behind the mountains, from icy mirrors on snowcaps and glacier.

The beauty of the place cast a spell of purity and peace. All this, with the quiet, smooth fjord, the good-night callings of the sea gulls, the clean, sweet air, was tempting me to linger indefinitely.

But we had to be moving shortly, and it was on the journey from Lofthus to Bergen that I had—I could hardly say enjoyed—the most spectacular bus ride I ever experienced. We were rolling along a shelf on the side of a mountain, dashing around juttings of the cliff and through cuts in the rock, wondering what would happen if we should meet someone approaching on this very narrow road. And around a sharp curve that is just what we did! We both stopped, precipitately. According to the rules of the road, since we were going up and they were coming down, they should back up to a passable place.

So they began backing up that precipice where a wrong move would have taken the car hundreds of feet through the air straight down! It's a shame Colonel Fishback didn't get a picture of the expressions on our faces as we watched that car backing. But after a half mile or so, it came to a place wide enough for us to get by, and we passed—and sighed a great concerted sigh of relief.

I realized when we were zipping along again that until we got past that little car, I hadn't even thought for a moment of handicrafts. But not for long, because while we stopped at a little country store, very much like the one at Penland, to get some cold drinks and sandwiches, we noticed a tiny church near by. Coming along the road toward it were three couples. The girls, I saw, were dressed in costumes of that province, gaily done, beautifully fashioned products of hand-weaving, I was confident. And so, once again I was back in the groove, our perilous journey forgotten in the excitement of seeing these beautiful creations of the loom and the expert, flying fingers.

They told us that the young people were going to a wedding in the little church, and I wanted the bus driver to stop in front of the church during the wedding ceremony, for if there's anything in the world I enjoy seeing as much as beautiful weaving, I suppose it's a wedding. But the driver wouldn't wait, and we went on into Bergen.

We got there in time to take the funicular railway a thousand feet above Bergen, which we did in ten minutes. From there we looked down on the city; below us lay the Hanseatic buildings, all of Bergen, the fjord, the mountains. It was beautiful, breath-taking.

At dinner there we had fresh salmon poached in white wine, another delightful experience.

But Bergen was only a stopping point, and the next day we went on to Voss, an excellent place to shop for Norwegian handicrafts. We bought weavings, wood carvings and pottery, some of which landed in our Penland craft exhibit.

For the next several days, however, handicrafts had to give way entirely to scenery that was spectacular, awesome, utterly thrilling. From Gudvangan at the foot of a giant mountain that looked like one tremendous boulder we went by ship through the Sognefjord, the deepest, widest and longest in Norway, varying in width from four miles to a few hundred feet, to Flaam, a small village clutching at the foot of a rock cliff, where we saw not one automobile. There was no room for one actually; every foot of space was scenery! I do believe Flaam was farther removed from the modern world than even our little Penland.

From Flaam to Myrdal we skimmed mountain ledges for an hour on an electric train, and from there into Oslo we took the regular train. We arrived in time to accept an invitation from Iris and Carl Hugo to have tea in their apartment, and it was a beautiful smorgasbordish tea.

The next morning, shopping again with Ingeborg. We bought pieces of enamel on silver, which we think is done especially well in Norway. Then we went to a store that reminded us of our Guild shops where craftsmen bring their work for sale, and once again we bought for Penland's permanent exhibit. But the thing in that store that fascinated me most was a tapestry wall hanging; it was about three by five feet, and it depicted a wedding party, with the bride and groom, the musicians, the folk dancers. I just couldn't come away until I had bought that piece for Penland.

We were almost at the end of our stay in Norway. That afternoon our friends gathered at the railway station to see us off. The Hugos had brought us gifts and flowers. Ingeborg Hugo and Betty Johansen seemed wistful as we left for Penland without them. And we ourselves were almost in tears.

From Oslo we left by train for Copenhagen, and from there by Linjebuss for Basle, Switzerland. We had lunch at Heidelberg and stopped at Hamburg, and for the night at Frankfurt, where we saw Ruth Zechlin, who had been a student at Penland. Ruth had dinner with us, and she gave me a beautiful little deer made of raffia.

CHAPTER 27

IN DENMARK, Sweden, Finland and Norway, we had fairly gorged ourselves on handicrafts, scenery and smorgasbord! "It seems to me you would have been surfeited," someone said to me one day after I was home and telling about my tour. "It seems that you would have got tired of looking and eating!"

"Well, I didn't," I said. "I probably did eat too much, but it was wonderful. And I never could see too much, either of handicrafts or that gorgeous scenery."

And now, after a veritable feast of looking and eating in Scandinavia and Finland, I was in Switzerland, the land, the paradise, I might say, of scenery and handicrafts, and where the eating too is wonderful. I was to have this proved at the home of the Glattlis.

On May 17 we took the train from Basle to Lucerne, and as we neared the station I recognized Mr. Glattli on the platform waiting for us. There was no mistaking him, because he was very like his twin brother Rudolph back home. I went right

254

up to him and addressed him without even asking if he were Mr. Glattli. He introduced me to his wife, his college son Hans and his eleven-year-old Fritz. Hans spoke English fluently, Mr. and Mrs. Glattli only a little, and Fritz none at all. Fritz though would learn it later in his school.

The Glattlis wanted to do anything we wished toward making our visit to their beautiful country most enjoyable. We suggested that they come to our hotel after we had got settled. At that point Colonel Fishback and his harem, all their baggage they had brought to Europe, and all the things we had purchased were all in a conglomeration on the station platform. But we got the situation in order and all of us piled into taxis that took us to our Hotel Balances, which was very well named, we found. It was on the Reuss River, and our rooms had balconies overhanging the water where we could have breakfast if we wished; but I preferred mine downstairs on a dining balcony where white swans came up to ask for crumbs from our toast.

Soon the Glattlis came and we went into a huddle on plans. They gave the Colonel directions for getting where to see what, and they invited me to drive with them out to their home in Zug, some twenty miles from Lucerne. Their house overlooks Lake Zuo, and immediately across from it are comparatively low Alps that looked like solid rock, though there were buildings on top. To the right and in the far distance were the high Alps, white and jagged against the blue of the sky. These mountains were just as different from any others I had seen as our Blue Ridge are different from the Rockies. Again, as with the Norwegian mountains, the Alps did not to me look cold and forbidding but rather unreal and unbelievable.

255

Mr. Glattli was director of the Swiss Brown Cattle Federation and the offices of the federation and his home were in the same building. As we had driven along we had seen many cattle of that breed, very beautiful, though more of a dove color than brown, I thought.

At the Glattli home Mrs. Glattli served us tea, and the best little thin crisp cookies I had eaten in many a day. She had made them herself. Then she showed me over the house, and I was entranced with her pictures, especially one showing a green foreground and the snow-covered Alps in the distance with a flat glow that Hans said was sunset and his father insisted was sunrise! I did enjoy seeing the cameraderie of that father and son, their mutual understanding, their quiet bouts of humor, which needed neither English nor German for expression. And I was entirely captivated by Mrs. Glattli's twinkle. She didn't speak English but I was confident that she had understood everything as we all asked and answered questions through Hans.

After our evening meal, served on Swiss china, we drove back to Lucerne in the sunset glow; I clutched a bag of those delicious cookies that Mrs. Glattli had done up in a dainty gift parcel. We drove by the Lion of Lucerne, of course, but I never would have recognized it from the pictures I had seen, for no picture could give the feel of the place or show all the setting that is so much a part of the sculptured figure. It was twilight as we approached, and as I got the first glimpse of the stone cliff through the trees and shrubbery, I thought there was a pale floodlight in the whole cliff. But as we came closer I could see that it was not artificial light but instead the warm beige color and glow of the cliff from which is carved the figure of the lion. Framing the figure on each side and above are the natural shrubbery and trees and at the foot is a pool. We instinctively spoke in muted tones, for the place seemed indeed like a shrine, which it really is, commemorating the bravery and loyalty of those Swiss Guards who in the French Revolution lost their lives attempting to defend the French king.

At Interlaken we found our rooms in Hotel Eden had tiny balconies from which we could see the Jungfrau in the dim distance when there was not too much mist. The next morning we took a train for Jungfrau and after two hours of traveling, much of the way by cog railroad, we had covered some 9,000 feet toward the 12,000-foot-high Jungfrau station. The train went slowly; I didn't know whether it was because the grade was so steep or because they were allowing the passengers time to get accustomed to that tremendous height.

Before we reached the snowfields we saw many wild flowers blooming: violets, buttercups, cowslips, worlds of wild narcissus, a white daisy, white thick-petaled anemones, and a very blue flower, one to the stem, that some thought was a kind of gentian. Many of these flowers were blooming right up to the edge of the snow.

I shall not attempt to describe the scenery, for I'm certain I would overwork the word ethereal. On the landscape there was usually a mist that made everything seem a little unreal. Often because of billowing clouds just back of the snow peaks it was difficult to know where the mountains ended and the clouds began. And much of the time we were on lakes where water, mountains and sky were so blended into tones of misty blue and white that one was never completely separated from the others.

The hotel at Jungfrau station was built into a side of the

mountain, so perched that it seemed to hang out over space. When we had eaten our lunch there, we were ready for more sight-seeing. We went through a tunnel, took a lift—it's hard for me to say lift instead of elevator—to the Tower and walked along a balcony that hung out over Jungfrau glacier. Down below, miles and miles it seemed, two skiers were racing down the glacier; we were told they would ski to the next station below and ride back on the train. Soon most of our group said they'd had enough activity for the day in that altitude, but Ellen, the Colonel and I went through other tunnels and after a while came out upon five dark brown polar dogs hitched to a sled. We bargained with the dogs' owner and with our guide went for a dogsled ride. That was indeed a new experience.

Next we saw the Ice Palace, a fairyland of electric lights sparkling on ice walls, with signs everywhere cautioning visitors: GO SLOWLY. That was because of the altitude; some persons we met were almost overcome by exertion in that rarefied air. But we got on. Perhaps living in our Blue Ridge, though our mountains aren't comparable in height with the Swiss Alps, helped.

At Brienz we would get back into our chief interest, craftsmanship. There, in the greatest wood-carving section of Switzerland, which boasts some of the finest work in that craft in the world, we saw a wood carver at work, and we visited stores filled with carvings. We had hoped to attend some classes at a wood-carving school, but it was not then in session because the carvers had gone to Berne for a special exhibition. But we had an enthralling time browsing about in the shops, and we bought some carvings.

We had left Hotel Eden with regret. We liked the hotel,

and we were delighted with Interlaken. Not only was it a place of amazing scenery on every hand, but it was also a center from which one could make endless trips to places of surpassing beauty, and to craft centers, to excellent shops selling craft products, watches, countless beautiful things made by the ingenious Swiss. And it was likewise a city of friendly, hospitable people.

Our train for Montreux went through incomparable Swiss country—lakes, snow-covered precipitous slopes, Alpine houses with over-hanging eaves, painted and carved decorations, gorgeous, color-splashed flowers everywhere. At Montreux we found another hotel with balconies overlooking the beautiful Lake Leman, and across and beyond it, through the ever-present mist, were the quiet and awesome Alps. We chartered a boat and crossed the lake to the Chateau of Chillon and went through the castle where Byron was inspired to write "The Prisoner of Chillon."

Two days in Geneva brought us back to the stir and noise of a large city. I missed the quiet beauty of rural Switzerland. And then we were off to an even larger and more stirring metropolis filled with tourists, and rather hot, we thought, after days in the rarefied atmosphere of the northern countries and the Swiss Alps—Paris. There we saw the sights over which countless thousands and millions have ooh-ed and ah-ed as they followed Napoleon or the Bourbons from palace to palace.

Then we were off for Penland!

Both of Penland's craft tours to Europe had been big events for our little school. The first had had the thrill of newness; it was my first trip abroad. The second had provided that great thrill of seeing friends we had met on the first tour or had known as students at Penland; and because of Europeans who had been to Penland in the four-year interval between the two trips, much more planning had been done in these various countries to make our visits happy and meaningful. This had been true especially in Finland, where we knew more people than in any of the other countries.

Who can measure the value of such experiences as these craft tours? Not the least of things gained are the friendships made and the happy relations established between schools and craft educators of those countries and our country, as well as between individuals interested in the crafts. And what does the world need today more than creative, constructive ideas, and a happy exchange of such ideas and ideals?

CHAPTER 28

I T IS PERHAPS fortunate that one cannot live always on the crests of thrills. Once home again, we settled back into the schedule of Penland, if one can say that we have a schedule. I was about to say that once more we had settled down to the humdrum of existence in our little mountain world; but I would err, because life at Penland is never humdrum, never prosaic. We live on change—on excitement, development and growth. Our existence is never dull, never the simple and orderly but uninteresting procession of the days.

Hardly had we returned from abroad when we began to approach 1954 with the realization that it would mark our quarter-century anniversary of having people from the outside world coming to work and play with us. It was difficult for us to realize it, despite the changes those years had brought.

We looked back twenty-five years to the Little Cabin and

to the Weaving Cabin, the neighborly meetings we had had through the years, the quiltings, the plannings, the despairings, the rejoicings, the discouragements and achievements. We saw many things.

We looked about us and saw now an international school, with neighbors reaching out across the world into thirty-five different countries. And we knew we hadn't planned it that way; we realized it had just happened. It frightened us, and at the same time it thrilled us. And it still does. Every opportunity, we know, entails a responsibility. Our opportunities have been tremendous; Heaven grant that we may meet worthily our responsibilities. After twenty-five years the opportunities and the responsibilities continue to expand and challenge. Each year is different, each brings a world of new experiences. We never know whom we are going to have visit us from where, and we await the arrival of each summer, and each Christmas season, with anticipation.

One day in December 1953 the telephone rang and the voice at the other end was that of Mr. Charles Babcock, whom I never met personally but with whom I had corresponded some months earlier. He wanted to come up to Penland the following Sunday. I invited him for dinner and asked how many there would be in his party. He said he would like to bring his daughter and Mr. Larson, an architect.

So they came. Mr. Babcock, I soon discovered, represented the Reynolds Tobacco Company, and Mr. Larson was their architect in charge of the great new project involving the moving of Wake Forest College to Winston-Salem.

Those two men, I saw at once, had the "seeing eye" and it was a joy to show them Penland. Architects, of course, must be craftsmen, and I saw that Mr. Larson felt as craftsmen do.

And I was confident that Mr. Babcock was likewise of the fraternity, for he had chosen Mr. Larson.

When Mr. Babcock began to inquire into my plans for Penland's future, I gladly listed the things I wanted to see done during the next ten years. (Every year I say I expect to be active at Penland another ten years!) High on the list were a heating plant for the Lily Loom House and the pottery, a new metal shop, a new maintenance shop, and sufficient funds to pay reasonable salaries to our teachers. I had to confess that we were paying our teachers less than we were paying our kitchen help.

Shortly after the two gentlemen left Penland, I received a letter from Mr. Babcock asking for figures on these projected improvements. Before his letter was cold in my hands I telephoned Mr. Biddix of the Spruce Pine Lumber Company, and in twenty minutes he was in my office. He and I figured and estimated, and the next day I went to Mr. Deyton, who perhaps has had more experience in building than any other person in Mitchell County, and he figured and estimated. And I sent the results to Mr. Babcock.

Very soon a letter came saying that we would receive a check for a heating plant for the Lily Loom House and pottery.

That heating plant was installed, and immediately the building was transformed. To know what that heating plant meant to us, one would have to have been acquainted with the Loom House and the pottery during winters, when all the heat we had was from stoves. A stove did make the office comfortable, but imagine one stove in one corner of that great weaving room, eighty by fifty feet in size! It was possible to move one's loom close to the stove and get warm on one side, of course, but the other side would be frigid; then one could turn the loom around and reverse the process. And think of those who couldn't even get near enough to bake one side at a time.

Imagine how the weavers feel now on cold mornings when, on opening the door, they are greeted with a warm, inviting atmosphere, and upon entering, they find that the entire building is warm and cozy. And it's the same way in the pottery. On winter days we used to congeal slowly; now we glow and purr.

Another gift we had during our anniversary year was from a friend of many years who had been to Penland when we lived in the old Pines. She had written me that she had been left a bequest of $2,000 that she didn't need, and she asked me if we would accept it and use it in supplying some of Penland's needs. The angel! Of course I answered, and quickly! But when the check came, it was for $3,500! I like to think that this gift made our friend as happy as it made us, and her letters indicated it did.

Each New Year we sent out letters to friends of Penland, reviewing the school year's accomplishments and listing our hopes for the coming twelve months. My New Year's letter that year had suggested that one way of making Penland's future secure would be for everyone who wanted to do so and could to give five dollars a year to what might be called Penland's living endowment. One gift in response touched me particularly. "I can give twenty-five dollars just as easily as five," she wrote, and she sent twenty-five dollars. For me it is unusual to know someone who can contribute twenty-five dollars as easily as five dollars and particularly to know somebody who says so.

264

One summer we had with us Cic Finc—whom we called Sis Fink—of Denmark, a designer and creator of special costumes. I yearned to weave two dresses for myself under her directions. Lily Mills gave me the materials for the dresses, and asked me for directions for weaving them; they wished to include these directions in a bulletin they put out called *Practical Weaving Suggestions*. Naturally I was happy to comply.

But they also wanted a picture of the dresses—on me. Harvey Chase took the pictures, but when I looked at the prints I realized they were so much like me that I just couldn't let them go into that bulletin, and neither could Lily Mills. In my thinking about myself, I am always young, and generally youth is not too hard to look at. But when I come face to face with reality, as I did when I saw those pictures, it is more than I can gracefully take.

So the situation was discussed and Lily Mills asked me to go down to High Point, where *Practical Weaving Suggestions* is published, to what appeared to be a Hollywood-type studio, and be photographed. And I did.

The first question asked me was, "Can you use lipstick?" Well, I did.

It took a lot of experimenting to get something that Lily's representative, Mrs. Hedrick, was willing to print.

During these efforts to get a presentable photograph of me, we had been in a studio that was under the same roof as a great quantity of furniture samples; High Point is the center of the furniture industry of the United States.

And it happened that I casually made the remark that our school certainly needed more furniture to make us more comfortable and better-looking for our twenty-fifth anniversary.

For instance, I said, some of our beds dated back to our beginnings in the Craft House, and even when that furniture was new it was anything but de luxe. I suggested that if we might relieve that studio of some of the samples that had had too much wear and tear to serve it properly but nevertheless were still good and quite usable, it would be quite a stroke of fortune for Penland.

"I have been to college with the presidents of some of these furniture companies," Mrs. Hedrick revealed. "While we are waiting for the photographic processing, why don't we call on several of them?"

Nothing could have suited me better. And though asking for gifts is not one of my favorite pastimes, Mrs. Hedrick made it an intriguing social diversion. She would go into an office, introduce me as a rare find, tell something of the school and then open the way for me to add a few details.

It was an experience.

And the presidents gave as if the giving made them happy. I believe it did, too. And there was no doubt about their making me a happy woman.

The Continental Furniture Company gave us six large plate glass mirrors and four benches and the president told us his contributions were not only for the anniversary year; he said he meant to contribute something each year.

Dallas, Incorporated, gave us two overstuffed davenports and two chairs to match, and even paid the express charges. The Dixie Bedding Company contributed four innerspring mattresses. Lucas National, Incorporated, gave seven beautiful and simple spool beds and three stools. And Mebane Mattress Company sent us six mattresses.

But more important than these valuable gifts the day had

266

brought us were the new friends the school had added. Each new group of friends adds new interest and new zest and extends our horizons. For me especially they add new courage and new hope for Penland's future. To us nothing approaches in value a friend, new or long tried and appreciated.

CHAPTER 29

WE HAVE FAIRIES at Penland. You doubt it? Fairies, you know, are craftsmen. They weave spells and wonders with their magic wands. And being weavers, why shouldn't they flit in and out of the coves of our Penland highlands?

You still can't quite believe it?

Then let me tell you about that very special loom that came to us as an anniversary year gift.

On both of our craft tours to Scandinavia and Finland we were especially charmed by the perfection of their damask weaves done on a type of loom very different from anything generally used in the United States. Some of these looms were modified Jacquards, but most of them were types of the draw-boy loom. No two schools, we observed, seemed to use exactly the same model of these looms, and the looms at each school seemed to have been made to order.

This kind of weaving is slow work and difficult, and we realized that it would not be considered practicable for us hurrying Americans. But I did yearn to have one such loom at Penland, and to be able to offer instruction in what seems to me the most beautiful of all hand weaving.

Colonel Fishback and I tried throughout our 1953 craft tour to find out how to own such a loom. We hardly dared risk trying to have one made in our country from measurements, specifications and photographs, and nowhere did we come upon one for sale.

We did know, however, that Mr. Edward Taggart, who had been a student at Penland, had later gone to Scandinavia and Finland to learn this very damask weaving and had also determined to own such a loom. He had brought back parts that he thought would not be obtainable in America, along with the most minute and detailed directions and drawings, and had found a friend who was willing to build a damask loom. It had taken them many months to complete the task, including sending to Europe for things they had thought they could get over here or make but had been unable to find or build themselves.

We at Penland figured we were unequal to the task of doing what Mr. Taggart and his friend had done.

But we were not willing to give up the idea of having such a loom. After we returned home we were still writing teachers we had met over there in the hope that they might discover one we could procure, when one day I had a letter from Mr. Taggart. He, by the way, did not know that we were trying high and low to find a damask loom.

269

And what do you suppose his letter said?

The damask loom he and his friend had built, he told me, had been of immense satisfaction to him and he had greatly enjoyed weaving on it. But with all the other interests he had, he said, he felt that he had invested too much in the loom to warrant his keeping it; he wanted it to be used more than he would have time to devote to its operation. But he did want that loom to have a happy home, and one in which it would provide pleasure and be of service. He preferred Penland as its home. He just wondered if by any chance we might like to have it. But if it would prove a white elephant, if it would take up more room than we felt we should give it, said he, then, please, Miss Lucy, don't hesitate to say so.

And you think I don't believe in fairies?

You can imagine what I wrote Mr. Taggart. We had things in mind.

The piece of damask we liked best of all that we had seen on our European trip had been done by Inga Werther, a student at Handerbetets Vanner outside Stockholm. She was completing her weaving course that same spring. So after I got Mr. Taggart's offer, I wrote to ask her if she would come to Penland and teach during the summer for the small amount we could afford to pay her. She replied that she would, and she came.

Before the time came for the summer session to begin, Mr. Taggart shipped his loom to us. Then with his friend who had made the loom, a Mr. Rhodes, he came to Penland, and with Colonel Fishback and Inga Werther, who soon arrived to advise and supervise, they got the damask loom assembled.

All summer Inga taught damask weaving, and at the end of

the summer she promised to return the following year. She has become a great favorite with us, and we like to think that she will return again and again.

But our tour in Europe was to have another result of much importance to Penland. It brought to us Martta Taipale of Helsinki, who designs and does tapestry weaving in her own special technique.

Martta also did something that we have to show visitors coming to our campus and that is a daily delight to us. She designed a wall hanging four and a half by nine feet that depicts Penland and its meaning. The weaving of this piece was done by Martta's interpreter and assistant, Sirkka Ahlskog, who has become another favorite among our students from other countries. The piece hangs on the wall in the Penland business office, and countless persons have admired it. The colors are glowing, and such as only Martta could produce. A modern artist working under Martta well described her beautiful pieces, I think, with the assertion that "Her colors are like music."

Colors in this Taipale tapestry blend into the coloring of the woodwork of the office and also into the colors of the rockwork of the walls. And too, there are contrasts in vivid tones which might be likened to the strains from some Wagnerian opera. The center portion of the tapestry shows peoples of many races and nationalities, such as those coming to Penland, and on each side of this panel are shown crafts, and people engaged in doing crafts—carding and spinning, weaving, pottery, metal work. It is unusual. It is modern. It is Marttan.

The climax of this eventful year came on July 25 with the official celebration of our silver anniversary. North Carolina's

271

Lieutenant Governor Luther H. Hodges, who has since become Governor, was the speaker, and I believe he made one of the finest speeches we've ever had at Penland.

Students, staff and neighbors had gathered on the lawn in front of the Lily Loom House. It was a festive occasion, and I suppose we were all rather proud of ourselves. Maybe that's why I so appreciated the Governor's address; more likely it's because of what he said about Penland:

"The greatest thing that each of us can do today is to make the most of the work we find to do. . . . In the midst of international tensions and worldwide uncertainties we need more than ever to go back to the fundamentals, as has been done here at Penland. . . . Here at Penland much has been done in improving our relations with countries around the world by exchanging with their handicraft leaders various handicraft skills. To me, that is one of the outstanding accomplishments of this institution that has done so much and gone so far."

On that occasion we looked for a moment at what we were twenty-five years ago and what we were on that day. We saw with pride that we had come a long way, but we also realized that we would not be satisfied until we had gone further and achieved more. And proudly, too, I introduced to the audience, most of whom knew them already, the members of the board of the school: Bonnie Ford, Clementine Douglas, Mr. Jason Deyton, Mr. Edward Fortner, Mr. Fred Biddix and Mr. Sidney Montague.

To me, at any rate, one of the most significant events of the anniversary day celebration was the reading by Mr. Deyton, superintendent of Mitchell County schools, of a letter from Maria Halva of Helsinki, who had been with us seven months during the 1952-1953 session, asking him to present to our

school two very choice craft books. With these books was a
beautifully hand-decorated little leaflet with the following
message to the Penland school from the craft educators who
had done so very much for our people when we were in their
country:

PENLAND SCHOOL OF HANDICRAFTS
25 YEARS 1954

The words Penland and Finland prove certainly that the Penlanders and the Finns are relatives.

By having the pleasure of knowing the student exchangers
between Penland and Finland, we have been acquainted with
the interesting craft and social education which Penland
School of Handicrafts, directed by Miss Lucy Morgan, gives
every year in many ways to an international group of students.

For these good reasons we want to congratulate the school
now and onward, joining the celebrators though here. Our
best wish is that the career of the School in creating the international understanding in the mankind will encourage and
inspire the people also in the future. May the School in the
Mountains always have the real success and happiness it has
from God.

As a sign that there are beautiful, beloved connections between Penland and Finland, take, please, the books *Ryï'jy-
Rugs of Finland* by U. T. Sirelius and *Design in Scandinavia*
by Remlov-Wirkkala.

Kasityonopetta Liitto—Handarbetslararinneforbundet:
  Karttu Aho, chairman   Pirkko Kilpio, secretary
  Taivaanvuohentie 3.B.   Lauttasaari.

Raili Seraste, supervisor for girls' crafts in Helsinki City ele-
  mentary schools

Maria Halva, supervisor for girls' crafts at the State Board of Education

The teachers of Helsingen kasityonopettajaopisto, Kulmak. 5. Helsinki:

Hulda Kontturi
Irja Teerisuo
Aino Ollila
Idi Lindholm
Eeva Grano
Aira Kilpia
Anneli Anttila
Martta Saarto
Pia Hypen

The teachers of Fredrika Wetterhoffin Kotiteollisuuso-pisto, Hameenlinna:

Alli Blomstedt
Helmi Adaltonen
Aili Henriksson
Laila Kartlunen
Viivi Merisalo
Ilma Neiminen
Helvi Pyysalo
Paula Tolonen
Rakel Valla

Maija-Liisa Suni, teacher at the Vocational School for Girls in Helsinki

Mrs. Noora Halva, Christmas-Mother to Irene and Ginny in Jyvaskyla, 1953

Toini-Inkeri Kaukonen, supervisor for crafts of women in the schools under Board of Agriculture

It's a long list, but I record the names proudly as Penland takes to her heart these gracious, friendly, accomplishing fellow craftsmen and neighbors across the waters in gallant little Finland.

Listing them brings to mind other world neighbors, many of whom have visited us. In fact, never have we had more interesting people from foreign lands than those who came to Penland during that anniversary year. Among them were Mr. Mendis and Mr. Serifaden from Ceylon, Mr. Gour from India, Mr. Hourme from Finland, Mr. Hellkaas and Ingeborg

274

Hugo from Norway, Lady Noon, Mrs. Minwalla and Miss Mowla from Pakistan, and Mrs. Bloom and Dr. Wunderlich from Germany. It can very reliably be promised anyone coming to Penland that he'll most likely "meet such interesting people."

Through the years I have especially enjoyed the philosophy of our Indian students, and Mr. Gour was no exception. I like what he wrote in my guest book. I wonder if anybody has better described our school than this man from far away India. This is what he wrote:

While I write a few words about this wonderful place, I am fully conscious, in fact more conscious than anyone else, of my own limitations to correctly assess the value and importance of an institution like the Penland School of Handicrafts. But I cannot help recording my spontaneous reactions to what I saw here during this one week of my stay on the campus.

Two things have impressed me most: One, the entire emphasis is, as should be, on the learn-by-doing method of instruction. The beginners don't have to confront the baffling explanations of how things happen; but they just see all that happens (in their own hands) as they work and can easily correlate the different stages in the process of doing their job. Second, the open-door system of making the craft instruction available even to casual visitors and transients is one of the most wonderful I have yet seen. It is a very broad-based technique of mass-education, where by education we understand enriching the minds of the people. No formal admissions and discharges; one could stay in the school as long as one felt like staying. One has to choose what one wants to make, and is straightway helped to put his or her hand to the job. One is thus enabled to utilize even a couple days' leisure to learn some craft, or at least the rudiments of it. He can improve upon his accomplishments as and when conditions allow. No system can be more conducive to the dissemination of knowledge among the people at large, nor another more capable of arousing the learner's enthusiasm to such a high pitch.

While the school has done outstanding service to the community (of which I saw quite a deal during my visit to a number of homes, far and near), I feel an institution of this type has an additional significance, too, specially in relation to the staggering speed at which machines are conditioning the day-to-day life pattern of the people of this country. These machines are being permitted to ride roughshod over the potentialities of the human mind and the subtle capacity of the human hand, while they give us comfort and more leisure to enjoy life. Schools such as this one stand for teaching how to fill in that leisure so that it may be a real joy to them. Popularization of craft education and craft workshops, like the Penland one, will be more and more needed to help the communities to meet the challenge of a machine-ridden civilization threatening to choke up the very springs of creativity and power of expression of the human mind. I hope thoughtful people have already realized the value of handicrafts and their place in the social set-up of this progressive country.

I have to thank Miss Lucy Morgan, who is herself all this school stands for, for looking after me so well, and I am grateful to the entire staff for treating me with such kindness and courtesy. My stay here will be an unforgettable experience to me, and if I ever have another chance to come to this hospitable and friendly country, I shall not like to miss visiting the Penland School of Handicrafts. Thank you, all.

Uma Shanker Gour
8/29/54

Mr. Gour in this letter expressed so well what we were wishing and shall always wish to do and be at Penland, and it makes us particularly happy to know that we can do even a small part toward making foreign visitors see the United States as a hospitable and friendly country.

The visit of Norway's Mr. Hellkaas was particularly fruitful, for it was through his efforts and interest that we obtained Mr. Sigurd Alf Eriksen of Oslo to teach metal enameling and general metalwork at Penland for a short while the following summer. He had described Mr. Eriksen as one of the most famous and cleverest men in the field of enameling work, "I suppose he is one of the best enameling artists in Europe," he said of the Oslo artist. "He is a master craftsman, and is teaching enameling at the big school of applied and fine arts in Oslo. I think you will find Sigurd Alf Eriksen excellent for the job. And I think, too, you should be happy to get him connected to your school."

And we were indeed. Mr. Eriksen has studied in Norway, Vienna, Paris, and Germany. He has been teaching some twenty years in Oslo, where he has his own workshop. He has works on exhibit at the Trienale in Milan and at the Scandinavian exhibition in this country, as well as many other places. He was a find for us.

Three ladies from Pakistan were our first visitors from that country and we were captivated by them. I hope that they learned as much from us as we did from them, for then I would know that Penland had been a rich experience for them.

Lady Noon is the wife of the Premier of Pakistan. We all gathered in the Craft House lounge one evening to hear her tell about her country and the work she and her two fellow countrymen at Penland were doing toward bringing about better conditions of health, education, economics and the general business of living, particularly for the women.

Afterward we asked questions until the poor lady was practically speechless, and we went to bed that night with a warm feeling for Pakistan and much admiration for the strides its citizens are making and for the progressive thinking of her leaders, as represented by these three interesting and charming women.

It was just before Christmas when Mrs. Bloom and Dr. Wunderlich came to us. Our school family was small then and there was more time to share them with our neighbors of the countryside.

Mrs. Bloom was superintendent of a school district in Hamburg, Germany, that embraced seventeen schools. Of particular interest to us was the fact that she had written several books describing her method of "learning by doing." She visited a number of the grades in the Spruce Pine schools, and a special assembly of all the high school students was arranged so that they might hear her speak of her work among the children of Germany. The students, I was happy to observe, demonstrated their interest by asking her many questions about German students and schools. We are always pleased when opportunities are presented Penland to do any small things toward improving international relations and bringing about better understanding among the peoples of the world.

If the hours we spent with Dr. Wunderlich in the evenings around the open fire were samples of what the young people of free Germany had been enjoying with him, we could easily understand why Dr. Wunderlich was a successful director of a youth center in Westphalia. We looked forward eagerly from one evening to the next to having him lead us in singing German and American folk songs; often we acted them out in pantomime.

In sharing Dr. Wunderlich with various civic groups in our county, including the Rotary club and the Woman's Club of Spruce Pine, we felt that we were further advancing our world brotherhood ambitions; we understood that when we know people we like them, and that liking people and having them like us is one of the greatest joys that anyone may attain.

But of all our anniversary year visitors, none brought us more joy in coming to see us, I'm sure, than a beloved friend of many years who was coming back to a Penland he had done so much to help set on its course, Mr. Allen Eaton, author of *Handicrafts of the Southern Highlands*. I think of him as a guiding star in the days when the Southern Highland Handicraft Guild was making its way through its period of growing pains and joys. He is a choice person, one whom it is a privilege to know.

CHAPTER 30

THROUGH THE YEARS at Penland we have lived and thrived on responding to challenges, on taking dares, as we used to say when I was a child. We have had problems that for us certainly were tremendous ones; some we have shed tears and much sweat over, some have been sheer joy in meeting and solving. Most have been intriguing, some even romantic.

So I'd like to relate briefly a story of challenge and accomplishment that I refer to as the romance of reproducing the green baize cloth for the tables in Independence Hall.

The challenging task came to us; in fact, it literally walked in one day. That's how many of our most interesting experiences have been introduced. Perhaps it was the case of the man looking for the mousetrap-maker.

The occasion was the dedication of the new North Carolina Minerals Museum, located on the Blue Ridge Parkway at Gillespie Gap not so many miles from Penland. Many dignitaries were there, including Governor Hodges and other state officials, Congressman Charles R. Jonas, and several National Park and Museum officials, among them Superintendent Sam Weems of the Blue Ridge Parkway.

It was after the dedication festivities were over that Sam Weems brought the parkway and museum officials to Penland. He had telephoned that he wanted to bring them over, and when I asked him what they wanted to talk about he said we'd know when they came.

We did. It was an interesting story, and quite a challenge they gave us.

They told us of the restoration project for Independence Hall sponsored by the General Federation of Women's Clubs, which had raised the money with which to finance the undertaking, and the National Park Service, which is supervising the work.

"What we want Penland to do," one of these gentlemen declared, "is to reproduce one hundred yards of green baize cloth for the table coverings for the fifteen tables of the first floor of Independence Hall."

They had brought with them a little half-inch square of green baize for us to match in color and weave.

"Is this a piece of the original cloth that covered the tables when George Washington and Benjamin Franklin and the other founders of our country sat around them, and when the Declaration of Independence was signed?" I asked.

I was told that it was not, that the only way they knew what those original coverings were like was from the study of a picture and a printed description. So they had sent to England for a sample of eighteenth-century baize cloth, and this half-inch sample they were giving me had been clipped from a table covering in a museum there. And of course the original coverings in Independence Hall had been homespun.

For our Mrs. Conley to card and spin enough wool for one hundred yards of cloth—and they wanted it forty-five inches wide—in her spare time would take years, I knew.

The original cloth, I was confident, was likely dyed with vegetable dyes, and if we did it the same way it would take months of gathering hickory bark, boiling it, dyeing the yarn in the ooze to make it yellow, and then dipping it into the blue-pot to make it green. And because of the time involved and the many dyeings we would have to make to dye all that cloth, we were quite certain we would come up with many different tones of green. And that would not do at all.

But we agreed to undertake the job.

The first thing to do, we decided, was to have our friend Mr. John Littlewood over in Ashe County do the dyeing, carding and spinning.

Mr. Littlewood has a one-man factory in his own back yard, a building in which he does all these processes. His machinery for picking, carding and spinning has been in use since 1900, and the "mule-spinner" duplicates the hand-spinning processes, thereby giving the finished yarn the same kink and general characteristics of hand-spun yarn.

So after the museum and parkway gentlemen had departed, we got busy on plans, and a few days later Bonnie Ford, Ginny Munford and Katie Lewis went off to have a talk with Mr. Littlewood. It was nothing new for us to go to him; we had been going to him over some thirty years for homespun yarns for our vegetable dyeing.

Mr. Littlewood, too, was intrigued. But like us, he knew it was no small task that we had undertaken to accomplish. There was no dye he could get, he told us, that would produce just that old mellow green of the eighteenth century, and he would have to experiment until he obtained it.

But he worked at it and he worked at it, and after a while he sent us a sample, which we sent off to Philadelphia. They approved it, and soon afterward Mr. James Mulcahy, museum specialist from Independence National Historical Park came down to Penland to discuss final details.

It happened that the day after Mr. Mulcahy arrived was the day Mr. Littlewood had set to do the dyeing—a whole one hundred pounds at the same time, so that it would all match. A hundred yards of the cloth would not require a hundred pounds of yarn, but he wanted some extra pounds for experimenting. So we went over to the Littlewoods—Mr. Mulcahy and a group of us from Penland, including our two photographers, Harvey Chase and F. B. Marchialette. Some persons may wonder why we took photographers along. Well, we thought it would be a fine story, quite a romance, we felt, to get down in pictures the record of processing wool from the time Mr. Littlewood brought it to his shop fresh from a sheep's back to the time it would be ready to spread on the tables in Independence Hall.

When we got to the shop we saw a huge copper vat with the hundred pounds of wool boiling merrily in it. It was stirred not with the usual punch stick we use at Penland but with a huge sapling, because stirring that much wool is a man-sized job.

We made pictures of the dyeing and arranged to come back two days later to see and photograph further processes. This we did, and for our instruction and the photographers' picture-taking, Mr. Littlewood climbed a ladder to the roof and with a tow sack considerably larger than Santa Claus's pack and filled with wool, showed us how he had spread out the dyed wool on the hot roof to dry.

When the wool was dry, Mr. Littlewood explained, he had to prepare it for the picker in the same manner that he would make a layer cake. He pointed out that boiling the wool during the dyeing process removed from it all the natural oil, and this oil condition had to be restored before the picking, carding and spinning could be done effectively.

So he and Mr. Mulcahy spread a layer of wool on the oiled floor of the picking room and then sprinkled it with oil. I shall always remember the can he used for the sprinkling. It was a tin coffee can, with nail holes in the bottom of it; but the oil would not leak out until he shook the can. After he had sprinkled it carefully, he and Mr. Mulcahy took poles and beat the wool, just as one would beat a cake, until the whole batch was thoroughly oiled.

Now the wool was ready for the picking machine, into which it was fed. This machine has picks on a huge roller and it opens, unpacks and fluffs up the wool so that it is ready for carding. This machine does for the wool what the hand spinner does when she separates the wool fibers in the matted wads of washed wool; it's essentially the same process.

The fluffed wool was then ready for the carding machine, which mixes the wool so that any unevenness in the dyeing will be harmonized into the whole with the result that the batch becomes one even color. It is from this process that we get the term "dyed in the wool"; anything thus described is considered genuine through and through.

The carding machines are large rollers set with wire teeth

that comb the fibers of the wool into uniform bats, just as our grandmothers did by hand. Just as they made this wool into bats ready for spinning, so the carding machine prepares it for the same purpose by turning it into rolls in proper size to provide the correct grist of yarn. Mr. Littlewood had set his to produce a grist that would make the yarn the right size for weaving into the green baize cloth.

But before the yarn is of correct size, the wool has gone through three carding machines, each with a different set of teeth, so that the rolls are twisted into ever finer yarn as the wool moves through them. As the rolls come off the first two machines, they are slightly twisted and rolled onto cones; as they come from the last machine they are rolled onto long spools ready for the "mule" spinning frame. Actually, what Mr. Littlewood's machines do is almost identically what Mrs. Conley would do by hand, but they speed the operation.

And now to get to the weaving.

When the museum and park officials were here, I suggested that the person I would most prefer to have weave this cloth was Colonel Fishback. But at that time the Colonel was on a good-will tour of the south and west for the Lily Mills. The park people knew Colonel Fishback, for he had been with the National Park Service before he went into the Army.

If we could but get him.

The Colonel is a perfectionist; he would do as perfect a reproduction of that green baize as would be humanly possible. And he was the only weaver associated with Penland School who would have the time to devote to this challenging job, because ordinarily he spent his falls, winters and springs fishing in Florida. I sent an SOS to him on the West Coast.

He wrote that the proposition would require thought. By the time the Lily tour should be finished, he said, he would be in sad need of rest, and besides, he was yearning for his Florida home and his fishing rod.

Lily Mills was interested, too, in seeing us accomplish our unique assignment and they co-operated—as they always have—by permitting the Colonel to end his tour.

So Colonel Fishback, descendant of that first John Fishback to come to this country from the Black Forest of Germany at the request of Governor Spottswood to help set up the first iron foundry in Virginia at Culpeper, was about to undertake a craft project also related to the early history of this nation.

One of the first problems we had to meet was that of obtaining a loom on which to weave the baize cloth. The material was to be forty-five inches wide and our wide looms are thirty-six inches. We wanted the Colonel to have the most efficient loom possible, and we knew that his preference would be a Macomber. So we wrote and telephoned the Macombers in Saugus, Massachusetts, and they promised to build a special loom for us which they would ship in two weeks. When the Colonel reached Penland and heard the news of the Macomber loom, he was delighted; I think any worries he might have had evaporated then.

The Colonel arrived just in time to go to Ashe County and watch Mr. Littlewood complete the processing of the Independence Hall yarn. In fact, he brought part of the material back with him so that he could begin his experimenting in order to get the exact weave of the eighteenth-century baize. He did his experimenting in narrow widths while he was awaiting the arrival of the Macomber special loom.

In order to get the identical effect of the cloth of almost two centuries ago, our material would have to be not only dyed, carded and spun in the same fashion, but would also require similar processing. For instance, in those days there was no steam pressing and flattening down of the nap, and so we had to avoid doing things that were not done to that original green baize cloth. We wanted nothing incongruous in our material, no anachronisms. And the Colonel was determined in this undertaking, as he was in all the things he did, to approach, at least, absolute perfection.

One of the first things he did was to get Barney Marchialette to make him a frame with small wire nails in the side. Then he washed one of his two test pieces in warm soapsuds, rinsed it very thoroughly and hooked the edges onto the drying frame. Even before the last bit was hooked over the nails, the upper portion of the cloth was dry, and in a very few minutes in the sunshine and breeze the entire piece was dry.

He used another method to test the second piece of his cloth. Mr. Littlewood had feared that there would be globules of oil in the cloth that would be hardened by the washing and thereby spoil the appearance of the material. He suggested that perhaps the cloth should be dry-cleaned and then washed. So this process was followed with the second piece.

Then we studied the two pieces carefully, and we could see no difference in them. When Mr. Littlewood was over at Penland a few days later he agreed that the washing had done all that was needed.

So we made plans for constructing a long drying frame, with tenterhooks instead of nails, so that the tension could be adjusted after the cloth was hooked on.

Then Colonel Fishback went to weaving in earnest. And this task was to be increased, because the order was increased from one hundred to one hundred and thirteen yards.

When the cloth comes from the drying frame it is smooth and requires no pressing, and as far as we can determine from descriptions of the old eighteenth-century green baize, along with that little half-inch sample from the museum, our cloth is a true replica of that which was used when the Declaration of Independence was signed. Certainly Mr. Mulcahy and the Independence Hall authorities approved it.

After the cloth was woven there was the business of making the table covers; they wanted us to do that too. So we set about that task. The green baize was forty-five inches wide, as I have said, but the Independence Hall people wanted the table covers to reach clear to the floor on all four sides of the tables. They said that the original covers were made that way so that the men in knee breeches sitting about the tables would be warmed somewhat by them; the covers served to keep off the drafts in the often poorly heated building. So we sewed the lengths together, making a cover of sufficient width to serve their purpose.

When the work was finished and the covers placed on the historic tables, I must confess I was very happy with the result. And so were the folk in Philadelphia. It had been a hard job, but an interesting one and certainly a challenging one. And we live and thrive on challenges at Penland, as I have already pointed out.

But we weren't finished with Independence Hall.

"Now," they said to us, "you have made us one set of covers; will you make another just like it? We want a set to use when these are cleaned and also should some of these from time to time be damaged in some way."

We agreed to make another set. And now Colonel Fishback, who wove every foot of the first one, is working on the second set. He has already done a part of the big order, and he will resume his weaving when he returns from his Florida sunning and fishing.

CHAPTER 31

THE REPRODUCTION OF all that yardage of green baize cloth for the Independence Hall table covers constituted, in my opinion, the one most interesting and challenging task the Penland School has undertaken in the producing of a single piece of handicraft—of a tangible character, I mean, something one can hold in his hand, a product whose texture one can feel, whose coloring he can study, whose excellence of workmanship he can feast his eyes upon.

Penland students, of course, in the more than a quarter-century of the school's existence, have turned out literally thousands of beautiful things in many different crafts, and some may be disposed to argue with me about the baize cloth's being our most outstanding product. Nor would I press the point, for I feel that, after all, our greatest achievements at Penland have not been the beautiful and useful things we have made there.

I am quite convinced that we cannot hold in our hands, we cannot run sensitive fingers over, we cannot study with discriminating eyes the textures or forms or colorings of our most beautiful and most useful Penland productions. I say these are the Penland intangibles, the wondrous handicrafts of the spirit, things impossible to feel in your fingers or examine under a magnifying glass but real, nevertheless, and tremendously important and of value inestimable. These are the things not made, but won, earned—received, at any rate—in the making of things.

Maybe I'm obscuring rather than clarifying. But listen to black-haired, vivacious, ever so clever young Aida Zahran, who has charge of the home economics program of Jordan, sitting in my living room in The Pines during the visit of some sixty foreigners to Penland for Christmas 1957:

"Penland! Ah, Miss Lucy, you ask what Penland means to us, to me, if it has done anything for us who have come here from so many different lands, so many different cultures, different faiths, different languages? And how do I say, how do I make you an answer? We came to America with one thing in mind, and that was to better ourselves, to gain as much knowledge as we can so that when we go back home we can help our lands and peoples. Some of us have been to America before, some have studied here, but others have come for the first time.

"And in Washington they say to us, 'Go to Penland,' and where is Penland? we say. But we come to Penland, and we leave behind us those differences and we are working for just one aim. And we learn to know one another, and for us most of the countries were just dreamlands; we didn't know the people there and we didn't know they did the things we do.

And here at Penland we meet these people and we say, 'Well, they do the same things that we do at home,' and now it is more a reality than a dream. And it shows that the world actually is not so far apart, that the people are not so different after all; it shows that the world can be joined in some form when the various peoples know each other."

Aida was waving her arms and her black eyes were flashing and her quick smile lighted her quite serious expression. She looked through my window toward old Bailey, and she turned back to me and shrugged her shapely shoulders and thrust forward a long-nailed forefinger.

"And, Miss Lucy, we have learned that all the United States is not New York and Coney Island and Washington, D. C., and San Francisco. We have learned that all the United States is not the taxicabs scurrying and the people rushing and the money being counted out in the great stores, and everything quite mad and everyone quite rich. And we have learned that you Americans are very much like all the rest of us." She narrowed her black eyes, and her face was deadly serious. "And we who have come to Penland have realized, Miss Lucy, that though our nations may be unfriendly and even considered almost enemies, we individuals who have come together at Penland are quite friendly. Is it not so?" She gesticulated with palms up, shoulders shrugged. "We are working together and playing together quite happily, is it not true? We are—let me see—we are working and playing, but—I cannot just express it—but we are sharing—that is it—we are sharing things; we share everything that we see, we look at things together, we work together at the same bench, we eat at the same table together, our looms are neighbors. And, Miss Lucy, when people share things, when they see

291

things and do things together, can they long be enemies?" She answered her own question with a pert toss of her pretty head. "They cannot, is it not so?"

Aida is but one of countless foreign visitors to Penland who have sought to describe what I feel is our community's most important product, a product, like those material ones produced on our looms and in our various shops, shaped by the people out of their traditions, their history, their inheritances, their cultures, their hopes and ambitions, their very lives. I think virtually all who have come here, worked together, played together, shared things, as Aida said, together, have felt as she felt; perhaps she was better able to express it.

I have told of a number of our visitors. But I must speak, if briefly, of the gentleman who was perhaps Penland's most unusual guest. It came about this way:

We had a student at Penland, Prong Song-Saeng-Term, whose American study was being directed by one of the government departments in Washington. Some time before the Christmas holiday season of 1956 I had a call from Washington inquiring if we could keep Prong over the holidays. We said we would be happy to do so and that we would be glad to entertain any other foreign visitors during that season.

A few days later we had another call to inquire of us if we could entertain a Buddhist monk from Cambodia, the Venerable Huot-Tath.

We had entertained notables from many lands, of many races and tongues, but we'd never had a Buddhist monk. I thought a moment, as the man on the other end of the wire awaited my answer.

"Yes," I said, "we'll be happy to have him. Just send him down."

I was reminded that the Venerable was quite a personage.

The monastic rules by which a Buddhist monk lives are quite different from those of the other guests we had entertained, I knew, but they did not sound too difficult, and we made preparations for his arrival.

I wanted to go to Marion to meet him, but I didn't know whether it would be just the thing to do, so I asked Mr. Sidney Montague, the chairman of our board of trustees, to meet the Venerable. Before the visitor's arrival the United States Information Service had telephoned to ask that we make a tape recording for the Voice of America of any speech the monk might make and that we take a series of pictures of him, particularly of his observing crafts being taught at Penland. We were also requested to send to Washington all newspaper articles we could obtain that related to his visit. The pictures and newspaper articles, it was explained, would be sent throughout Asia.

The monk, we realized anew, was indeed a personage.

Mr. Montague and a reporter-photographer were at the station in Marion at 7:13 Sunday morning when the Venerable Huot-Tath's train was scheduled to arrive. But the train was five hours late. Our emissaries telephoned me to report, and as the hours dragged toward the noon hour and there was still no train, I began to be concerned. I had been told that in accordance with the monastic rules to which he gave obedience, the Venerable was not to eat between noon and the following sunrise. When noon came and still no monk, we stopped saving his breakfast and ate it ourselves.

The Venerable Huot-Tath was to be at Penland only four days, Washington had informed us, and Sunday afternoon, we had thought, would be the only convenient time for him to speak to us. We had arranged to have his speech at three o'clock. But wouldn't the poor man be starved?

It was two o'clock when he arrived at The Pines. And he had had nothing to eat since eleven o'clock Saturday morning. But the moment I saw him I knew that, important and hungry though he was, he was a serene, kind, gentle person mindful of the good around him and quietly willing to accept any inconvenience. We allowed him half an hour to relax in his room and then we ushered him down to the dining room, which had been converted into an auditorium and furnished with a tape recorder. Photographers and an audience of civic and religious leaders of the county were assembled. We even had a greeting from Governor Hodges to pass on to him; the Governor was unable to be present.

The Venerable Huot-Tath sat in a cushioned chair, swathed from neck to floor in his great yellow robe, and talked to us. As he does not speak English, his disciple and interpreter, Mr. Chea-Ton, stood beside him and interpreted his speech. He spoke on Cambodia and Buddhism, and the group listened with rapt attention. After the talk was finished, he permitted us a question and answer period, and there were so many questions and answers that we asked our Mr. Prong Song-Saeng-Term of Thailand to aid Mr. Ton with the interpreting.

We were told that a Buddhist might belong to any church, and that the general rule governing his life is to do no harm to anybody but on the contrary seek to do everything possible to make others happy. We had at that time five Buddhists in our household, and certainly they were as kind and helpful and eager to be of service as anyone we had ever known. The five, including the Venerable and Mr. Ton, spoke the Thai language; the three others were from Thailand.

Mr. Prong was quite pleased that the Venerable was in the United States and having an opportunity to see much of the country, to talk with educators and religious leaders, to visit in the homes of the people, to become for a while a part of the everyday life of the nation, particularly of the rural country such as our little Penland community. He felt that the Venerable's impression of this country would be reflected not only in Cambodia, but in Thailand, Viet-Nam, Burma, Laos and that general area of the East. Mr. Prong had long and earnest conversations with the monk, and he told us that he had gained the impression that the Venerable Huot-Tath would carry home with him a good report on America; his messages to his own people would have great influence in insuring their continued friendship and loyalty to our standards of democracy and peace. We sincerely hope and trust that our treatment of him helped to insure his making such a report.

The Venerable Huot-Tath was our most unusual Christmas guest, his strange garb contributing to his uniqueness. But during that holiday season we had twelve students from six foreign countries—Cambodia, Thailand, Formosa, Pakistan, Indonesia and Brazil. All of them were educators, and each was seeking to learn as much as he could about American life, particularly the way Americans—ordinary Americans like us—live.

To help them do this we took them on visits to local industries and mines, school officials (the schools had recessed for the holidays), the homes of our weavers and other neighbors who entertained graciously. The visitors constantly asked discerning questions. We felt that they were enjoying themselves as much as we were enjoying them, and that is saying much, because they were a fascinating group. Indeed, the whole experience was a rare privilege for us, and from it we gained a higher plateau of tolerance, an enlivened eagerness to help make our world, our whole earth, a happier place. And out of the experience we determined we would do something like that every year, because of what it would mean for our community and our own happiness and because of what it might mean toward the promotion of international understanding and good will.

We were to have further opportunity to advance this purpose with the arrival the following April of a group of nineteen Libyans with their two interpreters and an escort from Washington. They had come to Penland not to study crafts, but to observe the public schools of our county.

Immediately we realized that their visit would give our community, and particularly our school children, an opportunity they had never before enjoyed, one that few schools in the nation would enjoy. The Libyans had come to the United States to obtain help in formulating an on-the-job rural teacher-training program in their own country. We were told that the presence of Penland School had been one of the factors in selecting Mitchell County for study.

Penland School of Handicrafts has in fact become a magnet that has drawn to our little Toe River Valley engaging persons from every part of the world, not only those who are interested in studying and exchanging ideas in handicrafts but also many who hold important positions in government or education and find at Penland an example of how handicrafts may be used to improve economic welfare, education and morale in rural areas. We know that handicrafts by themselves would not necessarily accomplish these purposes. But at Penland we have been for many years quietly fashioning a pattern of work that has begun to attract worldwide attention. Various reasons have been given. Some say it is organizational skill, strict

296

standards of workmanship, ingenuity in meeting difficult problems. Some add that it is our simple loving concern for human beings of all races, nationalities, religions. I'd say that perhaps it's all these things and maybe more, but I like most the last reason suggested.

The public schools of Mitchell County, like those in many areas throughout the nation, especially our mountain regions, have had less to work with in the way of facilities than have the schools in richer and more metropolitan areas. Consequently, the Libyans, Washington knew, would be able to find more in our schools that they could adapt to their own institutions' teacher-training programs.

The Libyans went everywhere, visited every public school in the county, observed 4-H Club programs in action, were entertained at turkey dinners in homes of the community, attended a fellowship meeting in the Spruce Pine Methodist Church—which one member of the church later termed "a rich experience in fellowship with persons of a different race, religion and culture, which increased our desire for appreciation and understanding of a people from another land."

In fact, Penland is coming to be known as a little United Nations. And we would like to think that our community and the students and teachers who come to us from every part of our nation and the world are making a contribution toward world understanding, which means world friendliness. When you understand a person, you are very apt to have a friendly feeling for him.

CHAPTER 32

Bᴜᴛ ɴᴏᴛ ᴏɴʟʏ has the Penland School been a
magnet that has attracted persons from all
over the world who have come here to study.
Penland has also sent emissaries to the other side of the world
to help demonstrate to foreign peoples the American way of
doing things.

In April 1952 our own Tony Ford, who had been such a
tower of strength through our years of struggle, was called to
Washington to talk with Point Four officials who wanted him
to go to India as a craft specialist under that program. Tony,
the Washington people knew, was one of the foremost craftsmen in the nation and they urged him to accept the assignment. If he did so, he would be gone two years.

India is halfway around the world from our little Penland,
and two years is a long time. When Tony came home, he and
Bonnie and the children talked it over all the remainder of the
spring and that summer. It would be a responsible assignment; it would take Tony all over India, observing crafts as

they were being performed by the Indian workers and suggesting materials, equipment and methods that would enable these craftsmen to do better work with less effort and time spent, and thus increase their earning power. It would be an opportunity, too, for Tony to learn a great deal himself, to broaden his own life considerably. It would be an opportunity for him to serve his country by carrying to the Orient its message of good will and brotherhood.

Would he go?

We wanted Tony to have the chance of doing a valuable work for Penland and America. Our state supervisor of vocational education shared our opinion that there was no other man in the country who would be able to do the job as well as Tony could. But at the same time we were reluctant to see him go so far away for such a long time.

But as the summer waned, the Fords decided. He and Bill, who by now was seventeen, would go to India; Bonnie and eleven-year-old Martha would help us hold the fort at Penland. Bonnie, of course, has always been one of our mainstays.

Tony was called back to Washington in November for several weeks of indoctrination. After Christmas he and Bill left Penland for the long trip to the other side of the world.

Penland has been proud of Tony's work and the recognition his achievements have earned. His work in India took him from the snow-covered Himalayan peaks to the green tropical lands in the southern area around Cochin and Cape Comorin by the Arabian Sea, and to beautiful Ceylon. He was flown to Bangkok, Thailand, where he represented the United States as a delegate to the United Nations conference on small industries. In India Tony, usually accompanied by a group of Indian government employes, used virtually every sort of conveyance in traveling over that tremendous country. Sometimes they would leave New Delhi by plane, transfer first to a railway coach, then to a river boat, then to an ox cart and finally walk for miles to reach their destination.

Tony's work was of an advisory nature and his title was technical adviser on Cottage Industries and Handicrafts for the Point Four program; he worked directly with the Ministry of Commerce and Industry of the government of India. One of the mammoth tasks in which he was involved with a team of Indian experts was the making of a complete survey of handicraft production in India. When one learns that there are more than two million hand looms at work in that land—and weaving was only one of the many handicrafts embraced in the survey—one appreciates better the enormity of that task.

In India Bill too had opportunities to travel much, but he spent a considerable part of his stay there as a student at the Woodstock School in Mussoorie up in the foothills of the Himalayas, a beautiful and wild section of India. Students from twenty-three nations were there, the Fords wrote us. Almost another Penland at Christmas time!

The year 1953 was gone and much of 1954, and we began to look forward to Christmas and the return of father and son. And then news came that Tony was being transferred to Lebanon to supervise crafts in the educational institutions of that country. And Bill entered a school in Beirut.

But there was considerable excitement at Penland when a big crate arrived at the Spruce Pine Station—it was a veritable miniature house—and after much maneuvering it was put on a truck and brought to Bonnie's home. There she and Martha, with several willing helpers, got out the boxes, parcels and cases and separated those that said "Open Now" from those that said "Don't Open Till I Come." Then came the unpacking of the treasures Tony and Bill had sent from India—beautiful prints, gossamer saris, huge and handsome copper trays. These, along with what the Ford men brought when they did get home, were enough to have a wonderful Indian exhibit months later in the Craft House.

They returned from Lebanon in July 1955. But in December Tony was assigned to Korea and he left shortly before Christmas. The following Christmas Tony did get home for the holidays, though he was here only until February, when he returned to the Korean assignment. There he represents the United States government as an attaché to the Office of the Economic Coordinator of the United Nations Command, with the Industry Division of the Rehabilitation Engineers Office—which means, to cut through this gobbledygook, that Tony is assisting in the program of rehabilitating old industries and establishing new ones. These industries include tire plants, fertilizer plants, steel mills, textile factories, chemical plants, tanneries and many others. And with it all he has not neglected to help promote in Korea his first love, handicrafts and cottage industries, built around community life and rural trade centers, with emphasis upon the use of indigenous materials and native skills. In other words, Penland in Korea!

We are hoping to have Tony with us again early in 1959. When he does arrive, he will find another member of the Ford family, Mrs. Bill. Our Bill—I claim him as my grandson— was married in July 1957 to Miss Barbara Young, whose parents lived at near-by Micaville until they moved recently to High Point, North Carolina.

It will be wonderful to have Penland's ambassador to the world home again. After all that he has seen and experienced, Tony will, I am sure, have some tremendous ideas for Penland.

301

CHAPTER 33

WHEN I BEGIN discussing the activities of beloved, longtime Penland friends like the Fords, I become retrospective; I start looking back to our beginnings. Yet that invariably leads me to project myself into Penland's future. Thinking of Tony and Bonnie, I always think too of Bonnie's mother, dear Mrs. Henry Willis, and the time I sent the loom out to her to inaugurate our revival of interest in an almost forgotten art.

That was in 1923, I remember, and it doesn't seem so long ago, though already over a third of a century. It was back in those years that the Weaving Cabin was built in an all-day log-raising, and this same little log structure is still headquarters for our community organization, the Penland Weavers and Potters. It is to this building that the weavers still bring the work they have done in their homes and here they get their checks, and from this little cabin the finished

302

products are mailed out to gift shops and friends in many parts of the country.

We do not have meetings of our community weavers every week, as we once did, but they do come in when they need extra help with special techniques, and they come to get materials and directions for their next weaving assignments. They may come at any time, too, for instruction in other crafts. No charge is made for such instruction. Generally the weavers need no further instruction in the type of weaving they do for sale, for after all these years many of our neighbors are experts, and the daughters learn from their mothers.

Six years after I sent that loom to Mrs. Willis marks the beginning of our school, the way I reckon it. Although no plans had been made to bring students from distant places to Penland to learn weaving, in the summer months we had seven students here from about as many states, and when Mr. Worst came to us in August 1929 to spend one week, the Penland School of Handicrafts was born.

And how the years do speed by as I review the first quarter-century of our existence, and within one mountain leap I am enjoying again the lively and exhilarating experiences of our 1954 anniversary year. That, I suddenly realize with a start, was four years ago.

Often someone—someone from California or Bolivia or Thailand or Norway or half a hop away over in Spruce Pine— will say after I have sketched with starry eyes the story of Penland, "Miss Lucy, I just don't see how you all did it."

And looking back, sometimes I wonder myself.

We've never had any money. I mean by that, no endowment, no backlog, no rich angels with opened moneybags held out.

But we have managed to get along. We've never been hungry. We've always had a shelter over our heads, even if at times it did leak a bit. And we have taught handicrafts literally to the world. We have had a gloriously wonderful time doing it, too.

We now have a plant conservatively valued at more than two hundred thousand dollars. We have on these hillsides some thirty acres of land, two deep drilled wells, a reservoir and two electric pumps, septic tanks and drainage fields, and twelve buildings, three of them three stories high, two of them of native stone and the other, the Craft House, of logs and stone. And we owe on the entire property considerably less than a tenth of its value.

We do need an endowment fund, of course, and we have hopes, even plans, to establish such a fund, which we hope can be enlarged as the years go by. Our trouble—and it has actually been a blessing—is that we have grown faster than we could keep up with financially. We are confident that soon we will be entirely debt free and have that backlog started.

We are confident.

Maybe that answers our friends'—our many friends'—question. Maybe we did it on confidence.

I choose, however, to enlarge that word. I believe we have accomplished what we have in these quickly passing years by testing liberally the verity of that great admonition of the Apostle Paul, that man should live well and fruitfully through the possession and exercise of that great triumvirate of virtues—faith, hope and love.

Through the years we have had a lot of faith at Penland. Sometimes, too, we were forced to keep a desperate grip on it. And, of course, we have always had hope. Of the three, hope is easiest to have and hold onto. Perhaps Paul was talking of a hope that confidently looks toward fulfillment. We have always had that sort of hope.

But truly the greatest of these is love.

Searching my heart, I can say that we have possessed love and given it freely at Penland, for how can one possess it unless he gives it without count or measure? And how can one multiply his own share without dividing it with lavish hand?

We have loved the creative arts, particularly within the fields of our handicrafts at Penland, and these fields have widened with the years until now we teach from the middle of March to the middle of December perhaps fifty or sixty different crafts to students who come from here, there and everywhere. And we teach many of these crafts to the special groups here during the Christmas season. We have sought diligently and with much zeal to revive and cherish these almost-lost arts of our forebears. Our methods of instruction have been unique in that they are adapted to the needs of our students, who may come for a few days, several weeks—our courses normally run over three-week periods—or may stay with us virtually throughout the year, as some do.

We have been made happy in seeing our hopes materialize as others have gained and shared our interest and have added their enthusiastic support to our efforts. We have watched dreams become realities.

But greater than for the revival and nurturing of the crafts and for the products of our craftsmanship, I am quite sure, has been our love for all of the people themselves—the creators, the planners, the skillful craftsmen.

CHAPTER 34

So AS I COME abreast of today's Penland in my relating of our school's story, I reassert my conviction that the most beautiful products, the most valuable, the most certain of survival, are not those works of art woven on our looms or beaten out on our metal-shop benches or turned on our pottery wheels.

I say again that as wondrous as these things are, and I exult in them, they cannot compare with those intangibles compounded at Penland out of the materials of understanding, mutual respect, a feeling of world fellowship, and love. These truly have been our most important products.

Throughout the years since those seven outsiders came into our mountains to study under Mr. Worst and share his joy in creating beautiful things, we have been welcoming handicraftsmen literally from everywhere. They have come to us from our forty-eight states, the District of Columbia,

Alaska, Hawaii, Puerto Rico and some fifty foreign countries; I haven't made a new check lately.

They have come during every month of the year that the school operates, and that is almost the year around. We normally close in December to have our vacation until about the middle of March. But we reopen before Christmas and we often have guests until well past the beginning of the new year—special guests sent to us by the various agencies and divisions of the State and Agriculture departments. So Penland is never dormant long.

They come as craftsmen interested in learning new ways, perhaps, of doing things in their fields. They may wish to learn other fields. They may be coming to learn for their own profit and pleasure; or they may be seeking to acquire skills to carry back to their schools, if they are teachers, or to their various communities if they are vocational leaders of one type or another. They may come from our immediate section of the state or the other side of the world; roommates may be a Baptist from Belmont, North Carolina, and a Buddhist from Borneo.

But here at Penland they are brothers in the joy of making together beautiful things with creative minds and agile fingers. Here, as Aida Zahran so well described the Penland spirit and atmosphere, they share everything they see and do and enjoy; they work together, play together, create together, and their differences, their prejudices perhaps, are left far behind them.

So we make things here, but the most wonderful things we make cannot be weighed or measured or counted.

Pimolphan Kaehacharoen sensed it before she had been here two days. Gentle, friendly little Pimolphan—isn't that a pretty name?—is supervisor of the English department of the Vidhara School in Thailand. She was one of the group at Penland for the Christmas holidays.

She said: "At first, when I came to New York I thought all this is America; people are rushing, they scarcely talk with each other, even though they live close together or are the next door neighbors. But when I came here, they saw me and greeted me, and I felt very warm when I was here. And to myself I said, 'But this is actually America, rather than New York. New York is a hodge-podge of all the world, but Penland is America. And when I go back I can tell my people that America is not the same everywhere. According to the community or the section is its own typical culture.'

"When I heard of Penland I could scarcely believe that there could be a school of handicraft; I thought that everything in America was made by machinery and so fast! When I came here, I felt warm and as if I were home again. Here the person's thought is not every minute how he can get the money, but here it is so much friendship and love. That is why I feel warm in my heart."

Oscar Ontimare is a Manila lawyer, a graduate of the University of the Philippines. He was a member of the group of agricultural leaders from the Philippines sent to Penland for the Christmas holidays. He was brought to the United States by the International Co-operation Administration for a six-month tour during which he visited colleges of agriculture, including our North Carolina State College at Raleigh, and conferred with American agricultural economists.

Oscar had come into the living room of The Pines from the Craft House, where he was entranced by the task of making a very handsome leather pocketbook for his wife. He had run

308

out long enough, he explained, to get a pack of cigarettes.

"Why was I interested in coming to Penland, you ask, Miss Lucy?" His black eyes danced. "Well, I was interested in seeing how people living in the rural areas are able to supplement their income, and I have seen with my own eyes already the answer to my curiosity. I have seen how your rural people in this community supplement their income by weaving in their homes, for one thing. And this I can use in the Philippines, where we have what we call the home industries."

"Oscar, are they very much like our home industries, as far as you have been able to observe?" I asked him.

"As far as weaving is concerned, yes. But—" he held up a hand, palm out—"no leather working, no metal, no enameling. And in the few days I have been here, Miss Lucy, already I have done all these things except the weaving. And now I am making the bag for my wife and already I have made the little copper ash trays for my wife, with her name on one and our son's name—his name is Teddy—on the other in the enameling. And now I am in a great hurry to get back to the bag. Inez—" Inez Blevins was his instructor—"says it is the most advanced work that has been done among these foreign visitors here for Christmas." He grinned. "Miss Lucy, I have decided not to go on the tour with the group tomorrow to Fontana Dam. I know it is a great dam, but I have seen dams already, and I wish to get finished with the pocketbook. I have little time; I must soon go back to State College at Raleigh and then to the University of Florida and from there to Puerto Rico, Japan, Taiwan. Our focus is studying the relations between landowners and tenants, and our goal is the lifting of the standards of living of the farm people of the Philippines."

For a moment his eyes were fixed on the stark limbs of the mimosa beyond the terrace outside the south window. "Miss Lucy, we don't learn much about the population of the United States, how the people live, what they think, how they go about their work, we don't learn much about them by staying in the cities. The Americans in the cities, for one thing, don't have much time to enlighten us, and if we would see only the city life we would be getting an incomplete picture."

He paused, and his pleasant face widened into a sheepish grin. He said, "Miss Lucy, I must confess to you that I was reluctant to come to Penland. I was pessimistic about coming here. 'Penland,' I said, 'where is Penland? Why should I go there? I have little time. Why should I waste any of it? What can there possibly be at Penland that could be of help to me? A little isolated community back in the mountains—what does Penland have to teach me?' I confess freely that I did not wish to come.

"But now I reveal to you, Miss Lucy, that I am having the best time of my life in the United States right up here in Penland. And why do I like it here?" His lawyer's flair for asking questions dramatically and then answering them in the same manner was easily evident. "I like it, for one thing, because here I have learned something very tangible that I can take home to my people—I have already sent one on the way to my wife, as I said, and I am missing the enjoyable tour tomorrow because for me it is more fun to remain here and work on the pocketbook, which will be another thing tangible that I have learned. These things I make here are diplomas of the knowledge I have taken, are they not? I have done something that I can hold in my hand and look upon and it is not only beautiful but useful. And I know that I can teach many of our

310

people, whose great curse is too much idleness, to keep busy with their hands and make things useful and beautiful. And I have seen more than sixty persons from eighteen different foreign countries working here and having a good time together in fellowship and good will. And so, Miss Lucy, I bless your little Penland, and I am thankful so much I was sent here."

And we of Penland are "thankful so much" that we can share our crafts, our homes, our mountain people, our wonderful rural Americans with our friends from every area of our shrinking world, a world that must shortly come to live in the spirit and atmosphere of our Penland, I am convinced, if it is to continue to exist at all.

We always have a Christmas tree and a Santa Claus, and to me it was a marvelous thing to see Buddhists and Moslems joining with Christians—Baptists and Roman Catholics, Methodists, Lutherans, Presbyterians—in singing Christmas carols on Christmas Eve around the tree and sharing with evident delight in the festivities of the season.

As Santa Claus, Bartolme Aspino of the Philippines required no pillows stuffed under his belt. He was perfectly built to do the honors of the beloved old saint. With a little bow he handed out presents to each, and his black eyes twinkled behind his white whiskers. But it was his speech that had for me a special appeal.

"Dear children," he said to the assembled Cambodians, Indonesians, Bolivians, Brazilians, Japanese, Taiwanians, Thailanders, Chinese, Greeks, people from Jordan, Pakistan, Turkey, Korea, Viet-Nam, folk from the Philippines, Guatemala, Lebanon, Nepal, Morocco, Washington, Spruce Pine, Penland, "you are indeed fortunate to be under the hospita-

311

ble roof of the Penland School of Handicrafts this Christmas season. With the motherly love of Miss Lucy Morgan—" and I *did* have the feeling that all these delightful folk were actually my brood—"everything is made possible for you to feel at home and enjoy the celebration of the birth of the King of Kings, who saved us from sins and taught us to love one another.

"The happy assembling here tonight of representatives of so many different nations is a realization of the great ideology of peace on earth," Bart went on. "Be therefore cheerful and enjoy a better understanding with each other for a wonderful fellowship and brotherhood irrespective of creed, color or social standing. Then and only then we can claim that we have that 'peace on earth.' "

As our chubby Filipino Santa Claus was making his little speech, I sat in rapturous wonderment. Never, I'm sure, has the joyous anniversary of the birth of the Prince of Peace meant more to me. Where on earth but at Penland, I silently asked myself, could such an utterly simple but sincere celebration of Christmas be held? Where could one see more vividly evidenced the truthfulness of the Galilean's bold and beautiful declaration that all men are brothers?

When a few nights later we assembled in the dining room of The Pines and pushed back our lazy-Susan-topped big round tables for our international stunt-night program, I had a similar great lift of the spirit as I sat and watched these eager young people—they were all young in heart if not in years—present typical entertainment from their homelands.

Everybody performed in one way or another; if they were not on the floor dancing or otherwise entertaining, they were clapping their hands in unison to add authority to the timing

312

of the record-player music. The Bolivians did a native dance, lively and amusing. One of the boys and one of the girls from the Philippines—I call all my international children boys and girls, regardless of their ages, but these were young people—did the unusual barefoot rice dance of the Philippines. A fan dance was performed by petite Yoshie Iwaki of Japan. This dance, I perhaps should explain to those uninitiated in Japanese customs, has no resemblance to what we Americans generally consider a fan dance to be. Miss Iwaki was clothed in a beautiful Japanese costume and the dance was actually a symbolic and graceful presentation in various meaningful positions of the handsome Japanese fan she held. There was little movement of the feet, though the dance ended with the dancer kneeling to bow to the floor with oriental grace and charm.

Nor did it seem incongrous that our evening's program should include a song by our Martha Ford that detailed in mournful tones the sad fate of one Barbara Allen. This preceded a unique dance by Yim Thong Dy of Cambodia and Clotilde Togle of the Philippines, which seemed to me more a rhythmical walking, gesticulating exercise in gentle gymnastics than a dance.

I say I had a great lifting and soaring of the spirit as I watched. I had the distinct feeling that here was a group of students, high school seniors or perhaps boys and girls home from their various colleges in our own state, happily vying with each other in representing their respective institutions at a community stunt night. Yet these folk had come together in our dining room from every side of the earth.

How our world had shrunk!

Of a truth, here in the dining room of The Pines at Penland

313

School of Handicrafts hidden away in the Blue Ridge Mountains of North Carolina we were having a stirring and joyous demonstration of the *fact* that all men indeed are brothers.

So I close my story of our Penland School with an emphasis upon what I consider our greatest achievement. I am looking at the map which John Morgan made that dramatically shows our world outreach, and I am amazed at the miracle of Penland. I ask myself what has brought it about, and these are the things that come to mind: a singleness of purpose in working toward the accomplishment of things that seem worth while; the joy of creative occupation; and a certain togetherness—working with one another in creating the good and the beautiful, working together in love.

The growth of the school has ever been a stimulating and invigorating challenge. Its growth has been my growth, its people my people. My privilege has been great and my reward abundant. Now in my sixties, I feel younger and much more hopeful than I felt that first year at Penland. My challenge now is to do what I can to plan for Penland's security in the days when my joyful service has ended. My hope and prayers are that Penland will continue to grow in strength and spirit, carried forward by those who have shared or who will come to share my dream.

Heaven grant that we may never lose those things that in our little mountain school have brought about miracles.

EPILOGUE

We haven't lost them yet.

And those words that ended the story of Penland with my expressing the hope that they would never be lost were written more than a dozen years ago. In the years since *Gift from the Hills* was first published in the spring of 1958, the growth of our little school in strength and spirit, as I comprehend it, has been a continuing miracle.

I shall never forget that day the book was officially released with a momentous celebration—momentous for us surely—at Penland. It was on May 13, indeed our lucky day. To bring his and the North Carolina citizens' compliments and to help us celebrate, Governor Luther Hodges flew over from Raleigh, and even the director of publicity of a rival New York publishing house joined scores of Penland's friends and neighbors for the festivities. For all of us at the school it was a great day. I gloried in it. I have never been prouder, even after the generous newspaper articles and reviews carried the Penland story across the nation. But I was prouder of the school and its accomplishments than I was of the book I had written about it.

It was that pride, I suppose, and the absorbing interest I had in the school, the utter delight to me of the nights and the days lived in its modest friendly buildings and walking the rolling majestic acres—to me, at any rate—of its sprawled campus, that held me there years longer perhaps than I should have stayed.

The office of director of the Penland school is a hard job to give up, particularly when one is not being asked to leave but on the contrary is being urged to remain. But I had been looking toward the day when I would resign from the directorship. Before I reached sixty—and I was into the sixties when the book came out—I called members of the board of trustees together and told them that I wanted never to be a burden to the school, that the school meant so much to me that I feared I might be tempted to stay beyond my years of usefulness. For that reason, I told them, I wanted them to make a ruling and record it in the minutes that I be allowed to remain as director until I was sixty-five, and that if I did not choose to retire by that time that I be required to retire at seventy.

But the board refused to follow my recommendation. Instead, it voted unanimously that I should remain director as long as I should live. I knew then that it would be up to me to make and carry out my own decision.

But it was the fall of 1963, more than five years after the book came out, before I actually did retire. It wasn't altogether my reluctance to relinquish the directorship, however, that had kept me at Penland. One of the problems had been finding a successor. Who, we wondered, would be foolish enough to want to become director of a school as large as Penland had become, when it had no financial backing?

Fortunately, we found such a man.

Bob Grey of the Southern Highland Handicraft Guild had written his friend William J. Brown, who was teaching at Worcester Craft Center, of the search we were making; he suggested that Bill might wish to consider coming to Penland. Bill decided to have a closer look. So he excused himself from classes for one day, flew down to Asheville, and was driven to Penland, where he spent a whole day with us before flying back to Worcester. During that day he learned a lot about Penland and we learned a lot about him. I remember, for instance, as we were walking from building to building we came to the little outdoor shrine whose history included a touch of sadness and much of faith, hope, and charity. I recalled that when the school was ten years old we thought we had reached a great milestone and had observed it in a variety of ways. For one thing, we had had my clergyman brother Rufus conduct a "craftsman's service" that our Reverend Peter Lambert had compiled from the Apocrypha, which has much to say about a great variety of crafts. I suggested to Bill that he might want to continue this custom and that if he did he would of course want a priest of his own church to conduct the service. "I believe in evolution," he answered, "not revolution."

During that day the two of us met with the board of trustees. "I happen to know," I said to Bill as we were meeting, "that you were offered a generous salary"—I mentioned the figure—"to teach in another school. How then do you happen to be interested in Penland when you know that Penland has no money?"

"The position offered me," he replied, "was to teach sculpture for so many hours a day. The rest of the day I could

317

work on my own. Sculpture is my craft and I could have done that job almost without effort. This job at Penland is big, hard, and scares me to death, and I like the challenge."

Bill sold himself to me then and there. The board of trustees had told me that they would never hire a new director without my approval. I assured them they had it. Bill is an artist and a master craftsman. I am no artist, and I'm a mediocre craftsman. Another advantage that Penland has in having Bill Brown as director is that there are two of him, for he has his wife Jane. One day when Bill's praises were deservedly being sung, someone observed, and truthfully too, "Yes, but he couldn't do it without Jane."

So, forty-three years after the train had deposited me beside the tracks at Penland station and I had begun the long trudge up the twisting trail to the school—that day was June 1, 1920, and now it was September 1963—I turned the directorship over to Bill Brown and started down the long slope, this time in an automobile over a road paved all the way to Penland station.

I had planned to have a little cottage built on the school grounds, for it had not occurred to me to live anywhere else. But during that first week of Bill's directorship I realized this would never do. For forty-two years students and staff had been coming to me with their questions, criticisms, suggestions, problems, proposals, and this they were continuing to do, though meticulously I had told them that I appreciated their devotion and loyalty and that I was depending upon them to be just as helpful and cooperative with the new director. I emphasized the fact that for a time the job would be infinitely more difficult for Bill than it had been for me, because I had had the opportunity of being an integral part of the school from its inception, learning day by day, with the growing school being my teacher. But Bill was being plunged into the directorship of an internationally recognized craft

318

school; he was being permitted no apprenticeship in preparing himself to lead Penland, for his responsibility as director was immediate and complete. And I urged everybody to support him loyally and with enthusiasm.

Bill himself, in fact, had asked me to stay around until he could get the hang of things. But during that first week I realized that I should get away. People coming to me with comments such as "Miss Lucy, I'm working for you" told me clearly that I should build no cottage on the grounds. I should be far enough away from Penland that the people there wouldn't be able to reach me with their day-to-day problems and concerns.

Fortunately, I had an excellent, perfectly valid excuse for leaving. My dear friend Mary Clark, whom I have long called my fairy godmother, had invited me to spend the summer with her in California. So off I flew to her, all the way across the country from Penland.

I had known Mary longer, in fact, than I had known Penland, even though it does seem that I have lived at Penland for an entire incarnation. She calls my nephew Dr. Ralph Morgan "our nephew" and they are devoted to each other. He is a cardiologist whose office is in Sylva and whose home is in the country out of Webster. We had several telephone conversations with him from California during which we talked plans with him for building a house for me on a knoll just above his home. For years he had suggested that if I ever considered building a home of my own I might like to build it on that knoll. I agreed that his knoll, rather than some knoll or hillside at beloved Penland, should be the site of my future cottage. I had a savings account in the bank at Spruce Pine, I told Ralph, and I would make it available for building the house. Little did I know then that my small savings would not build a house such as I wanted!

But in my perplexity when I discovered I needed more

money I found help and support, just as I had invariably found help in meeting the expanding needs of Penland.

It had been Mary's custom to live six months of the year in California, where her son Peter and his family live, and six months with her daughter Wendy in Switzerland. But Mary, bless her, said she might like to vary that arrangement perhaps from time to time; at any rate, she would like to have a place of her own to which she could come whenever she chose. Would I allow her to plan and finance the addition to my cottage of a bedroom and bath that would be hers when she came to Webster? Would I *allow* her to do that!

When I came back from California to Ralph's, I telephoned my widowed sister Laura and asked her if she would like to come and live with me. She came, and she added her contribution to the building fund, and we built a workshop where she does her hand-hammered pewter.

So with Laura's help and with Ralph and Mary putting in as much as I did, and more, we have a comfortable home within hollerin' distance of Ralph and his sweet wife and family.

And we are in the high hills, of course. We have a wonderful view of the Great Smokies, Clingman's Dome and Mount LeConte, two of the highest peaks in eastern America, and a view of the Balsams just across the valley. And in that valley below us flows the Tuckaseegee River. Below, beyond, all about us are beauty, immensity, serenity, peace.

Mary lost her daughter Wendy about a year ago. Mary's son Peter and his family live in Santa Monica and Mary visits them on special occasions. But in general she prefers living in our little mountain cottage the year round. Her granddaughter Renée lives with us. Our house has grown, too, along with its growing family.

Often we have visitors, sometimes from distant places.

Two of the especially choice people who have visited us in our Webster home are Sam Weems, superintendent of the Blue Ridge Parkway, and Michael Frome, nationally known author of books, one of which is *Whose Woods These Are,* and magazine articles about America's great outdoors. I always love to see them come. Mr. Weems is a friend of many years. I remember particularly our attending years ago a meeting of the Southern Highland Handicraft Guild in Asheville. He had driven me to Asheville over the Parkway, which at that particular season was closed to the general public. Because of another appointment, though, he could not drive me back to Penland. But over the telephone in his car he talked to the various park rangers and gave them instructions to see me home by relaying me from one to another until we met the ranger at Gillespie Gap, who took me into Penland. That was an experience I called romantical. There may be no such adjective in the dictionary, but it's a good one for me. Those rangers did not treat me as if I were for them a duty to be performed. They talked about crafts and about the various people who came to them for directions for reaching Penland; they made me feel as if I were in their age group as far as interests were concerned.

I was especially pleased, too, when Mr. Weems brought Michael Frome to our home in Webster. And if it didn't make me appear too boastful, I would quote the beautiful inscription Mike wrote in his book for me. Anyway, all who are interested in what our national government has done to protect our national forests should read his book, and also his later one, *Strangers in High Places.* And look in the index for Penland!

Among my greatest joys of the years since I resigned the directorship are my visits to Penland. Our new director and my best of friends, Bonnie Ford, both make me feel not only wanted but needed. Of course I know I'm not necessary there, but I like to be made to think that I am!

We at Penland and Webster have had our lives touched by interesting personalities, individuals, rare souls. Bill Brown has had a special flair for spotting and luring to the Penland hilltop special personages especially equipped for finding ways of filling Penland's needs. Two recent such visitors were from Chapel Hill, Lambert Davis, at the time director of The University of North Carolina Press, and Dr. Warner Wells, author of *Hiroshima Diary*, a best seller published by the Press. I am the proud owner of a copy of that book, with a special message inscribed by the author to me. I was at Penland, too, when these men were there.

Bill Brown's genius in taking over leadership of the school and advancing its program has been shown further in his planning and building of the new metals and lapidary shop. Funds for the shop grew from a multitude of small gifts given in memory of Edward Fortner, one of the first trustees of Penland. Ed was one of the local business men who gave me confidence and courage during the years when the school was evolving from an idea, a hope, a vision into what it is to-day. Except for his faith, I often wonder, how could I have made the long grade?

The late John E. Lear—Pop Lear to us—had been our first teacher of lapidary work. He had come to Penland in our early years when he was head of the department of electrical engineering at The University of North Carolina. Lapidary work was his hobby, and he had shared his skill and his enthusiasm with us. A lapidary fund had been established in his memory at the time of his death. In planning the new metals shop, which would include working in metals, lapidary work, jewelry making, and enameling, Bill showed his usual genius in having the shop built between the Lily Loom House and the pottery, so that the east wall of the pottery became the west wall of the metals shop. Thus he saved from the building fund to add to the John E. Lear fund enough money to equip entirely the shop. He achieved at the same time an interesting as well as useful continuous building—pottery, metals shop, woodworking shop, loom house—as you look at it from the upper entrance. From the lower entrance the long building provides working areas for all but the loom shop.

Bill pleased me mightily, too, when he asked my clergyman brother Rufus to come over for the annual craftsman's service and to dedicate the John E. Lear metals shop and its equipment. The service was held outdoors and we all sat in folding chairs. It was a sweet service, held just at sunset, and nature and man participated in joyful harmony.

Through the long years I was director, and now under Bill Brown's leadership, we have had from time to time interesting and significant events at Penland. One of the great occasions, for me certainly, was the wedding of my goddaughter Martha Ford, at Trinity Church in Spruce Pine. Her father, Howard Ford, whom everybody around Penland calls Tony, flew home from Saigon and gave the bride away. Martha met her husband, William Waters, when they were working for the State Commission for the Blind and living in Raleigh, where they planned to continue making their home. Martha, I was sure as I joined in the festivities of the wedding, would be another to help carry the spirit of Penland outward from our mountains just as her father had carried it with such enthusiasm and success to the other side of the earth.

And today, when our world is in such turmoil, when our scientific achievements have so outstripped our spiritual growth, what is more needed than that creative thinking and creative activity so stimulated and encouraged at Penland? This is indeed a beautiful world, and if the peoples of the world could realize the joy of working and playing together, then surely wars would cease and the millenium might be attained. As for me, I get great satisfaction from the feeling I have that waves of creative helpfulness emanate from Penland to circle the world. Considering the fact that people from more than seventy different countries have been to Penland, might not this indeed well be true?

In returning to Penland to visit I meet topnotch instructors in every department. On one of these visits I talked with Bill about it. "How do you get them?" I asked. "I wouldn't even have known the names of all these persons. And if I had known them, I wouldn't have known how to get the money to pay such high rankers."

"That's easy," Bill said. "I got the first one by telling him what a privilege it would be for him to have the opportunity to teach his craft in a place such as Penland, which is in a most beautiful setting, away from the turmoil of the world, and to be with congenial people, all intent on creativity. After he accepted our invitation, other topnotchers were eager to come in order to rub elbows with him."

"Then was he willing to teach half a day for his board and room in order to do what he wished the other half?" I inquired.

"No, he works all day," said Bill, "and is usually teaching these eager beavers until the wee small hours of the morning."

One day I was talking to an instructor there. "I understand that you were offered a hundred dollars a day to give a ten-day course in your special technique," I said to him. "Do you regret coming here instead for little more than your expenses?"

"If I regretted it," he said with a grin, "I wouldn't be planning to come here next summer."

Indeed, it is Penland's experience that great personalities

and congenial atmospheres attract others of like tastes. If you have a Penland brochure for 1967 you will find under MUSIC FACULTY a dozen names with notations of the musical instrument played by each instructor. As I run down the list I find these instruments named: guitar, cello, violin, oboe, recorder, viola, flute. And I am impressed by biographical data such as this—John Ferritte: conductor-composer, bachelor of music in piano, Cleveland Institute of Music; master of music in composition, Yale University School of Music; formerly conductor of the U.S. 7th Army Symphony; violinist with various orchestras; numerous composition awards; formerly executive assistant of the Music Center of the North Shore, Winnetka, Illinois, and lecturer in music at the University of Chicago; currently director of the Greater New Haven Youth Symphony.

I am always amazed at the work of the stitchery class, too, for although I had done things with needle and thread ever since I was a little girl, I had never seen anything that could compare with things designed and created by Martha Mood and her class. They made wall hangings that seemed to me akin to tapestries, and made them of scraps of cloth. One student, Adelaide Chase, made Bailey's Peak with rhododendron in the foreground. This is the view from her own front porch. Beautiful, the view and her recording of it! Of Adelaide's work, Robert Winn of the American Craftsman's Council reports, "In the last ten years her tapestries have been acquired by many collectors, including President and Mrs. Lyndon Johnson . . . Mr. and Mrs. Winthrop Rockefeller . . . ." I note that Mr. Winn calls them tapestries, too.

The work in pottery likewise excites me. Although pottery has been taught at Penland many years, and both the instructors and the articles produced have been all that could be desired, under Bill's leadership a new venture has been planned and successfully undertaken. The students under the supervision of their instructor have built two salt-glazing kilns back of the long structure in which are housed the weaving and woodworking operations, pottery making, and the enameling studio. One of these is called a "hound dog" kiln; it is especially meaningful, since each student brought one or more bricks and did the actual construction work under the supervision of their able instructor.

One night Bill announced at dinner that there would be a grand opening of the salt kiln that evening at eight. So at eight we gathered about the kiln, fired with gas and all aglow, and the show began when the potter, who had huge asbestos gloves on his hands, started removing the glowing bricks one by one from the kiln's opening. The bricks glowed, the pots glowed, we all glowed from the warmth of the hot kiln. I wish I had a panoramic picture of that whole scene, for people were hanging out of the windows on every floor of the building; indeed, it looked to me as if the entire enrollment of a hundred and twenty-five students, plus their instructors, plus the visitors—I was a visitor—composed an interested audience watching the glowing scene.

A course in plastics, a field entirely new to me, was introduced at Penland during the summer of 1967. It was described for me by Byron Bristol, the instructor, this way:

"In the 1967 August session it was our pleasure to introduce to Penland a course in reinforced polyester plastics. We are convinced that the basic knowledge in the creative use of plastic materials can be a valuable aid to the artist and craftsman. The interest and enrollment of students, two of whom traveled all the way from Canada to attend, seemed to bear out our conviction.

"The course was structured to teach the fundamental processes of fabricating translucent and opaque laminates and

326

three dimensional forms. From this starting point the students then launched into their own adventures of experimentation, to discover for themselves how the plastic could best serve their creative desires. The results were cast and free form sculptures, laminated art objects, and translucent windows and plaques."

I was surprised, actually spellbound, at what to me seemed like real stained-glass windows, all done by students in this class in plastics.

The development of the Penland program in the creative arts under my energetic and innovative young successor, both in the number and novelty of the crafts taught and the number of instructors and students participating, I am happy to observe and report, is advancing steadily, and I'm confident that the years ahead will record continued and accelerated advancement.

But though few friends of Penland perhaps know it, our little mountain campus has also been the site selected by the United States government from which to launch a scientific study involving the collecting of weather data.

In September 1962—not long before I resigned the directorship—we had this most unusual experience. Two government scientists, Mr. William Cobb, a meteorologist, and Mr. H. G. Wells, a meteorological technician, were sent to Penland by Dr. Gilbert Kinzer, director of technical research in Washington and long a friend of the school. Their assignment was to collect weather data high in the air above Penland, which would be sent to the United States Weather Bureau's Washington laboratory for study and evaluation.

Penland was selected, they told us, for two principal reasons, the air was clear and clean and the Penland area was free from static. The bureau, they added, especially wanted data about winds above a valley surrounded by mountains, and

Penland with an elevation of almost three thousand feet and peaks surrounding it seemed ideal for the purpose.

The two weather scientists sent up balloons from the knoll just in front of The Pines. The balloons, made of latex, they said, measured about eight feet in diameter. They carried certain telemetry equipment high into the stratosphere, in excess of ninety thousand feet, we were told. The balloons had attached to them, by what I thought of as a kite string, a parachute to which was attached a radio set that transmitted to the receiving set on the knoll a mass of data on altitude, temperature, humidity, wind velocity, and other weather factors. One of the balloons, said the men, ascended more than ninety-six thousand feet; that's eighteen miles!

When a balloon reached these very high altitudes, it expanded and after a while burst. The parachute then opened and lowered the telemetry equipment back to earth. I asked one evening where that descending equipment likely was at that moment, and Mr. Wells said that it probably was somewhere over the Atlantic. When I asked him how they might retrieve it, he said they wouldn't, that experience had taught them that it was less expensive to buy a new set of equipment than to try to retrieve the one sent up. I asked if similar experiments were being made in other places; Mr. Wells said that Penland was the only place in the universe where this particular phase of weather information was being gleaned and recorded.

What place in the universe, what place so small, at any rate, draws people with as great a variety of interests as Penland!

That September day of greatest balloon activity, incidentally, was my birthday. I thanked those Washington gentlemen for giving me such an original, interesting, and unique birthday party. Indeed, one never knows just what may happen, and likely will, any day on our beloved little knoll-top!

As I'm writing this final chapter with which to close the new edition of *Gift from the Hills*, I have been away for seven years from my daily looking through the front windows of my living room on the second floor of The Pines to ponder the gently rounded loveliness of that friendly small knoll. But in those years I've never for long been away physically, and never, never, never in my loving thoughts. Nor will I ever be. In fact, the board most generously and graciously set aside for me for my lifetime that apartment I occupied for so long as director, and often, as often as I can find a satisfactory excuse for it—and sometimes, I'm sure, hardly satisfactory—I slip away from Webster and head happily for Penland. You can take a mountaineer out of the mountains, they say, but you can't take the mountains out of a mountaineer. Surely no one will ever, ever, be able to take Penland out of me.

Every time I go to Penland I find new and thrilling changes and expansions. On a recent trip I saw that the two barns that had belonged to the Appalachian School had undergone a face lifting and an entire regeneration. With weatherboarding, sheet rock, paint, and plumbing alterations, Bill had made some attractive studios and apartments. The two barns were on different levels; the upper level now consists of attractively arranged studios where resident craftsmen work the year round, and the lower level comprises three apartments used by teachers. Not long ago Bonnie Ford and I were invited over by one of these teachers for a sip of sherry.

Wouldn't the cows be surprised if they should return and see their former home!

On another visit I had as classmates in metal enameling Mr. and Mrs. William Plafson. One day when he was recounting to me what Penland had meant to him, I suggested that he write down what he had told me. He said he would. This is what he wrote:

"Came to Penland three years ago looking for peace and quiet and to get away from the smog and the usual turmoil of the city's activity.

"We did find peace, quiet, and the most lovable people we have ever met in our lives. I must mention we are so busy with our activities we don't have time to be quiet; we stay busy all day and night long and by the end of our day's pleasure we drag ourselves to bed with contentment. We knew after our first visit to Penland that we wanted to be a part of this scene permanently.

"For two years we looked for something to buy in the area and we finally found a home about a mile from Penland, and, we are very happy to state, we bought it. Now we feel like a dream's come true.

"P.S. We wish we could tell you in words how we really feel about Penland."

Another time on an earlier visit, I was walking toward the Lily Loom House. As I drew near it, I saw a gentleman standing in the doorway looking toward the knoll in front, the valley below, the mountains beyond. As I came up to him, he swept his arm outward as if to embrace it all. "Does all this property belong to this school?" he asked.

"No, it is part of the Appalachian School property," I answered. "That school is closed permanently, and I understand that the knoll right here in front of us is to be sold as building sites. And that would break my heart!"

He held up two firm fingers. "That will never happen," he declared. "This is a religious atmosphere up here. You feel it as soon as you get to the top of the hill. God will never let that happen."

"What church do you belong to?" I asked.

"That doesn't matter," he answered. "You and I both believe in the same God. And He will never let that happen. You *hold* that in your mind. I will *hold* it in mine!"

Bill Brown told his friend Philip Hanes about the Appalachian School property, revealed that its three hundred acres and eighteen buildings were for sale. Phil Hanes made Penland School a big gift. With it and many small but happily contributed gifts from appreciative friends, Bill bought that property, which adjoins our school, and his plans for using it, some already developed, are thrilling and expansive. I'm proud of that young fellow. No one, I'm sure, even a doting grandmother, could be prouder. He has been good for Penland; he will be better and better.

I do wish I knew the name of that gentleman who told me to hold in my mind that the knoll would never be sold away from us, that he would hold that conviction in his. I'd like personally to report to him the good news. Maybe he knows it. Maybe he's known it all the time.

Anyway, there's an idea. If enough people *hold* in their minds the right thoughts, what couldn't the whole world accomplish!